The Dynamics of American Jewish History

The Dynamics of American Jewish History

Jacob Rader Marcus's Essays on American Jewry

Edited, with introductions and notes, by
Gary Phillip Zola

BRANDEIS UNIVERSITY PRESS

Published by University Press of New England

HANOVER AND LONDON

Brandeis University Press
Published by University Press of New England,
37 Lafayette St., Lebanon, NH 03766

Library of Congress Cataloging-in-Publication Data
Marcus, Jacob Rader, 1896-
The dynamics of American Jewish history : Jacob Rader Marcus's
essays on American Jewry / edited with introductions and notes
by Gary Phillip Zola.— 1st ed.
    p.   cm.
Includes bibliographical references (p.) and index.
ISBN 1-58465-343-4 (cloth : alk. paper)
1. Jews—United States—History. 2. Judaism—United States.
3. Marcus, Jacob Rader, 1896- 4. Marcus, Jacob Rader, 1896—
Bibiography. 5. Jewish historian—United States—Biography.
I. Zola, Gary Phillip. II. Title.
E184.35.M37 2004
973'.04924—dc22   2003021957

Brandeis Series in American Jewish History, Culture, and Life

Jonathan D. Sarna, Editor
Sylvia Barack Fishman, Associate Editor

Ilana Abramovitch and Seán Galvin, editors, 2001
Jews of Brooklyn

Ranen Omer-Sherman, 2002
Diaspora and Zionism in American Jewish Literature: Lazarus, Syrkin, Reznikoff, and Roth

Ori Z. Soltes, 2003
Fixing the World: Jewish American Painters in the Twentieth Century

David Zurawik, 2003
The Jews of Prime Time

Judah M. Cohen, 2003
Through the Sands of Time: A History of the Jewish Community of St. Thomas, U.S. Virgin Islands

Ava F. Kahn and Marc Dollinger, editors, 2003
California Jews

Naomi W. Cohen, 2003
The Americanization of Zionism, 1897–1948

Seth Farber, 2003
An American Orthodox Dreamer: Rabbi Joseph B. Soloveitchik and Boston's Mamonides School

Amy L. Sales and Leonard Saxe, 2003
"How Goodly Are Thy Tents": Summer Camps as Jewish Socializing Experiences

Gary P. Zola, editor, 2003
The Dynamics of American Jewish History: Jacob Rader Marcus's Essays on American Jewry

To the graduates of the

Hebrew Union College-Jewish Institute of Religion . . .

past, present, and future

whom Jacob Rader Marcus regarded as his legacy

Contents

Part III—Marcus's Bibliography

Acknowledgments

It is a pleasure to recognize the many individuals and institutions who lent their support to the publication of this particular volume. If any scholar in the field of American Jewish history can be said to have succeeded Dr. Marcus as the proverbial "Dean of American Jewish historians," the laurel would undoubtedly belong to my beloved teacher and colleague, Jonathan D. Sarna. In reading my work, Professor Sarna never fails to insure that the final draft is significantly improved as a result of his critical eye and his vast warehouse of knowledge. I am grateful for the encouragement, help, and support he invested in this particular publication. I am also deeply indebted to Professor Pam Nadell of American University and Dr. Lance J. Sussman of Knesseth Israel Congregation in Philadelphia, and Dr. Henry Winkler, President Emeritus of the University of Cincinnati for their excellent suggestions that, no doubt, made this a better volume in the final analysis. A special word of gratitude goes to my colleague and friend, Dr. Frederic Krome, academic associate at The Marcus Center and managing editor of *The American Jewish Archives Journal*. Dr. Krome's support, guidance, and editorial advice has been both unstinting and invaluable.

No level of eloquence could properly salute the wonderful historical and archival work that is be carried out by my colleagues at The Jacob Rader Marcus Center of the American Jewish Archives (AJA). The Marcus Center's archival professionals, Kevin Proffitt, Dorothy Smith, Melinda McMartin, Christine Crandall, and Alison Stankrauff never falter in their helpful efforts. It is their responsibility to archive all of the photographs and documents that appear in this volume, and they located each one in the spirit of helpful support that has become synonymous with The Marcus Center's name. Several Marcus Center interns contributed their efforts to the publication of this volume: Claire Krome, Rabbi Geri Newburge, and Rabbi Jeff Wildstein. The archivists and I would be remiss if we did not recognize the loyal efforts of Ina Remus, the AJA's project historian and support staffers Camille Servizzi, Elise Nienaber, Ruth Kreimer, and Phil Reekers. It is a special pleasure to acknowledge Ms. Eleanor Lawhorn, The Marcus Center's executive secretary, and Ms. Lisa B. Frankel, director of programs and administration, for their indefatigable loyalty and much appreciated encouragement over the past many years.

Without the Hebrew Union College-Jewish Institute of Religion, there would not be an American Jewish Archives. The school's Board of Governors deserve much praise for their decision to respond affirmatively back in 1947 to Dr. Marcus's appeal to expand the institution's archives into "a national institution" that would seek to collect, preserve, and make available for research materials on the history of Jews and Jewish communities in the Western Hemisphere, but primarily in the United States. For more than fifty years, HUC-JIR has supported and generously endowed the AJA's efforts. Special thanks are due to HUC-JIR's president, Dr. David Ellenson, and Dr. Norman J. Cohen, HUC-JIR's provost, who have been unflagging in their support of my professional endeavors.

I wish to express my sincere appreciation to Phyllis Deutsch and Jessica Stevens, able editors at University Press of New England. Their guidance, counsel, and attention to detail facilitated the successful completion of this volume.

Finally, I wish to acknowledge the loving contributions that my precious family make to any project in which I am involved. I thank my dearest, Stefi, and my darlings, Mandi, Jory, Jeremy, and Samantha, whose love and affection make life so joyous and fulfilling. Ultimately, it is their love and support that fuels my desire to create and contribute.

Cincinnati, Ohio   G.P.Z.
September 2002
Rosh Hashanah 5763

Introduction

Jacob Rader Marcus and the
Dynamics of American Jewish History

— GARY PHILLIP ZOLA

Jacob Rader Marcus (1896–1995) was a scholar, professor, and rabbi. He played a leading role in the development of American Jewish history as an academic discipline. Unquestionably, he was one of the field's seminal figures. His long professional career spanned most of the twentieth century. When Marcus began to concentrate his efforts on the history of Jewish life in North America, American Jewish history had not yet become a defined field of academic specialization. In fact, his doctoral thesis was in general history as the authorities at the University of Berlin were unwilling to approve a dissertation that focused on Jewish history. During the early part of his academic career, Marcus published books on German Jewish history and Medieval Jewish history. Nevertheless, as the essays in this volume demonstrate, the first sparks of interest in studying the American Jew appeared when Marcus was still in rabbinical school. A major shift in focus began to occur in the late 1930s and early 1940s, when Marcus recognized the fact that the American Jewish community was destined to become—in the wake of the Nazi regime's bestial annihilation of European Jewry—the most important Jewish community in the world. This realization spurred his desire to retrieve, preserve, and conceptualize the history of the heretofore unacclaimed heritage of United States Jewry, an interest that immediately became a lifelong passion.[1]

During the course of his long and productive career, Marcus published more than three hundred books and articles on the history of American Jewry.[2] In addition to the prodigiousness of his historical writings, Marcus was among the very first trained historians to apply a modern critical methodology to the writing of American Jewish history (a methodology he referred to as "the scientific approach"). Moreover, as Jonathan D. Sarna points out, he was the first trained historian of the Jewish people born in the United States and the first to devote his scholarly energies full-time to

1. See Jonathan D. Sarna, "Jacob Rader Marcus (1896–1995)," in this volume.
2. A complete bibliography of Marcus's publications appears as an appendix to this volume.

the field of American Jewish history. In 1941, he began teaching what was, most probably, the first required university-level course in American Jewish history.[3] He not only studied and taught the history of North American Jewry, he churned out scholarly volumes on colonial and early American Jewish history. He also labored strenuously to publish books of primary documents so that those interested in the subject would have access to the basic source materials that they needed to gain an even keener understanding of the American Jewish past.

In 1947, Marcus—with the support of his friend and classmate, Nelson Glueck, the newly elected president of Hebrew Union College in Cincinnati (HUC)—convinced HUC's Board of Governors to establish an American Jewish Archives (AJA) on the school's Cincinnati campus. Marcus became the AJA's founding director, and he directed the institution from its fledgling beginnings until his death in 1995, during which time it grew into one of the world's largest and most significant catalogued collections of archival material documenting the history of Jewish life in North America.[4]

When the AJA was only one year old, in 1948, Marcus launched a biannual periodical wherein he promised to publish "at least one article of scientific calibre" as well as a listing of the important documents that the AJA was acquiring.[5] For nearly forty-seven years he edited this "bulletin" which evolved into a major academic publication. Today, *The American Jewish Archives Journal,* which is mailed to more than six thousand individuals and institutions, is one of only two scholarly journals in the world devoted exclusively to publication of articles on the entire scope of American Jewish history.[6]

3. See *HUC Course Catalogue,* 1941, p. 44, copy in The Jacob Rader Marcus Center of the American Jewish Archives, Cincinnati, Ohio.

4. Current information about The Marcus Center can be found at its Website: www. AmericanJewishArchives.org.

5. Jacob Rader Marcus, "The Program of the American Jewish Archives," in *American Jewish Archives* 1 (1948): 5.

6. Since volume 49 (1997), *American Jewish Archives* has been called *The American Jewish Archives Journal.* On the history of the AJA, see Randall M. Falk, *Bright Eminence: The Life and Thought of Jacob Rader Marcus: Scholar, Mentor, Counselor, for Three Generations of Rabbis and Lay Leaders of American Jewry* (Malibu, Calif.: Joseph Simon Pangloss Press, 1994: 87–97). See also Kevin Proffitt, "The American Jewish Archives: Documenting and Preserving the American Jewish Experience," *Ethnic Forum: Journal of Ethnic Studies and Ethnic Bibliography* 5 (Fall 1985): 20–29; Stanley F. Chyet, *The American Jewish Archives* (Cincinnati: American Jewish Archives, 1972); and Jacob R. Marcus, "The American Jewish Archives," *The American Archivist* 23, no. 1 (January 1960): 57–61.

Just as Harry A. Wolfson's (1887–1974) name became professionally linked to Harvard and Salo W. Baron's (1895–1989) to Columbia, so too did Marcus's name become synonymous with that of Hebrew Union College in Cincinnati. He was barely fifteen years old when he matriculated to HUC in 1911 and, with the exception of his two years of military service during World War I and his years of graduate study in Europe, he spent the entirety of his life either as a student or a faculty member at HUC in Cincinnati. Ordained a rabbi in 1920, Marcus had no desire to pursue a career in the pulpit.[7] He jumped at the opportunity to work at HUC as an instructor in Bible and Rabbinics. When his teacher, HUC history professor Gotthard Deutsch (1859–1921) died unexpectedly, Marcus was asked to take charge of the curriculum's courses in Jewish history. He quickly realized that if he hoped to secure his future in the field of higher Jewish education, he would need to pursue advanced graduate studies. He left Cincinnati in the summer of 1922 to spend four years earning his Ph.D. from the University of Berlin. Just before his return to Cincinnati in the fall of 1926, he spent several months visiting Palestine, where he had hoped to master spoken Hebrew. Once Marcus resumed his duties at HUC in Cincinnati, he never left and never retired. To the very year of his death, he taught Jewish history to rabbinical students.

Marcus was always one of the most popular figures on the HUC faculty, and for many of the school's alumni "the Doctor" (as he was often called) became "the rabbi's rabbi."[8] In later years, he explained his popularity by pointing out, with tongue in cheek, that he was the only HUC faculty member who spoke intelligible English! He was, in fact, a good listener and a loyal friend. Although he was deeply devoted to his scholarly pursuits, he was mindful of the fact that his graduate students were preparing themselves to enter the American rabbinate. No matter how large his reservoir of knowledge and erudition grew, Marcus never lost touch

7. In 1920, Rabbi Max Heller of New Orleans was looking for an assistant. He asked his friend, Dr. Gotthard Deutsch of the HUC faculty, which ordinee he would recommend. Deutsch identified Marcus as the most outstanding man in the class, and he tried to persuade his protégé to go to New Orleans. Marcus demurred, and Deutsch reported the news to Heller saying "[Marcus] will not go, for he wishes to be my successor." See Gotthard Deutsch to Max Heller, 18 March 1920, Box 2, Folder 2, Max Heller Papers, Mss. Coll #33, The Jacob Rader Marcus Center of the American Jewish Archives (AJA), Cincinnati, Ohio.

8. As early as 1926, the year that Marcus returned to Cincinnati, HUC student Perry Nussbaum told his hometown rabbi that "the fellows like [Marcus] very well." See Perry E. Nussbaum to Ferdinand Isserman, 22 October 1926, Box 6, Folder 8, Ferdinand Isserman Papers, Mss. Coll. #6, AJA, Cincinnati, Ohio. For additional information on Marcus's popularity down through the years, see Falk, *Bright Eminence.*

with the active rabbinate. From his perch in Cincinnati, he advised hundreds of rabbis on a wide range of problems. In fact, he himself was intensely involved in the affairs of the Central Conference of American Rabbis (CCAR) and, from 1949 to 1951, he was CCAR president, the first HUC faculty member elected to that office since Isaac Mayer Wise founded the rabbinical organization in 1889.[9]

Marcus's influential role in the CCAR provided him with a valuable platform to enlist rabbinic support for the field of American Jewish history in general and the AJA in specific. Each year, he wrote a letter to his students asking them to contribute monies from their discretionary funds to support his work. In themselves, these annual solicitations convey a great deal about Marcus's remarkable personality and wonderful sense of humor.[10] Equally important, he urged his former students to be on the lookout for primary source materials that deserved to be preserved in the AJA. His love for the subject he studied was infectious; he inspired many rabbinic students to complete important research projects in American Jewish history.[11] A select group of his students went on to earn doctorate degrees and join their teacher as major scholars in the field.[12] The growth of scholarly research in the field of American Jewish history as well as the remarkable burgeoning of the AJA's collection owes much to Marcus's role as a beau ideal to a large number of HUC rabbinic alumni. In 1978, the CCAR named Marcus its "Honorary President." The honorific title, Marcus gratefully acknowledged, was ". . . the greatest honor that a rabbi can receive in the [Reform] movement."[13]

Jacob Marcus's roster of professional accomplishments is as impressive

9. Isaac Mayer Wise (1819–1900), founder of both the College and the Union of American Hebrew Congregations, was the CCAR's president from the year it was founded (1889) to his death in 1900.

10. See *All Hail to a Prince of a Schnorrer: The Collected Schnor Letters of Dr. Jacob Rader Marcus* (Cincinnati: American Jewish Archives, 1996).

11. Examples of the work that Marcus's rabbinic students carried out include Earl A. Grollman, "Dictionary of American Jewish Biography in the Seventeenth Century," *American Jewish Archives* 3, no. 1 (1950): 3–10; Joseph R. Rosenbloom, *A Biographical Dictionary of Early American Jews: Colonial Times through 1800* (Lexington: University of Kentucky Press, 1960); Joseph Buchler, "The Struggle for Unity: Attempts at Union in American Jewish Life: 1654–1868," *American Jewish Archives* 2, no. 1 (June 1949): 21–46.

12. The rabbinic disciples who have published in the field of American Jewish history include Stanley F. Chyet (1931–2002), Bertram W. Korn (1918–1979), Malcolm Stern (1915–1994), Lance J. Sussman (1954–), Allan Tarshish (1907–1982), and Gary P. Zola (1952–).

13. Falk, *Bright Eminence*, 76.

as it is long. He participated in numerous scholarly organizations and he associated with many other pioneering figures who contributed to the field of American Jewish history, including Salo W. Baron, Oscar Janowsky (1900–1993), Max Kohler (1871–1934), and Lee M. Friedman (1871–1957). For many years, he served on the Board of Directors of the Jewish Publication Society of America (JPS), where he chaired the influential Publications Committee from 1949 to 1954. This post provided him with the opportunity to influence the direction of Jewish book publishing in the United States. Marcus also played a prominent role in the American Jewish Historical Society (AJHS), and served as that organization's president from 1955 to 1958.[14] In 1954, American Jews took note of the fact that three hundred years had passed since the first Jewish community took root on the North American continent. Marcus served as a member of the tercentenary's academic council, which sought to use the anniversary as an occasion to advance the study of the American Jewish experience.[15]

Though Marcus never occupied a pulpit, congregational rabbis never hesitated to ask him for help when they found themselves in a political quandary. He also proffered strategic advice to executives and other influential figures who led the various organizations in which he was active. Although possessed of a warm countenance and charming demeanor, Marcus almost always had a distinct point of view. He expressed his opinions frankly, and he typically dispensed advice that was directive as well as diplomatic. Historians who explore his personal papers in greater depth will be better able to analyze the full extent of Marcus's influence on affairs of organizations such as the CCAR, HUC, the AJHS, the JPS, Cincinnati's Jewish Community Relations Council, as well as many other organizations with which he was associated. As a result of the many posts he held and the many influential individuals he counseled and advised, Marcus unquestionably influenced the course of American Jewish life during the last half of the twentieth century.[16]

14. Jonathan D. Sarna, *JPS: The Americanization of Jewish Culture 1888–1988* (Philadelphia: Jewish Publication Society, 1988).

15. On the significance of the tercentenary, see the essay by Arthur A. Goren, "The 'Golden Decade': 1945–1955," in *The Politics and Public Culture of American Jews* (Bloomington: Indiana University Press, 1999), 186–204.

16. For an example of how Marcus counseled HUC president Nelson Glueck, see Jacob Rader Marcus, [Memorandum to President Nelson Glueck concerning Latz Family contribution, 11 February 1960], Box 1, Folder 8, Nelson Glueck Papers, Mss. Coll. #160, AJA, Cincinnati, Ohio. For an example of advice that Marcus offered to rabbinical colleagues,

Little wonder that students and colleagues dubbed Marcus the "Dean of American Jewish historians." He lived a long life and maintained his scholarly productivity into his late nineties (with two major volumes appearing posthumously). As he approached the centenary of his birth, he became fond of declaring that he not only studied American Jewish history, he *was* American Jewish history! In light of his significant scholarly and academic accomplishments in the field, few would quibble with the assertion.[17]

The Evolution of an American Jewish Historian

The first decade of Jacob Rader Marcus's career served as a training ground that laid the foundations of the perspective he would eventually bring to his study of the American Jew. His earliest writings on the American Jewish experience, those that appeared before he traveled to Berlin to earn his doctorate, concentrated on the social and religious challenges that confronted the life of the American Jew. These early writings evince the impact of Marcus's formative personal experiences. He was the child of East European Jewish immigrants, raised in the American heartland of West Virginia, and became a rabbinic student at a liberal Jewish seminary in Cincinnati. During the course of his rabbinical studies, he enlisted in the United States Army and served in Europe during World War I. All of these experiences contributed to the shaping of his character and perspective on the world.[18]

In retrospect, it is an intriguing happenstance that one of Marcus's

---

see Jacob Rader Marcus to Norman Gerstenfeld, 29 September 1953, Washington Hebrew Congregation (Washington D.C.), Nearprint Geographies File, AJA, Cincinnati, Ohio. With regard to Marcus's influence on the field of history, see his remarkable exchange of correspondence with Cecil Roth, Box 71, AJA Collection, Mss. Coll. #687, AJA, Cincinnati, Ohio. Finally, it is a little known fact that Marcus was one of the founders and leaders of the Jewish Community Relations Council in Cincinnati. See Jewish Community Relations Council Collection, Mss. Coll. #202, AJA, Cincinnati, Ohio.

17. *United States Jewry, 1776–1985*, 3 vols. (Detroit: Wayne State University Press, 1989–1993), vol. I, 14.

18. It is important to note that during this early stage in his career, Marcus's modest financial circumstances drove him to compose articles for periodicals that paid their authors by the word. See Joseph Jacobs to Jacob Marcus, 27 January 1916, Box 1, Folder 1, Jacob Rader Marcus Papers, Mss. Coll. #210, AJA, Cincinnati, Ohio.

first publications, written more than two decades before he turned his scholarly attention to the history of American Jewry, constituted a manifesto on the prospect of Jewish life in America. This inaugural essay—written while he was yet a student rabbi at HUC—champions a theme that would ultimately become a leitmotif throughout the course of Marcus's writings on American Jewry: Judaism in the America nation will be able to thrive and distinguish itself as long as Jewish education and Jewish cultural life become a high priority on the Jewish communal agenda.

Similarly, the essays he wrote during and immediately following his period of service in the United States Army bespeak the lessons he learned as a Jewish soldier in a predominantly Christian milieu. These experiences aroused his concern over how quickly Jewish soldiers—many of whom were children of East European Jewish immigrants—were willing to abandon their Jewish associations under the influence of secular American culture. He observed how powerfully the Young Men's Christian Associations (YMCA) attracted the participation of Jewish soldiers who had no comparable Jewish outlet. Stressing the critical importance of an indigenous American Jewish culture, Marcus calls on American Jewry to intensify its commitment to Jewish education and to enhance the community's organizational infrastructure. All in all, this early phase of Marcus's career was characterized by the young rabbi's efforts to reform the American Jewish community through the creation of organizations that would serve the educational, religious, and cultural needs of American Jewry.

By the early 1930s, Marcus entered what might perhaps be termed a "second phase" of his career development. Having completed his graduate studies and established himself as a capable teacher and promising scholar, a maturing Marcus focused his attention on the emerging role that American Jewry was destined to play in the worldwide struggle for Jewish communal continuity and survival. He wrote about the historical forces that influenced Jewish mass migrations and their subsequent impact on the creation of Jewish communities around the world. It is during this period that Marcus first introduced his concept of "omniterritoriality": the enduring necessity of maintaining numerous centers of Jewish life around the globe. Jews, Marcus believed, must never place all of their survival eggs in one territorial basket. As long as there were many centers of Jewish life, Jewish existence could never be completely eradicated.

Here it is interesting to note in passing that Marcus's notion of omni-territoriality was not synonymous with Classical Reform Judaism's vision of "the mission of Israel." Marcus's concept was based on history rather than theology; it reflected experience not ideology. This is why, though not himself a Zionist, Marcus was able to appreciate the efforts of those who sought to create a vibrant Jewish center in the Middle East. The continuity of Jewish life depended, he believed, on the coexistence of flourishing Jewish centers in various corners of the globe.

In light of his notion of omniterritoriality, it is easy to understand why the utter devastation of European Jewry during World War II led to a third phase in Marcus's career as a Jewish historian. The annihilation of the great European centers of Jewish culture turned his historical interests inward to American Jewry—its past and future. While many may regard this period as the point at which Marcus "switched" from German Jewish history to American Jewish history, it may be more accurate to view this stage in Marcus's development as a time of "shifting" focus. Marcus insisted that his courses on Jewish history at HUC never ignored Jewish life in the American nation. By the late 1930s, the ideas and concepts that he had been developing from the earliest days of his career now congealed to shape his consuming interest in the history of American Jewry.[19]

In the aftermath of World War II, the United States of America had become a superpower. The American nation was thrust onto the main stage of world events. What was true of America was true for American Jewry. The tragic results of the Holocaust had, in a few short years, transformed the American Jewish community into the largest and potentially most important center of Jewish life in the world. Marcus, now an experienced and sophisticated scholar, instinctively recognized that United States Jewry was in need of a history that suited its emerging prominence. The phrase he coined articulated a conviction that animated his work in the field of American Jewish history: "a people that is not conscious of its past has no assurance of a future."[20]

Consequently, in this "third phase" of his scholarly development, Marcus devoted practically all of his energy to retrieving and reconstructing an American Jewish past. His prospectus outlining the mission of the American Jewish Archives elucidates this point, as does his address

19. See "A *Moment* Interview with Jacob Rader Marcus," by Elinor Grumet, in this volume.
20. Jacob Rader Marcus, "The Archives Story," publicity pamphlet from 1959, a copy of which can be found in the collections of The Jacob Rader Marcus Center.

on the tercentenary of Jewish life in North America. Simultaneously, he called on American Jewry to meet its obligations as the preeminent Jewish community during the last half of the twentieth century. This is the core of his message to the JPS; Marcus told the JPS that it must now conceive of itself as a world class cultural reservoir whose mission it is to enrich Jewish culture around the world. It was also during this period that Marcus emphasized his belief that Judaism in America—in the American synagogue and in American Jewish institutions—must embrace the "ethos of Americanism" that now characterized most of America's Jews. As an influential voice that urged American Jewry to embrace its place in a new post-Holocaust world Jewish order, Marcus played an important role in the ascension of American Jewish scholarship as a whole during the last half of the twentieth century.

Finally, it is important to remember that this man's career was fundamentally an alloy composed of two cardinal elements: Marcus the rabbi and Marcus the scholar. The essays in this volume contribute to our understanding of how "Rabbi Marcus" and "Dr. Marcus" matured and evolved concomitantly. His writings demonstrate that his concept of history was informed by a religious perspective; a secular critical historian would not have written about the past in the way that Marcus did. Toward the end of his life, Marcus embraced this tension; he made no apologies for it. The historian, he noted, could not "jump out of his skin." He insisted that he was "devoted to the critical method" of scholarship, but simultaneously he declared himself a loyal partisan of his subject matter: "I like Jews," he wrote, "I am convinced that they are an unusually gifted lot." Throughout the chronological flow of the essays in this volume, a reader can discern the author's evolving struggle to find a proper balance between what Marcus himself once called a "pardonable filiopietism" and "the desire to create a new American historiography which will more truly reflect the growth of the American people."[21]

∼

Although Jacob Rader Marcus's contributions as a historian have received a modest degree of recognition—most recently in a series of essays in *The American Jewish Archives Journal*—to date there has been no attempt to analyze the ideological foundations that shaped his pioneering ideas about

---

21. Jacob Rader Marcus, *United States Jewry*, vol. I, 14; and *idem*, *Memoirs of American Jews, 1775–1865*, vol. I (New York: Ktav Publishing House, 1974), 5.

the American Jew and the American Jewish experience. Moreover, little has been said about the various contemporary influences that shaped Marcus's perspective on the history of the American Jew. The essays selected for this volume are intended to serve as an initial effort at filling this gap.

By gathering together a collection of Marcus's thematic essays, it is possible to shed greater light on the scholar's foundational ideas about the character of American Jewish history. Some historians have suggested that a large portion of Marcus's work, particularly the numerous documentary collections he published, have proved to be largely descriptive and, at times, short on historical analysis. Marcus himself once admitted that if he "leaned over in the direction of detail," he did so purposefully. He disapproved of historians who were "long on generalizations and short on data." Moreover, as a pioneering scholar in a relatively unexplored field of research, Marcus recognized that without a massive supply of "the *stoff*" of history, the primary source material, a historian's ability to offer useful analysis and meaningful interpretation was severely hampered. Yet Marcus bluntly rejected any suggestion that the fact had any value in itself. "Interpretation of facts," he wrote, "is imperative, for history is the precipitate of interpretation." Clearly, he devoted a massive effort to quarrying the raw materials with which any analysis of American Jewish history must necessarily begin, but as the essays in this volume exemplify, Marcus was continually occupied with the task of interpreting the past even as he was building up a repository of documents that would be an indispensable resource for any serious student of the American Jewish past.[22]

It should be noted that Marcus did not view himself as an essayist. In fact, he counseled his students to focus their scholarly energies on books and not articles. Books, he insisted, offered authors their only hope for immortality. In Marcus's opinion, stand-alone articles were, by their very nature, ephemeral. Generally, he followed his own advice, though as a very young scholar he (like most academics of modest means) wrote articles for journals that paid their authors by the word.[23] At some point in

22. With regard to the observation that Marcus's history is fact-based, see Moses Rischin's necrology, "Jacob Rader Marcus: Historian-Archivist of Jewish Middle America," *American Jewish History* 85 (June 1997): 175–81. For quotations, see Jacob Rader Marcus, *The Colonial American Jew, 1492–1776*, 3 vols. (Detroit: Wayne State University Press, 1970), vol. I, xxvi–xxvii.

23. It seems likely that Marcus's first publication for pay, "Mendele Mocher Seforim," appeared in the *American Hebrew* (18 February 1916). On the *American Hebrew*, see Robert Singerman, "The American Jewish Press, 1823–1983," *American Jewish History* 73 (1983–1984): 424.

the late 1930s or early 1940s, Marcus began the practice of publishing in pamphlet form many of the major addresses he had been invited to deliver. He distributed these pamphlets to students and colleagues. Each of the articles in this volume was written for a specific audience and, oftentimes, for a particular occasion. Consequently, each essay stands on its own merits. Yet all of the essays in this book contribute to our understanding of Jacob Marcus's ideas about the dynamics of the American Jewish experience. When read collectively, the foundational values that influenced Marcus's thinking about the American Jewish experience come into bold relief.

This volume begins with Jonathan D. Sarna's important necrology on Marcus, which originally appeared in *The American Jewish Year Book* (1997). This essay provides the reader with a broad evaluative overview of Marcus's life and career. Following Sarna's essay, we have reprinted Elinor Grumet's revealing interview with Marcus, which originally appeared in *Moment Magazine* in 1981. Grumet's interview, which took place when Marcus was eighty-five years old, sheds light on how Marcus himself analyzed his life and career. The bulk of this volume consists of eleven historical essays written by Marcus over a period of seventy years, ranging from one of his very first publications in 1916 to what he conceived to be his farewell address to the rabbis of his beloved CCAR in 1989.

The Dynamics of American Jewish History

In light of the fact that the articles in this volume span nearly three quarters of a century, headnotes have been supplied in an attempt to provide readers with a historical context for each article. These introductions also strive to summarize the central themes that appear in each article. When these essays are considered in totality, a unifying framework emerges. Five broad themes informed Marcus's conceptual approach to the study of American Jewish history:

1. *American Jewish history is consistently influenced by the total historical experience of the Jewish people.*

The essays in this volume repeatedly emphasize the view that the American Jewish experience is inextricably linked to the totality of Jewish history. "The Jews [of America] are heirs of a great culture;" Marcus once wrote, "their fathers wrote the Bible . . ." He first encountered this idea during his years at the University of Berlin in the early 1920s when he studied with Germany's leading Jewish scholars and was exposed to the historical writings of Heinrich Graetz (1817–1891) and Simon Dubnow (1861–1941). Marcus was deeply impressed with the various ways in which these Jewish historians attempted to conceptualize the broad sweep of Jewish history. Later in life, he applied many of the ideas he learned during this period to the study of the American Jewish experience.[24]

In his necrology on Marcus, Sarna notes that Marcus was especially influenced by Simon Dubnow's notion of "Diaspora nationalism," an ideology that asserted that in spite of the fact that Jews have lived within other civilizations and without a land of their own, a knowledge of their own distinct history enabled them to successfully maintain a national consciousness. Marcus adopted this ideology, and it undoubtedly fueled his drive to make American Jewry cognizant of its own history. Also following Dubnow, Marcus believed that Jewish history in the Diaspora is inextricably bound to the history of the civilization within which Jews lived. Marcus taught that the "interrelationship and interaction, within the life of the individual Jew and the Jewish community, of the Jewish heritage and the American environment" constituted the essence of American Jewish history.[25]

The extraordinary breadth of Marcus's Jewish education and, especially, his knowledge of Jewish history made him keenly aware of the fact that the study of American Jewish history must be seen as part of a Jewish historical continuum. Thus he began his account of American Jewish history with the story of how Jewish life "took root 3500 years ago in a Near Asiatic environment":

> This religion and its followers have lived through a variety of cultures and tremendous inner changes down to the present day. The American Jew with his composite background, stemming from Slavonic East Europe, or Germanic Central Europe, or Iberian Southwestern Europe, is now in the process of evolving a type of Judaism in this new Anglo-Saxon, Christian environment which will permit him to be all-Jewish and all-American.[26]

24. Marcus studied with many prominent scholars, including Ismar Elbogen (1874–1943), Leo Baeck (1873–1956), and Fritz Baer (1888–1980).

25. On Dubnow, see Michael A. Meyer, *Ideas of Jewish History* (New York: Behrman House, 1974), 1, 247–69. See also Sarna, "Jacob Rader Marcus," in this volume. For the quotation, see Marcus, "The Program of the American Jewish Archives," 3.

26. See "The Program of the American Jewish Archives," 3.

To fully understand the American Jewish past, Marcus insisted, the historian must bear in mind that this community is in fact another link in the long chain of Jewish history.

2. *American Jewish history has a practical benefit; it illuminates our understanding of contemporary issues in American Jewish life.*

In the Baccalaureate Address he delivered to the students graduating from State Teachers College of the State University of New York, Marcus reminded his audience that there is a "pragmatic value" in the study of history. "The student of history can learn from the past not only what to do, but also what not to do. History has something to teach us." For Marcus, the study of American Jewish history was didactically useful. He maintained, again following the ideas of Graetz and Dubnow, that a knowledge of the Jewish past serves as a pivotal factor in maintaining the Jewish people's national character even when living as a subgroup of a larger host culture. His earliest essays demonstrate that he was inclined toward this view years before he first read Dubnow as a doctoral student.[27]

In addition to the practical role it plays in the corporate survival of the Jewish people, the study of history also provides Jews with a "perspective" on their own contemporary realities. This "perspective," he maintained, provides Jewish leaders with an enhanced ability "to assess what is happening, to sense the direction in which Jewry is moving." The ability to assess and prepare for the unfolding future is a critical factor in safeguarding the continuity of Jewish life. Whether he was arguing for the establishment of social service organizations for Jewish soldiers in the aftermath of World War I, or rationalizing why the Zionist movement played a significant role in defining the future of Jewish life, or motivating the Jewish Publication Society of America to expand its mission, Marcus's essays repeatedly insisted that "a perceptive community can then plan socially and, if successful, assert itself as the subject, not merely the object, of history."[28]

Finally, the study of American Jewish history has a practical value for members of the general American society as well. Summarizing the history of Jewry during the colonial period of American history, for example, Marcus reminded his readers that the American Jew, "together with

---

27. See *Pedagogue's Progress*, 2. See also Marcus, *United States Jewry*, vol. I, 20–21.
28. Meyer, *Ideas of Jewish History*, xi; Marcus, *United States Jewry*, vol. I, 20–21.

all dissenters . . . helped teach his neighbor religious tolerance. The fruit of this tolerance was respect for the personality of the individual." In this way, Jewry's achievements during this formative epoch of the American nation shed light on the cultural and social evolution of the nation as a whole. Just as Jewish history during the colonial period illuminates our understanding of American history during that same epoch, so it is with every chapter of the American Jewish experience.[29]

3. *American Jewish history possesses inspirational value; it enhances Jewish pride and strengthens Jewish identity.*

In addition to the utilitarian function of American Jewish history, Marcus emphasized the inspirational value of American Jewish history. Historians have noted that for the modern Jew the study of the past is hardly an academic matter alone; history for the modern Jew serves as a cornerstone of self-understanding. Marcus consistently underscored the important role that history plays in helping to strengthen the individual's awareness of and pride in his or her Jewish identity.

If there is one idea that runs like a thread throughout his essays in this volume, it is Marcus's dogged insistence that the study of the past maximizes the likelihood that Jews will become "proud exponents of the best in our Jewish heritage." In the first essay in this volume, he calls upon American Jewry to study its heritage. This knowledge will kindle a spirit of pride that, in turn, will sponsor a renaissance in American Jewish life: "Oh, that we could realize . . . our debt to the past; the debt we owe of continuing the great work that has been going on for the past three thousand years . . ." Forty years later, Marcus reiterated this same appeal in his essay commemorating three hundred years of American Jewish history. Responding to his own question as to how the American Jew can secure his or her own future, Marcus insisted that the answer lies in the study of the past. The Jew who takes pride in the past will absorb its ethical lessons: "Every Jew should so live and conduct himself," he wrote, "as if the future welfare of his people were dependent upon his own personal moral activity."[30]

In feting the centennial anniversary of the Hebrew Union College, Marcus again urged his readers to take pride in the institution's remarkable academic, spiritual, and educational achievements. A tiny school that began with barely a dozen students had managed to foster the "larg-

29. Marcus, *Colonial American Jew,* vol. I, 1341–42.
30. "America: The Spiritual Center of Jewry"; "Three Hundred Years in America."

est liberal religious group in the world" with rabbinic alumni who teach and inspire in all corners of the globe. This same idea reappears in the last essay in this volume: "We Jews pride ourselves that we are a civilized humanitarian folk. Let us manifest it in all of our actions. Our history demands that we continue our quest for Zion. Zion is our highest Jewish self in projection; it is the ideal we seek but we can only glimpse."[31]

American Jewish history, Marcus believed, evokes a sense of pride that, in turn, spurs a commitment to Jewish survival. As one American Jewish historian recently observed, "in order for a community that develops within the culture and space of another nation to survive, it needs to be aware of its special historic experience, which contains a sense of its worthwhileness."[32] According to Marcus, the Jew's historic experience, "what the Jew has learned after 3,000 years of bitter experience," constitutes a spiritual lesson for the whole world. By taking pride in their history, he maintained, the Jewish people can be summoned "to heroic achievement." This realization makes American Jewish history a critical factor in American Jewry's survival. Through the study of their past, Marcus repeatedly emphasized, American Jews would become intelligently conscious of their future as Jews and as Americans.[33]

4. *American Jewish history is, at its core, the study of how the lives of individual Jews have interrelated with their ethnic-religious community in America.*

In the preface to his four-volume magnum opus, *United States Jewry,* Marcus declared: "I am committed to the thesis that the story of the Jew in this land lies not in the vertical eminence of the few but in the horizontal spread of the many." As a twenty-year-old rabbinic student, Jacob Marcus had already begun to discern this idea that would ultimately become a cornerstone of his historical methodology. Though there have been many prominent American Jews, Marcus's historical eye was constantly fixed on the common Jew's efforts to "create and further a distinct community with its synagogues, schools, and charities."[34]

---

31. "Genesis: College Beginnings," 17; "Testament," 6.

32. Henry L. Feingold, *Lest Memory Cease: Finding Meaning in the American Jewish Past* (Syracuse: Syracuse University Press, 1996), 7

33. Marcus, *United States Jewry,* vol. I, 14; "New Literary Responsibilities"; and *American Jewish Archives,* 5, no. 1 (January 1953): 4.

34. Marcus, *United States Jewry,* vol. I, 15–16.

In his first essay on American Jewish life, he exhorted his readers to be mindful of the fact that each individual Jew was critically important to the future of Jewish communal life: "The American Jew must, if he would save himself, awake and take an active, all-absorbing interest in all things Jewish . . ." Marcus's essays on the Jewish soldier during World War I, also written early in his career, expressed his fears that the organized Jewish community was missing a crucial opportunity "to step into the lives of myriads of Jews." Marcus repeatedly returned to this idea, insisting that the Jewish experience in America consisted of a symbiotic relationship between individual Jews and the larger Jewish community with which they associated.[35]

In later years, Marcus articulated this theme with ever greater clarity and certainty. The primary mission of the American Jewish Archives, he wrote, was to assemble the documents and records that would furnish the historian with data needed to study the lives and careers of "individual Jews." Yet the total understanding of the American Jewish experience emerged through the interaction and interrelationship of these individual Jewish lives with the American Jewish community.

During his career, Marcus published many volumes of primary source material on the history of American Jewry. This initiative was spurred, in part, by a desire to make these documents widely accessible. Yet Marcus's interest in publishing individual memoirs and personal correspondence was also rooted in his conviction that these records exposed the "heart of the Jewish experience" in America. From an aggregate of personal documents, the historian garnered knowledge about the realities of crucially important historical trends such as immigration, business life, the emergence of Jewish communal life, and so forth. As Marcus wrote in the introduction to one of those volumes, "American Jewish history is the story of *all* that happened to the Jew as an American."[36]

This focus on the individual in relation to the whole may have guided Marcus in the art of reconstructing history from a string of fetching anecdotes about the lives of Jews both outstanding and obscure. He employed these engaging illustrations to exemplify a specific characteristic of American Jewish life. For instance, his essay honoring the Hebrew

---

35. "America: The Spiritual Center of Jewry"; "Lost: Judaism in the A.E.F."
36. "The Program of the American Jewish Archives," in this volume, pp. 108–15; Marcus, *Memoirs of American Jews,* vol. I, 5.

Union College on the centennial of its founding constitutes the apotheosis of this style, filled as it is with humorous tales about individuals who attended the school.[37]

In his 1989 address to the Central Conference of American Rabbis, Marcus reminded his colleagues that sustaining the involvement of the individual Jew within the community is a critical factor in the survival of Jewish life in America. "When you survey your congregation on a Friday night," he preached, "don't count bodies, count souls." He assured them that all of Jewish history testified to the fact that ultimately the individual Jew was the most important statistic in Jewish life. "If we raise but a handful of disciples who treasure our ideals, we will survive." Yet, the Jewish individual can never be cut loose from the community. "In Jewry," Marcus wrote, "where there is no community there is no history."[38]

5. American Jewish history lends support to the historically based assertion that the Jewish experience is immortal.

At the conclusion of his essay titled "Mass Migrations of Jews and Their Effects on Jewish Life," Marcus abandons his academic tone and invokes a more exhortative style. He calls on the leaders of American Jewry to "build while others destroy, to seek for light while others writhe in the darkness of despair, to strengthen the bulwarks of civilization while others seek to shatter them." Jews are relentless in their determination to survive because they have been "trained in the crucible of the centuries to struggle with courage and dignity." To validate this assertion, he cites a verse from the Psalms as his proof-text: "I shall not die but live and declare the works of the Lord."[39]

"Jews glory in their survival," Marcus once observed, "they refuse to disappear." Undoubtedly, his views on this subject were influenced by the Jewish historians he studied—men such as Nachman Krochmal (1785–1840), Isaac Marcus Jost (1793–1860), Heinrich Graetz, and Simon Dubnow—all of whom believed in the Jewish people's immortality. As a young man, Marcus imbibed the writings of these master historians who

37. "Genesis: College Beginnings," in this volume.

38. Ibid., pp. 135–45; "Testament," in this volume, pp. 146–51; Marcus, *United States Jewry,* vol. I, 16.

39. Psalm 118:17. See also "Mass Migrations of Jews and Their Effects on Jewish Life," in this volume.

aligned themselves with the concept of an immortal Jewish people, and he made this idea his own.[40]

The notion that American Jewry constituted a great spiritual center for the Jewish people is a recurring theme in Marcus's essays. If American Jewry hoped to fulfill its destiny as a great spiritual center, then American Jews would need to create a vibrant culture. The moral lessons of their religious heritage were the source of Jewish survival—what Dubnow called Judaism's "living soul." Like many of the Jewish historians he admired, Marcus believed that civilizations and nations may rise and fall, but as long as Jews cling to their ethical legacy they can never be obliterated. Again following Dubnow, Marcus insisted that the total Jewish experience transcended territorial boundaries and the history of the land of Israel. The Jewish people's presence in all parts of the world ("omniterritoriality") was another key factor in its indestructibility.[41]

The antecedents of Marcus's concept of Jewry's immortality may be traced back to numerous sources. His thinking, for example, might be compared to that of Abraham Geiger (1810–1874) who—like Marcus—was simultaneously interested in *Wissenschaft des Judentums* (the scientific study of Judaism) and the active rabbinate. Geiger, whose religious orientation was decidedly universalist in character, believed in the spiritual union of the Jews and the other nations of the world. Marcus, too, emphasized that Judaism's universal teachings made the Jew a natural partner in the moral improvement of humankind. He regularly concluded his public lectures by pointing out that the core essence of American Jewry, indeed that of the Jewish people, had been distilled in the prophet Micah's famous maxim: "It is told thee, O man, what is good and what the Lord doth require of thee; only to do justice, love mercy and walk humbly with thy God."[42]

On the other hand, Marcus's rhetoric also mirrored the teachings of Nachman Krochmal, the man who devised the first systematic philosophy of Jewish history. Krochmal argued that in its unshakable commitment to monotheism, the Jewish people had become "teachers of the great multitude of nations." It was through this role of spiritual leadership that Jewry merited its immortality. With this contention, Marcus concurred. The American Jew has a lesson for the whole world, Marcus

40. Jacob Rader Marcus, *The American Jew, 1585–1990: A History* (Brooklyn: Carlson Publishing, Inc., 1995), 383.

41. Meyer, *Ideas of Jewish History*, 257.

42. Micah 6:8.

insisted in his final address to the Central Conference of American Rabbis, a message that is the distillate of a three thousand-year-old history:

> Our prophetic exhortations are the last and best hope of humanity. If we raise but a handful of disciples who treasure our ideals we will survive. We are an *am olom,* an eternal people; the world can never, never destroy all of us. And in that fateful moment when the earth begins to shatter, when the very heavens tremble, when the sun, the moon and the stars turn dark, when the last bomb falls and the last mushroom cloud evaporates, we, we will emerge erect, undaunted, dedicated to the hope that a day will yet come when "they shall not hurt or destroy in all my Holy Mountain, for the earth shall be full of the knowledge of the Lord as the waters cover the sea" (Isaiah 2:9).[43]

The field of American Jewish history has grown dramatically since Marcus began his work more than sixty years ago. Over the past two or three decades, hundreds of Jewish organizations, historical societies, and synagogues have established local archives in which historical documents are preserved and made available for research. Today, thousands of monographs, articles, and books have transformed what was once a barren field of study into a burgeoning academic enterprise. Where once no more than a half-dozen scholars specialized in the study of the American Jewish past, now there are hundreds of academicians and independent researchers who specialize in the field. For many years, American Jewish historians frequently overlooked the manifold contributions of the American Jewish woman. A half-century after Marcus turned his full attention to the task of reconstructing the history of American Jewry, a noteworthy number of women scholars have emerged and assumed a leading role in the field.[44] Researchers will undoubtedly continue to recover the history of American Jewry and, in doing so, exciting new research trends will certainly develop. Yet even as the body of American Jewish historiography increases, tomorrow's students will have no alternative but to make Jacob Marcus a critical point of reference from which the field's efflorescence will be gauged. In this way, Marcus's career and scholarly contributions will continue to impact upon the dynamics of American Jewish history for years to come.

43. See "Testament," in this volume, pp. 146–51.

44. This point may be illustrated by pointing to the works of this partial list of contemporary scholars: Joyce Antler, Dianne Ashton, Sylvia Barack Fishman, Naomi Cohen, Hasia Diner, Paula Hyman, Karla Goldman, Deborah Dash Moore, Pamela Nadell, Riv Ellen Prell, Shuly Rubin Schwartz, Ellen Umansky, Beth Wenger.

PART I
Marcus's Career

Jacob Rader Marcus (1896–1995)

—JONATHAN D. SARNA

Jacob Rader Marcus was the first trained historian of the Jewish people born in America and the first to devote himself fully to the scholarly study of America's Jews. Through the American Jewish Archives, which he founded in 1947, and through a parade of books—culminating in a magisterial, three-volume history entitled *The Colonial American Jew: 1492–1776* (1970) and an even larger four-volume history of *United States Jewry: 1776–1985* (1989–1993), completed in his tenth decade of life—he defined, propagated, and professionalized his chosen field, achieving renown as its founding father and dean. At the time of his death, on the evening of 14 November 1995, he was also the oldest and most beloved member of the Reform rabbinate and the senior faculty member at Hebrew Union College-Jewish Institute of Religion (Cincinnati), where he had taught for some three-quarters of a century.

Education and Training

Marcus was born on his father's thirty-first birthday, 5 March 1896, in the tiny village of New Haven, across the river from Connellsville, Pennsylvania. "New Haven was a village, the base from which all the Jewish peddlers in Southwestern Pennsylvania moved . . . to sell goods to the Slavs," he recalled in an interview in *Moment* magazine on the occasion of his eighty-fifth birthday. His father, Aaron Marcus (né Markelson, 1865–1932), and his mother, Jennie Rader Marcus née Reider, 1870–1971), were recent immigrants to America's shores, having grown up within a few miles of one another around Vidz (Widzy) in the Lithuanian province of Kovno. In the final volume of his *United States Jewry* (1993), as if to connect himself with the history that he had by then spent a lifetime researching, he recounted his father's story as an illustration of how East European Jews struggled to survive in the American hinterland:

> [Aaron] Marcus arrived in New York in 1889, worked in a brickyard and in a matzo factory, but determined to improve himself, became a

garment worker. He was discharged the first day; he had sewed two right sleeves on a jacket. Marcus then picked up a basket of notions and peddled his way to Pittsburgh. There he worked in a small machine shop for George Westinghouse at a time when this industrialist knew all of his employees by name. Then came the dreadful panic of 1893; Marcus worked for a time in a steel mill and finally when everything threatened to shut down he turned again to peddling.... Around the year 1900, now a horse-and-wagon "merchant prince," Marcus had saved enough to go into business as a shopkeeper. He moved to Homestead, set up a retail store, and within a few years a second store in the borough of Munhall. Spurred on by ambition he moved to Birmingham, Pittsburgh's South Side, the proud possessor of a small department store. Within a year or less he was bankrupt; the panic of 1907 destroyed him. By 1909 he was operating a small clothing and gent's furnishing store in Wheeling, West Virginia, unsuccessfully. Yet, ever-mindful of his religion, which was dear to him, he helped organize a congregation; he served as its president.... About the year 1915, in desperation, Marcus moved once more, this time into the mountains of central West Virginia where he operated a small general store for about seven years. He did well....

While his father struggled, young Jacob Marcus commenced his education. He attended public school in Homestead and studied Hebrew after school in an Orthodox *heder*. Homestead boasted a well-stocked public library, thanks to Andrew Carnegie, and it was there, Marcus later claimed, that his love for history first awakened, stimulated by the juvenile historical novels of George Alfred Henty. Marcus's wondrously retentive memory also displayed itself at this time, inherited, he was told, from a maternal ancestor who had been a prodigy in Talmud. But for the most part, the childhood Marcus recalled was unremarkable. Like so many children of immigrants, he experienced poverty and anti-Semitism at first hand, learned far better English than his parents ever knew, held odd jobs from a very young age, engaged in mischief, and endured the wrenching upheavals of moving each time circumstances changed and his parents set up shop in a new location, hoping that a change of place would produce a change in fortune.

During his short stay in Pittsburgh, Marcus received his first education in Bible and Jewish history at the Orthodox Sunday School of Rabbi Aaron Ashinsky's Beth Midrash Hagadol. Since Wheeling, West Virginia, his next home, offered no supplementary Jewish education under Orthodox auspices, he attended the Reform Sunday School of the Eoff Street

Temple, Congregation Leshem Shomayim. There he came to the notice of the congregation's rabbi, Harry Levi, who took him under his wing, taught him privately, and became a significant role model. It was he who first suggested to the Marcuses that they send their youngster to Hebrew Union College to study for the rabbinate, a nine-year course that in those days began in high school. When Aaron Marcus, struggling to make ends meet, found that rabbinic education at Hebrew Union College was free and that the traditionalist Jewish Theological Seminary accepted only college graduates, the die was cast. In 1911, at the age of fifteen, Marcus boarded the train for Cincinnati to attend high school and commence his rabbinical training.

Marcus grew intellectually during his student years in Cincinnati. He attended Woodward and later Hughes High School, continued on to the University of Cincinnati (B.A., 1917), and pursued his rabbinical studies in the afternoon. He also studied briefly at Lane Theological Seminary and at the University of Chicago. It was during these years that he de-cided to specialize in history. Hebrew Union College's professor of Jewish history, Gotthard Deutsch, served as his mentor, and Deutsch's approach to history—his skepticism, his reverence for facts, and his penchant for piquant details—left, as Marcus later admitted, a lasting impression:

> He became a great influence on me. In part, he influenced me because of his personality. For the most part, I was influenced by his method. He was essentially a skeptic, a realist. He believed practically nothing in history. He believed only in facts, and wanted to be pretty sure before he would accept the fact. He was in essence an annalist. . . . Deutsch em-phasized the anecdote, social history, and was very much interested in the details of the lives of individuals. I was influenced by this approach.

Marcus published his earliest articles while studying with Deutsch. The first, "America: The Spiritual Center of Jewery [sic]," anticipated what be-came one of his favorite themes: the "golden age" of American Jewry. He argued in later years that American Jewry "is the greatest Jewry the world has ever known." He also published some thirteen other articles and re-views prior to receiving his ordination. Most dealt with historical subjects; a few with the problems of Jewish soldiers in the American army.

This last subject was one that Marcus knew firsthand, for in 1917, three weeks after the United States entered World War I, he took time off from his studies and enlisted in the army. He spent two years in the service, most of it in France, and rose to the rank of second lieutenant and acting company commander in the 145th U.S. Infantry. "I am in charge of four large warehouses, not to say the supply of fuel for an area of about fifty square miles," he wrote to his classmate Morris Lazaron on 22 January 1919. "A couple of months ago I established a Friday night service and I have been able to have a minyan every Friday since." Marcus always believed that he had matured in the army. The skills that he learned there— administrative and human—served him well for the rest of his career.

Returning to Hebrew Union College in 1919, Marcus took a student pulpit in Lexington, Kentucky, wrote a long rabbinic thesis entitled "An Investigation into Polish Jewish Life of the Sixteenth Century with Special Reference to Isaac ben Abraham, Author of Hizuk Emunah," and in 1920 was duly ordained. At the suggestion of Rabbi David Philipson, the dean of Cincinnati's Reform rabbinate and an influential member of the college's board, President Kaufmann Kohler soon invited the new rabbi to join the faculty—an honor previously accorded only to David Philipson and Solomon Freehof, who had likewise joined the faculty immediately upon their ordination. Marcus held the title "instructor in Bible and Rabbinics," but in fact he served as "assistant to Dr. Deutsch in the history department." When Deutsch died unexpectedly in 1921, he took over all of his mentor's courses, earning praise from the students as "the youngest and one of the most popular members of our faculty."

A year later, in June 1922, Marcus took a leave of absence from his teaching in order to study in Germany and obtain a Ph.D. The *Hebrew Union College Monthly* reported that he was "urged on by an impulse kindled within him by his revered predecessor," but Marcus himself later claimed that he went because he felt incompetent, especially given his meager knowledge of German and modern Hebrew. Deutsch and most of the other illustrious professors at Hebrew Union College had studied in Germany; it was the acknowledged center of Jewish scholarship at that time. Only with "scientific" training and a degree from a German university, Marcus felt, could he be prepared properly for an academic career in Jewish history.

The four years abroad proved transforming and shaped Marcus's scholarship forever after. In Berlin, he sat at the feet of some of Germany's greatest historians, encountered many of Germany's foremost Jewish scholars, and even came in contact with "the essence" of Russian Jewry. "The intellectuals, the great Hebrew writers, poets, and dramatists are all here," he enthused in a letter to his friend Lazaron. Many of them, such as Simon Dubnow, Mark Wischnitzer, and Elias Tscherikower, were refugees from Bolshevism. After temporarily retreating to Kiel to immerse himself in German, Marcus returned to Berlin more resolved than ever to acquire "Sound Knowledge. Learning. Understanding . . . the ability to work scientifically . . . [and] the elusive thing that the Germans call Method."

He was "profoundly influenced" by the approach of historian Simon Dubnow, whom he read and probably met in Berlin, and decades later still identified himself, following Dubnow, as a "diaspora nationalist." Much of his understanding of American Jewry's historical role was shaped by Dubnow's model of "shifting centers." What Dubnow did for East European Jews, bringing their history "to the same plane of scholarly and scientific quality as that achieved by the *Wissenschaft des Judentums* in the West," Marcus eventually sought to do for American Jewry. He was also influenced by what he learned from Ismar Elbogen and Leo Baeck, and especially by his association with his tutor, Fritz Baer, whose scholarly techniques he never ceased to admire. Yet for all of his work in Jewish history, Marcus ultimately wrote his doctorate, at the University of Berlin, in general history, focusing on the mercantile relations between England and the Hanseatic League (1576–1585). The university authorities, he reported, declined to accept a Jewish subject.

Marcus dedicated his 1925 doctoral thesis to Antoinette ("Pretty Nettie") Brody, a young New York woman of Russian-Jewish parentage who was studying voice in Berlin. They were married in Paris soon after he received his doctorate, with his former Hebrew Union College classmate, Nelson Glueck, then a student in Berlin, serving as best man. Several months later, Marcus traveled alone to Palestine, where he attended classes at the Hebrew University and studied modern Hebrew. Near the end of his life, he told his biographer, Randall Falk, that he had been "very disappointed" with this experience, but at the time he wrote glowingly to Judah Magnes of Palestine's potential "to take upon its shoulders the task of stimulating World Jewry in a modern, progressive yet traditionally Jewish spirit," and exclaimed that "nothing in all Jewish life" was more important than the Hebrew University. In the afterglow of this trip, he wrote sympathetically in the early 1930s about "Jewish Palestine" and "Zionism and the American Jew" for the *New Orient* and the *American Scholar.* He never, then or later, became a card-carrying Zionist and always believed that America was the more important Jewish center. But he still cast his lot with those who brought about a change in Reform Judaism's attitude toward the Zionist cause.

Teacher, Counselor, and Rabbi

Marcus returned to Cincinnati in 1926 and lived there until the day he died. He spent all of his remaining years on the Hebrew Union College faculty, where he continued for almost seven decades to teach some of the school's most popular classes. He reorganized and extended the history curriculum, offered seminars in methodology, and began to focus on modern and contemporary Jewish history, even as he was frequently called upon to teach other courses far removed from his specialty. Whatever he taught, he combined careful preparation with a flawless, memorized delivery and a seemingly limitless supply of anecdotes and humorous asides that brought history alive. "The burden of stimulating interest falls on the teacher," he once wrote. "I interest my student; I never use notes. I persist in using eyeball to eyeball contact." Through the years, he taught students to read and analyze texts as well as to appreciate individual human beings, with all of their frailties and foibles. He made history relevant, entertaining, and inspiring, and students flocked to him.

Outside the classroom, Marcus became a rabbi and counselor to his students. "The most important thing in life is integrity," he preached. "Be a gentleman to everyone and remember to laugh; view the world, your work, and yourself with a smile." He was, as he put it, "psychiatrically oriented," and students quickly learned that in his study they could find sympathy, support, and guidance. Legions of students credited him with helping to sustain them through rabbinical school, and many of these same students turned to him again later, as rabbis, for help with their congregations or their personal problems. Into his nineties, he spent hours, often late into the night, counseling and consoling, finding jobs for his students, and helping those who were lonely find mates. This, he felt, was part of his rabbinic calling, and he considered it no less important than his scholarship and his teaching. His students reciprocated, electing him president of the Central Conference of American Rabbis in 1949—the first Hebrew Union College professor since Isaac Mayer Wise to be so honored—and lifetime honorary president of the conference in 1978, an honor he esteemed above all the others accorded him. During the final three decades of his life, he looked upon the Reform rabbis of the Central Conference ("his boys," as he called them, even after the college admitted women) as his own surrogate family. His wife, after years of illness, had died in 1953. His only daughter, Merle (b. 1929), to whom he was deeply attached, perished in a fire in 1965. From that time onward, he confessed in his *Moment* interview, "the world that means most to me is the rabbinical world. . . . When I lost my family, my daughter, the only child I had, people said to me in the funeral sermons, you now have five hundred sons. *That's my world.*"

Scholarship in Jewish History

Marcus's reputation as a scholar developed more slowly than his reputation as a teacher. He had a family to support—he also helped to provide for his parents and siblings during the Depression—so he spent long hours traveling on the lecture circuit, where he achieved great popularity. Teaching, too, took a great deal of his time, and he was also active in Reform Jewish affairs, in the Cincinnati Jewish community, and from 1939 onward in the Jewish Publication Society. His schedule left little room for creative scholarship. While his historical colleague at Hebrew Union College, Jacob Mann, secured his scholarly standing with an intimidating series of highly significant books on Medieval Judaism, and his rival at Columbia, Salo Baron, completed the first edition of his *Social and Religious History of the Jews*, Marcus's most important early publications consisted of a monograph on Israel Jacobson, "the founder of the Reform movement in Judaism" (1928), and a popular derivative history of German Jewry (1934), best remembered for its premature forecast that "Hitlerism will probably fall," and its too-hopeful prediction concerning German Jewry's destiny.

In 1938, Marcus published a far more important textbook, a volume of carefully edited documents dated 315–1791, entitled *The Jew in the Medieval World.* Here he displayed a singular mastery of primary literature and a prescient interest in usually neglected subjects and sources, such as women's history, the lives of Jewish laborers, and early American Jewish history. The textbook proved a great success and is still widely used. Continuing to work on neglected subjects, he embarked in the 1930s on an in-depth study of Jewish communal institutions—this at a time when communal institutions of every sort faced daunting challenges. As it turned out, Salo Baron was working on a related project, but as usual the two historians' approaches proved utterly different. Baron examined the Jewish community through a wide-angle lens, producing, in 1945, a three-volume synthetic study of its history and structure from ancient Palestine to the American Revolution. Marcus characteristically focused far more narrowly, allowing him to generalize based on all relevant primary documents. *Communal Sick-Care in the German Ghetto,* the fruits of this research and Marcus's last significant scholarly publication dealing with German Jewry, appeared in 1947. Signaling the great change that was, by then, redirecting his scholarship toward the New World, he concluded the volume with a brief appendix describing "the beginnings of the Jewish Hospital in Cincinnati."

American Jewish Historian

Marcus's interest in American Jewish history was perhaps natural, given his status as the community's first native-born professional Jewish historian. His popular writings and his surveys of "Contemporaneous Jewish History," written for the Central Conference of American Rabbis, frequently touched on American Jewish themes, and even his scholarly volumes, as we have seen, integrated American Jewish history in a way never before found in Jewish historiography. Marcus delivered a well-researched lecture on "The Americanization of Isaac Mayer Wise" in 1931, and a year later, when Rabbi Allan Tarshish became the first HUC student to propose writing a doctorate in American Jewish history, he and Tarshish "devoted much time and care to the preparation of a statement detailing the potential importance of the American Jewish community and the need for research in the field." The doctorate ("The Rise of American Judaism: A History of American Jewish Life from 1848–1881"), six years in the making, was a landmark contribution in which Marcus took a great deal of pride.

Throughout the 1930s, Marcus collected source material and urged his students to write papers in the field of American Jewish history; in 1942, celebrated as the 450th anniversary of the discovery of America, he offered what he later described as "the first required graduate course in an academic institution in American Jewish history." The 1940s saw other scholars, too, including Salo Baron and Oscar Handlin, strengthen their interest in American Jewish history. With the destruction of European Jewry and America's emergence as the undisputed center of world Jewry, the subject gained new legitimacy, if not urgency. What set Marcus apart was that he knew more than the others did, having come to the field earlier, and he alone decided in the 1940s to devote his full attention to American Jewish history; for him, Europe was now dead.

During the next half-century, Marcus worked systematically to establish American Jewish history as a scholarly discipline. He founded both the American Jewish Archives (1947) and the American Jewish Periodical Center (1956) on the campus of Hebrew Union College (Cincinnati). He served as president and later honorary president of the American Jewish Historical Society. He collected and published thousands of pages of edited primary sources. He created reference tools and a semiannual scholarly journal, *American Jewish Archives* (1948–). He encouraged students and young scholars by answering their questions and helping to fund their research. And he published book after book of his own incomparable scholarship. All of these projects sought to address the lacunae in American Jewish history that he set forth in 1951 when he published his pathbreaking two-volume study entitled *Early American Jewry:*

> [I]t is no more difficult today to write American Jewish history than it is to make bricks without clay. The clay, the sources, are still to be dug up. In this field there are no biographical or historical dictionaries, no atlases, no auxiliary works, few collected sources, no satisfactory union list of Jewish serials, no genealogical tables, not a single complete history of the American Jew that satisfies the canons of modern methodology and criticism. The basic tools with which every historian works are still missing.

He had singlehandedly created or inspired practically every one of these "basic tools" by the time his own life's work was finished.

Marcus, by his own admission, was "primarily a fact man with a capacity to interpret the facts properly." He worked whenever possible from original sources: the millions of documents and thousands of reels of microfilm reposited in the American Jewish Archives. "The fact scrubbed clean is more eternal than perfumed or rouged words," he believed, and his aim in writing American Jewish history was to "give the facts and document them" so as to distinguish "truth" from "ethnocentric schmoose." "I believe that in every discipline, every area, every subject, there has to be at least one work which supplies the *Stoff,* the raw material, if only for others to summarize, to reevaluate, and even to reject," he wrote in the preface to his *The Colonial American Jew.* Much of his life's work was directed toward that goal: to supply the *Stoff* that future students of American Jewish history might reliably build upon. When his own student Lance Sussman asked him why he did not do more with secondary literature, he replied, characteristically, that "you cannot ride two horses at the same time. . . . I dig out the facts. I don't have time for anything more than that." As a rule, he was suspicious of generalizations and theories. "I would gladly trade in all of my theories," he once told me, "for one new fact." Facts, indeed, were his greatest contribution to American Jewish history. Nobody commanded more of those facts than he did, and nobody could possibly have done more to make those facts available to succeeding generations.

Marcus never retired. He opposed compulsory retirement in principle and used his considerable political skills to win a contract from the Hebrew Union College Board of Governors permitting him to teach for as long as he wanted. He slept more as he advanced into his nineties, and his legendary sixteen-hour work days contracted. But even at age ninety-eight, he continued his lifelong habit of rising early, walking, and working at his desk far into the night. He also maintained regular attendance at the Hebrew Union College synagogue every Friday night and Saturday morning, only late in life moving up to the front row as a concession to his failing hearing.

Honors were showered upon him in his final years—awards, degrees, testimonials; in 1987 the City of Cincinnati even named the intersection where he lived Jacob Rader Marcus Square. What meant most to him, however, was finishing up his life's work. He published at least a book a year during his tenth decade, including the four volumes of *United States Jewry* and a two-volume *Concise Dictionary of American Jewish Biography*. Two more books were in press at the time of his death: *The American Jew,* a one-volume narrative history, and *The Jew in the American World,* a one-volume documentary history. Soon after his death, Brandeis University purchased his library. To help ensure that his life's work continued even after his passing, he left his entire fortune—almost four million dollars—in trust for the American Jewish Archives, renamed the Jacob Rader Marcus Center of the American Jewish Archives in his memory.[1]

---

1. Two substantial biographies of Jacob Rader Marcus have appeared: Stanley F. Chyet, "Jacob Rader Marcus—A Biographical Sketch," in *Essays in American Jewish History to Commemorate the Tenth Anniversary of the Founding of the American Jewish Archives Under the Direction of Jacob Rader Marcus* (Cincinnati: American Jewish Archives, 1958), 1–22; and Randall M. Falk, *Bright Eminence: The Life and Thought of Jacob Rader Marcus* (Malibu, Calif.: Joseph Simon Pangloss Press, 1994). In honor of his eighty-fifth birthday, he also gave a revealing interview to Elinor Grumet, published in *Moment,* March–April 1981: 75–85. *Biz Hundert un Tsvantsik,* edited by Abraham J. Peck and Jonathan D. Sarna (Cincinnati: American Jewish Archives, 1986), contains tributes and reminiscences from former students and colleagues. His 223 publications to 1978, as well as two festschrifts and other tributes are listed in *The Writings of Jacob Rader Marcus: A Bibliographic Record,* compiled by Herbert C. Zafren and Abraham J. Peck (Cincinnati: Jewish American Archives, 1978). Marcus's voluminous papers are housed at The Jacob Rader Marcus Center of the American Jewish Archives.

A *Moment* Interview
with Jacob Rader Marcus

(1981)

—ELINOR GRUMET

Editor's note:

Marcus eschewed memoirs. When Elinor Grumet interviewed the eighty-five-year-old historian for Moment Magazine *in 1981, Marcus told her flat out, "If you have enough strength to write a memoir, then you have enough strength to finish your scientific work." Ironically, this conviction which he shared with Grumet and to which, by and large, he remained loyal has made this interview so very unique and interesting. Though Marcus informed Grumet that he was "not capable of abstract or philosophic thinking," the interview is remarkably candid and revealing. Marcus insists that he aspires to "use no equivocation" and in responding to the questions posed he does not disappoint. This conversation, coinciding with the sixtieth anniversary of Marcus's appointment to the faculty of Hebrew Union College, provides us with a valuable autobiographical record in the historian's own words.*

Covering a wide range of interesting topics including his decision to study American Jewish history, Marcus discusses his thoughts on the history of the American Jewish woman, on anti-Semitism, and his outlook on the future of American Jewry. The interviewer also encourages Marcus to explain how and why he decided to establish the American Jewish Archives and the American Jewish Periodical Center.

This interview, a source document rich in content, highlights some of the central paradoxes in Marcus's life and work. He was a Zionist sympathizer but steadfastly refused to join a Zionist organization. He was a loyal Reform Jew, whose entire career was linked to the Hebrew Union College, but he defended Orthodoxy and described his own theology as being "closest to Reconstructionism." He was a man who adored his East European father, but still declared that pre–World War II German Jewry was the "cultural core of world Jewry." He confessed his disbelief in immortality, and nevertheless declared that the human soul lives on eternally somewhere ("assuming that the universe is infinite"). In short, he was at once progressive and old-fashioned—a skeptic and an optimist.

～

This spring, Jacob Rader Marcus, the iconoclastic dean of American Tenth historians, will be eighty-five, and will celebrate the completion of his sixtieth year as a teacher on the faculty of the Hebrew Union College in Cincinnati as well. He is the founder and director of the American Jewish Archives, and is Honorary President of the Central Conference of American Rabbis.

One day last summer, he was interviewed by Elinor Grumet at his office in his home in Cincinnati. They talked about his boyhood in the Ohio Valley at the turn of the century, the Reform rabbinate, and Dr. Marcus' latest book, on American Jewish women, which will appear this spring. Elinor Grumet is a Mellon Post-Doctoral Fellow in the Humanities at Brown University.

∽

∽ *What have been the major changes in Hebrew Union College since you've been there?*

At one time the College had a budget of around $100,000; today it's over eight million. We began, or I began, in the original college building; it was a private home in what by the time I came to school was already a slum. The private building had once been a mansion occupied by wealthy people who probably fled. It had three or four floors. And in those days the fourth floor was not the attic; it was a dance pavillion for guests and that was turned into a chapel for us.

∽ *So the college had the whole building?*

The college had the whole building. And the chapel was where people would come and talk to us back in 1911. It was there that I heard a talk by the first chairman of the Board of Governors. He had been appointed in 1875, and he was still alive. Isaac Mayer Wise probably recruited young men who would listen to him and take orders from him. This chairman of the board was Bernard Bettman. He was born in Germany, and was really a cultured, educated man—but he was reputed to have said in his heavy German gutteral, "I vant you boys to go out and to dissimilate Judaism." And the boys have been doing it ever since.

∽ *How did you get to the College?*

My father was a peddler, and in 1900 we moved to a steel town called Homestead where Carnegie had mills. It was in Pennsylvania. As far as I knew, my father was the only Jew living in this little village and he peddled out of this village as his base. Since then, a researcher has found the charter of an Orthodox congregation in the 1890s nearby. My father was one of the charter members. New Haven was a village, the base from which all the Jewish peddlers in Southwestern Pennsylvania moved into the coke ovens and the steel towns for twenty-five or thirty miles around to sell goods to the Slavs. My father spoke all the right languages. He spoke Russian because he had been a soldier in the Russian army for five years. He spoke a little German, he spoke Czech, and could get along with the Croatians.

∾ *Your family was Orthodox?*

Oh yes. We kept strictly kosher in the house, although we weren't Shomrei Shabbas. And they had a cheder in town, but it wasn't a commercial cheder; it was a congregational cheder where you learned to read Hebrew. They were supposed to teach you more but we never got beyond learning to read Hebrew and a few stories.

∾ *How many years did you go?*

Maybe two or three years there. Then we moved to Pittsburgh, and my father, being Orthodox, sent me to an Orthodox synagogue, the outstanding Orthodox synagogue in the city and the finest Sunday school, better than the Reform Sunday school of the elite Germans, because the rabbi had Vassar and Smith girls running the school and he had a man who was superintendent who was very eager to do the right thing. Everything in good English and good textbooks. And then I went to Wheeling, and I was confirmed at the Reform synagogue.

∾ *Why Reform?*

I was also Orthodox; I'd become a bar mitzvah. But my father wanted me to have a good education. He was a good Jew, but he was a Litvak, and Litvaks are not fanatical.

∾ *But why suddenly Reform? Was this the better school?*

Yes, although my father wouldn't go in the place. He objected to the prayer book, which he called a "consumptive" prayer book, it was so small. But there was no school at all among the Orthodox. All they had was a minyan, but no school, no cheder, nothing. Now in my days, the Reformers wouldn't even talk to the Orthodox people. I had come from the wrong side of the railroad tracks and I was never invited to a party of my colleagues in the confirmation class.

✺ *It was Harry Levy who was the Reform rabbi, wasn't it?*

It was Harry Levy who later on became one of the great liberals of New England. He was a fine gentleman, but he was of East European origin—though you wouldn't know it. He had a lovely accent, almost English, and he wrote a book on the Jew in English "Lit-er-a-tyure."

✺ *And it was he who told you that you were going to be a rabbi?*

Yes. So my father wanted to be sure I was going to the right place to become a rabbi. He consulted an authority. The authority was the solicitor for the *Morgen Journal,* our Yiddish paper. He came around to collect, and my father asked him, and he said: "You send this man to Cincinnati, he will come out a *mishummed,* or apostate Jew."

✺ *Your parents read the* Morgen Journal?

They read the *Morgen Journal;* they wouldn't think of reading the *Forwards,* which was socialistic. They'd want to spit when they pronounced the word *Forwards.* So, "Where shall I send my son?" said Mr. Marcus. "Send him to Schechter's school," said the solicitor. That was the only name they knew: Schechter's school. Solomon Schechter's JTS. This was in 1909. Schechter came to JTS in 1902.

So I wrote to JTS, and a young instructor by the name of Israel Davidson, who later on became one of the great scholars of America, was then the registrar. He wrote back a curt note: "We don't take freshmen in high school; write us eight years from now." JTS was only a graduate school. So, we told this to the rabbi and he said "No problem. You go to the Hebrew Union College, and when you graduate you become an Orthodox rabbi." In my day at HUC, at least half the boys, even more, were of East European origin. Native American, but of East European families. And some of them looked as if they had just come off the steamship, though they hadn't, but living in New York on the East Side, and having cultural ambition, they dressed like Yiddish intellectuals. And so when they came, I would think maybe they had just come off the ship out of the steerage. So in 1911, after two years of study and two years of high school in West Virginia, I came here. I was not prejudiced *against* Reform, or predisposed *toward* Reform. But Reform was associated in my mind with social rejection. A lot of the other boys, particularly the boys who were born in Europe, had the same idea. It didn't make as much difference to me, because I was just a kid going to school. I had no ambitions or anything, I was just like an animal hitched to a plow: Pull,—and I pulled.

∾ *So how did you evolve into a Reform Jew? Was it a violent or sudden transformation?*

It took me four years to eat nonkosher meat. I was one of the few boys who kept kosher, one of the very few. And almost all the boys lived in Orthodox homes, because the Germans wouldn't take them in. There were exceptions, there were German boarding houses too, but most of the boys stayed in East European homes, where they automatically ate kosher—and where they got garlic sandwiches. And some of the boys who were embarrassed would take the sandwiches, and when they turned the corner, would throw the sandwiches into the empty lot. That's what they did, and poisoned the poor birds, and then they'd buy themselves lunches. So we were exposed to various influences in the college. Every member of the faculty, with possibly one or two exceptions, maybe one exception, had been an Orthodox Jew, but they all had different stances. Some who came from very Orthodox homes despised Orthodoxy, and they were constantly attacking it, and the attack on Orthodoxy retarded my entrée into Reform because I was fighting for my papa and my mama. When they poked fun at t'fillin they were poking fun at my old man.

∾ *Do you perceive a change in the nature of the rabbinate or its function or the kind of people it educates or accepts? Do you see a change in the profession?*

What happened is that until at least World War II, and even after World War II, say to about approximately 1960, the ideal was Classical Reform. And the boys patterned themselves on that, and I guess that I have been profoundly influenced by that. My whole philosophy and theology is Classical Reform. I totally reject halachah. I maintain that peasants (and 99 percent of the people in Mesopotamia were peasants) have no right to determine what I am to think 1500 years later, and what I am to do and how I am to make my life.

∾ *What do you do about papa and mama now? What do you do about the historical connection?*

You can't ever reject papa and mama. The result is you make your own Shulchan Aruch. And that is why I have never consciously eaten any pork product—even with two years in the army and bacon every morning, which made me very popular at breakfast. I have never consciously eaten shellfish, and when I discovered that Chinese eggrolls have shrimp in them—I have never forgiven the person who told me the facts about eggrolls.

∾ *The facts of life.*

The facts of life. So I revered my father and because I revered my father, and because I'm conscious as an historian how Jews have died for kashrut. I observe biblical kashrut. Those are the only things that are forbidden.

∾ *Let me ask a different question altogether. What troubles you most about the contemporary Jewish situation in this country?*

This is going to shock you. Nothing troubles me. Why, Dr. Marcus, why is it that nothing troubles you? The answer is because I spent several years in Germany and Germany was going through in my time what we're going through here now. And a man named Felix Theilhaber wrote a book, I think it's called *Der Untergang des Yiddishchen, The Decline of the Jewish People,* and he pointed up all the statistics, showing that intermarriage is 33 percent, which is approximately what we have today. The Jewish people are going to disappear, he said, and I believe he also said that therefore our only salvation is our homeland in Palestine. Now, I am an historian and I know the history of Jewries. All Jewries are destined to die. No Jewry is permanent. There may be fragments that remain, as in Italy, and even in Egypt, and other places, but they die. I know that all Jewries will die. Jewry is saved not by numbers but by the saving remnant. The *she'erit hapleitah,* the *sh'ar yashuv,* the percentage that's going to persist. We are not going to be helped by a country of our own. We will always be a minority group.

∾ *You're saying that American Jewry is on the way out, because it's repeating the history of German Jewry in the 1920s?*

I want to modify that. It's certainly declining radically in numbers through defections of all types. But German Jewry, with 560,000 or whatever it had when I was there, was in my opinion the cultural core of world Jewry. There were five million East European Jews who were doing nothing but regurgitating Talmudic passages and interpretations that go back for centuries. They were making no cultural contribution. No single book of any value, of any world-humanitarian cultural value came out of Poland.

∾ *What about distinguished individuals like the Vilna Gaon?*

He made a critical contribution to the study of the Talmud, but no great book or anything came out of it. Everything that we know scientifically about Jewry came out of this group of half a million German Jews, and that is why in 1922 I went to see Julian Morgenstern, and I said, I'm going to Germany. It's the only place I could go. Now let me make my point in a sentence or two. Jewry will not disappear. American Jewry is destined to decline, very slowly, but it will decline. And the more it declines, the more to a certain extent you will have Jewish loyalty, and you'll have learning and scholarship, and we will exercise hegemony to a great extent culturally even over world Jewry.

ᴄᴏ *Isn't your understanding of history fatalistic: If there's no hope, if decline is inevitable, why bother, why be hopeful? Why found institutions if they are to decline?*

You see, Jews have declined in other countries where they had no general cultural opportunities. There was no cultural opportunity for the Jew among the Poles, nor in North Africa. They *did* have this cultural opportunity in Spain from approximately 1000 to 1300 and that's why they produced a Golden Age. The important thing is that we are going to become strong culturally because we are creating a synthesis here of American culture and critical Jewish culture. And it will be limited to a relatively small group who will have tremendous influence.

ᴄᴏ *I'm stuck on your parallel with Germany. You're saying then that German Jewry would have declined even without the Holocaust.*

It would have. Instead of 560,000, say a generation later, you might have had 450,000, but culturally it would have been and would still be the hegemonic center of world Jewish culture. And now I'm going to give you another suggestion: From a Jewish point of view, World War I was a great misfortune. Not only because it killed a lot of East European Jews who were crushed between the oncoming East Slavic armies and the German Austria armies, but also because if Germany had won and imposed its culture on the five million Jews of Poland and the Ukraine, we would have had the greatest efflorescence of Jewish culture—Hebraism and German culture—that the world had ever dreamed of. What happened was a major calamity.

ᴄᴏ *So you regret the culture of your father, too?*

My father was a man who loved Jewish things. He was not a scholarly man, but from the age of six or seven till thirteen he had had no secular training, only Jewish training. He knew the Tanach fairly well. And I must say *this* to you, I love Judaism. I'm leaving out something important:

Before or about the time that Harry Levy was speaking to me, I was already reading Jewish books. One of the books that profoundly influenced me was Israel Abrahams' *The Jew in the Medieval Period*. And I can still see my father in a rocking chair opening Isaiah and turning to me and saying, "This is wonderful." I never forgot that influence. I wanted to be a good Jew. And my brothers were pretty good Jews too.

∾ *Do you see any further parallels between Germany in the 1920s and America, say in terms of anti-Semitism? Do you think a holocaust is possible here?*

I would say a holocaust is possible anywhere. The Holocaust in Germany was an accident because there was less social prejudice, and less actual *expressed* prejudice in Germany than there was at the same time in America, and than there is today in America. I have a paperback in my library here that lists hundreds and hundreds of vandal attacks on cemeteries and synagogues in America, and acts of violence against the Jews. A hundred years from today, if God forbid there should be trouble here, people would take that book and would say that it was predestined that the Jews should be destroyed in America. Look at what's happening every day. Look at the Ku Klux Klan, look at this man in North Carolina, getting thousands and thousands of votes, look at this man in California, who got thousands and thousands of votes. And it's not at all impossible, if we have bad depressions, that we will have an anti-Semitic block in the Congress as they had in Germany since the 1880s.

∾ *Does it make a difference that between then and now there's been a fuller development of scientific anthropology? The dominant anthropology is no longer racial, so that anti-Semitism, if it ever has political power, could not have the full authority of an academic racial ideology.*

The people who are going to propagate hate, the Ku Kluxers, don't know race from schmace. They are the rank and filth of society. They don't care. They are people who are illogical, inconsistent, and full of hate. I'm a subscriber to *The Thunderbolt*. I get their periodical, under my name. They're glad to send it, they probably know I'm a Jew, they're probably glad to get my two or three dollars. I look through that thing. Those people believe everything and anything. So I believe that there is room for calamity here, and that's what the crowd hired by the American Jewish Committee never did. They never really, in my opinion, analyzed the psychopathology of the ignorant anti-Semite. They're at somebody like Henry Adams—cultured people. I believe that there is still room for a good book on the psychopathology of the anti-Semite, which would include also the motivations for the cemetery vandalism and its relationship to necrophilism.

ᔀ *Aren't the fairly enlightened mass media a major difference between our situation and that in Germany?*
It doesn't mean a thing. The Jews were very powerful in the German newspapers. You can't foresee an accident. None of these arguments applies. If times are bad, really bad, and people have to have a scapegoat, nothing will deter them, particularly if there's a chance to go down and to plunder Jewish property. When the movement takes form and shape then the clever, cultured, ingenious people who want to make careers, they'll join up. They'll have no conscience.

ᔀ *You once spoke, I remember, of omniterritoriality.*
That's my English word, which I created out of a German word.

ᔀ *—and what you mean by that is that the only hope for the ultimate survival of Jewry is that there should be Jews living everywhere on the globe?*
Yes, and that idea is also found in the Talmud in Pesahim, page 87A or 87B, with a comment of Rashi in the margin. Rashi says the Lord dispersed us so they couldn't destroy all of us at once. The survival of the Jews lies in a *minyan* in Patagonia. We have to have Jews everywhere. And we should make compromises socio-economically. If we can get a *minyan* who will be left alone in China, we should go to China.

ᔀ *So galut is a good thing*
Galut is a good thing, yes.

ᔀ *That brings us to your feelings about Israel. Does that make Israel a bad thing? Or Zionism a bad thing?*
I don't like the fact that so many people are there; three million Jews are there. And I dread and would not be shocked at the prospect of a holocaust in Israel.

ᔀ *You're saying that the idea of a coherent Jewish culture, on which Zionism is predicated, is fallacious?*
I think so, yes. There is no such thing as a universal Jewish culture. Every Jewish culture is a dual culture, a mix between the host culture and

the culture we bring with us. And Israeli culture is going to be dual culture: a blend of what the Israelis are developing and traditional Jewish culture.

∾ *So the Kingdom of David is irretrievable.*
Yes. What the Israelis are doing is developing an Israeli culture that is a form of civil religion.

∾ *Don't you think a Jewish state serves the purpose of being an* ir miklat—
a place to run to?
No doubt. The reason I give to Israel, and give very generously, is that there has to be a place where the Jew can go. I have no conviction, no absolute conviction, that we will live in America eternally and ride in our 8-, or 6-, or even 4-cylinder Chevrolets. My only worry is that if *we* go down the drain, I think Israel will go down the drain. I think Israel, to use a Talmudic phrase, lives by the breath of the United States. And if anytime Israel really annoys the United States, they can have resort to a device that was attempted in Eisenhower's day. We have confidential memo in the Archives written by Admiral Lewis Strauss. He met with the National Security Council when it was proposed that the government remove the tax exemption for all American Jewish gifts to Israel. That would have meant a loss of over half a billion dollars a year. And I think, fiscally, that would destroy Israel because how many Jews, if they couldn't get tax deductions, would give money to Israel? And when Strauss objected, they not only withdrew the proposal, but they apologized to him. We have the document at the College.

∾ *Are your feelings about Israel colored by your education in Classical Reform, which was anti-Zionist?*
I was never a hot Zionist. I never joined a Zionist organization. I lived for a summer in the 1920s in Mandate Palestine. I came back much impressed. I wrote two articles, one in *The American Scholar* and one in *The Open Court*. (*The Open Court* was the University of Chicago's liberal paper, a paper for cultured people.) In both of those, I was extremely sympathetic. But I never joined a Zionist organization because I don't want anybody to tell me what to do. I belong to only one Jewish organization, and that is B'nai B'rith. They never tell me what to do except to write a check. And I write the check. They do good work and they're innocuous.

∾ *So you stay away from ideological groups?*

Yes. Because I have my own ideology. I can't belong to a group if I don't agree with them.

∾ *And liberal Judaism permits the idea of being Jewish without subscribing to an ideology?*

That is correct. I am willing in my Judaism to reach out and to take ideas from everybody, as long as I can take them and use them as I see fit. I am closest to Reconstructionism in this sense: my theism is my own definition. I'm way over on the left. I am a humanistic theist, but I am a theist. But humanistic, with a more or less transcendental concept. I am a Diaspora nationalist, strongly. And therefore I have been profoundly influenced by the writings of Dubnow, particularly his philosophy of Jewish history. I am sympathetic to Orthodoxy in the sense that I observe some Orthodox customs. My kiddush, my mezuzuhs, my Passover haggadah—which is strictly Orthodox according to Minghag Maxwell.

∾ *Maxwell House?*

Yes. And in many respects I go along with the Conservative Jews. I believe in the doctrine of "salutary neglect" when it comes to certain observances.

∾ *Is there any sine quo non of Judaism then?*

Actually there are today in America close to 5,600,000 Judaisms.

∾ *All kosher? All permissable?*

All permissable. So now you want to ask what makes a man a Jew? This is the definition I use in all my classes: any man is a Jew who *says* he is a Jew. No matter his color or creed. And as long as he identifies with the Jewish *people* and contributes to causes concerning which there is a consensus for that decade.

∾ *So like Mordecai Kaplan, you put people first?*

Yes. But I didn't get it from him. I had these ideas in 1913 when he was just learning to be a modern American, long before his books.

∾ *Let's go back: What's your working definition of humanism?*

I believe there is intelligence in the universe. Intelligence. Beyond that I can say nothing. I don't believe in immortality. Although I can conceive that a man does have a soul and that soul lives on eternally somewhere. You can believe that if the world is infinite.

∾ *Why humanistic?*

Because I emphasize ethics. I am an ethical monotheist. People poo-pooed it in my day, people used to make a joke about it. He's a Reform Jew, he's an ethical monotheist. Well, that's what I believe. There is benign intelligence in the universe. Otherwise I would have to conceive of the possibility of accepting satanism instead of theism.

∾ *Was your acceptance of change and evolution hard to come by?*

There was a writer that I used to like as a kid, I think his name was Grinnell. He wrote boys' books, dealing with wild animals. And he referred to people who had all sorts of ideas about what animals did, rather fanciful ideas, and he referred to them as "nature fakers." I am not a nature faker. I don't really know what I believed as a child because I am not trained in abstract thinking, or philosophic thinking. I don't think I'm capable of it. I've had courses in philosophy and I minored in philosophy at the University of Berlin but I memorized the book of the professor who quizzed me and got through with flying colors. I was clever enough to get him to do all the talking.

∾ *The early essays you wrote were all about European Jewry. When did you become interested in America?*

I began to write in 1916 and I wrote six items in that year. I was twenty years of age. And the first thing I wrote that was published was called "The Spiritual Center of Jewry."

∾ *Meaning America?*

America. I wrote it for the Jewish Community Bulletin of Wheeling, West Virginia.

∾ *So in establishing American Jewish history as your main interest you were returning to an earlier preoccupation?*

I wouldn't say so. In those days I established that this was going to be the world center. But after that I wasn't working on any American material for a long time. Now, I'd like to know myself how I came to go into the American field. People ask me, and I answer rather superficially. But it might not be a superficial answer. I realized in the 1940s that Europe was dead as a great center. And I didn't want to concern myself with a dead Jewry.

∞ And you didn't feel that your task as an historian was memorializing the community?

That's correct. I wanted to work for the live community. Germany had been a live community when I determined to devote myself to it. The important event was in the summer of 1942. Then I gave the first required graduate course in an academic institution in American Jewry history. A required course. As far as I know I am the first scientist to work in the field, to make it a full-time job in an academic institution of caliber. And almost immediately, either that year or the next year, the American Jewish Committee called a conference on American Jewish history. So from then on, the ball began to roll.

∞ Was there any difficulty convincing the College that American Jewish history should be required?

Well, it was in the days of Morgenstern and he was very pro-America. And he was glad to have it, I'm sure. The boys were glad to have the course prior to 1942, all my modern history courses had considerable American material. I was never divorced from it. But things moved fast. I induced the head of the Jewish Welfare Board to take the American Jewish Historical Society and adopt it. I did a number of things like that. I had already gone to Rothman, the HUC librarian, and I said, "I want to start a collection of Americana," and he cooperated. Then in 1947, I went to Gleuck. I said we ought to start a national archives. I told him I want the building. He said, "Take the building." He didn't know and didn't care. But whatever I asked for was all right.

∞ Was that because you were friends?

Friends. And he knew that I knew what I was doing. Or he thought I knew what I was doing. And I thought I knew what I was doing. I didn't realize I had a tiger by the tail. Because then I got the building and I didn't have any money at first. Not a penny. Not one cent. And then I went to a member of the board, who a very difficult person, and yet, a very, very important person, and he thought it was a beautiful idea. He found out there was $10,000 in a book budget that wasn't being used. He had the $10,000 assigned to me. And I was in business. And then I got a famous female historian who's still living, Mrs. Eugene (Selma) Stern-Taeubler, very famous. A woman now about eighty, to be my assistant. The College paid her salary. And then I started writing for documents. And people were going to throw all this stuff out, things nobody had any use for. And their records began to pour in.

∾ *What kinds of things?*
The minutes of the congregations.

∾ *Is that where you started—with congregational minutes?*
Minutes. B'nai B'rith minutes. Anything. "Send it to the College; what do we need it for?"

∾ *When did the private collections start coming in? You know, the Schiff papers, the Warburg stuff?*
Very early. The minute they found out there was a place that would take it. I made some egregious errors. I didn't take certain papers I could have gotten. Egregious errors. But I learned.

∾ *Can I ask what?*
The Otto Kahn papers. Then in a period of ten years or fifteen years, American history had so caught on we began to have local societies all over the country. Today, there are about thirty of them. I gave impetus to it, through the American Jewish Archives.

∾ *The timing was good, wasn't it? Because of the three hundredth anniversary of the first settlement.*
That isn't the reason why it was 1954. The reason was there was a Holocaust. The Holocaust was beginning to come out in 1942. And came out in 1943. Europe was dead. This was obviously the great center. And here is a point I want to make: after fifteen years, congregations refused to send me their minutes.

∾ *Why?*
Because "These are valuable historic documents! We're not going to give them to you!" It was garbage before that. At the same time, or actually about a decade later, in about 1955, I created the American Jewish Periodical Center and I literally rescued Jewish periodicals that were about to be masserated. Thrown into the garbage heap.

∾ *From public libraries?*

No. From the owners who had closed the papers and had them lying around and wanted to get rid of them.

∾ *With an important collection, like, say the Schiff collection, what other options did the family have for donation? What does the Archives compete with?*

They could have given them to the New York Historical Society, which would have taken them. They may even have tried to give them, but they made a condition that all economic papers, fiscal papers of the banking firm, be destroyed. The banking, which is the core of the collection. I destroyed them. That was the deal we made, so I destroyed the banana, the fruit, and kept the peel. But a peel is better than nothing. The Warburg papers I got complete. No, except this. They spent weeks going through and picking out anything of a personal nature. But I still have 200,000 pages.

∾ *Didn't it bother you to destroy documents you knew were important?*

What choice did I have? I can get a half a loaf of bread and I'm starving, it's better than refusing the half a loaf because they won't give me a whole loaf.

∾ *Somebody would have destroyed them, whoever took them ultimately?*

Yes. It really was a revolution. I'm amazed—it grew like Topsy. Today we have five or six million pages.

∾ *What's the most significant paper you have in the building?*

That's a document that was issued to me when I came out of the United States Army. You've seen the document, haven't you?

∾ *Your honorable discharge?*

Oh, no, please! I've put my own picture in as a Lieutenant Acting Company Commander in the 145th United States infantry. And then there's a document underneath that. "This is to certify that Lieutenant Jacob Rader Marcus is entirely free of lice and venereal disease."

Actually, we have a letter signed by Daniel Boone to his employers who were the owners of the largest store in Richmond, Virginia—Korn & Isaacs. We have a signed letter of Weizmann given to Glueck in which he agrees to partition. We have a number of things like that. Nothing of *supreme* importance.

❧ *What is your principle for accepting or rejecting materials?*

That it should throw light on the Jewish social experience. Actually, we don't turn down anything. I'm interested in criminals just as I am in rabbis.

❧ *In the writing of American Jewish history, what needs to be done now?*

Nobody has yet written a scientific history of the American Jew. In all the one-volume histories, the elements are correct, but many of the facts are wrong. And they are not acceptable from the point of view of a trained historian.

I set out to do the volume, to do that book. About twelve years ago. I called it MOV—Marcus One Volume. I worked for a year or so, two years, and realized you cannot write one volume until you know the field. And I'm now working on the history of the American Jew. I have four volumes and manuscripts. From 1776 to 1921. I have to stop at the first immigration act because I'll never live to finish it. I'm not sure I'll live to finish it as it is, and I work on it all the time.

❧ *That's exclusive of the colonial work you've already done?*

Exclusive. That's been done. For a generation, nobody's going to touch it. I spent fifteen years on the colonial period. I think that's when I started to do the MOV and fifteen years later, all I had was the colonial period. And sixteen hundred pages printed. Now, I'm working on the revolutionary post-revolutionary periods to 1921.

❧ *Who's been your model? What books have been your models as you write?*

My model is Jacob Rader Marcus. There's no Irish history or German history to please me. I do not know of any ethnic history, though I've made no special study of ethnic histories, that is acceptable to me. I think that my approach will be unique, that the Jews are unique. You're dealing here with an extended middle class, the bulk of whom came as immigrants. They were either poor or impoverished, and have become the most affluent group in the United States today. Not the wealthiest, but the most affluent *group*. The differences is there are no Hunts with billion-dollar silver purchases.

❧ *How long will the book be?*

At least four volumes. Running about four hundred pages a volume. If I finish. I've got to have the *Kadosh Baruch Hu* with me. You see, we always have a partner. If you're a businessman you have a partner. A man with a long beard called Uncle Sam. He takes his share of everything. You're a literary man, your partner is always *Hakadosh Baruch Hu.* He decides whether you're going to finish it or not.

∾ *How did you have the spirit to keep on going in your career, after your book on German Jewry proved wrong?*
All that was proved wrong was one paragraph. Three lines. All the rest was correct. I was only extrapolating and I extrapolated wrong. But the facts were all right.

∾ *You didn't in any way try to recall the book, or—*
Why should I recall it? I simply said I can't imagine he'll kill the Jews. *He did.*

∾ *What are your feelings abut the Holocaust?*
I don't like the way it's been commercialized. I will not look at pictures of these dead Jews. I will not listen to the television because Hitler killed my father. Though my father did not die in the Holocaust. But the Jews in every picture I have seen of Jews about to be executed looked like my father. I refuse to go to Germany. I was invited to go to Germany, by a semi-official agency under the patronage of the State Department to talk to the German people, and I told the people who contacted me I wouldn't touch them with a ten-foot pole. When Miriam slandered Moses, they locked her up in a concentration camp for seven days, just for slander. And he killed six million; we could ignore them for a generation or two.

∾ *To go back to your work. You've just finished a book on the American Jewish woman.*
It will be out this spring. About 1,100 pages altogether, I guess.

∾ *What brought you to deal with women's history?*
This is a very important question. My secretary said, "You ought to do it." And I knew where the female bodies were buried. So, the book. That's how a book is written; you don't sit down and assume the East European intellectual pose looking off into space. Books are not written that way. Maybe Shelley had an itch somewhere and he wrote "To a Skylark."

∾ *How many years on the women's book?*
Less than two. In an hour, I could assemble half the documents. Then

I started to work as a scientist. There were two or three first-class essays with good bibliographies. I dug out every one of those articles. And the result is, I have a documentary that I think will last for at least forty years. My *Jew in the Medieval World* was published about 1940 and is still selling, still a textbook. If people are still interested in women, academically, they'll use that textbook. And the introduction is important. Two hundred pages. That's the history. Straight history.

∞ *The introduction is separate?*
A separate volume, no relation. It's the first time that anybody has scientifically taken the majority of American Jewry—who are females—and has attempted to study them. I had to begin with periodization.

∞ *Was it different from the periodization of general American history?*
Sure. These are women making history. They make it differently.

∞ *But aren't the waves of immigration—that sort of thing—the same?*
I don't deal with Germans and East Europeans. They are all in there. But that isn't my principle of organization. My organization is chronologically, continuously, sociohistorical. What were women doing? Who were their leaders? Did they have any "culture"?

∞ *What were the key dates when things changed?*
In the history, I began with 1654 when the first Jewish woman landed. And then I go to 1819. In 1819, for the first time we have a woman's organization, and I maintained it's unconscious consciousness-raising. I go from 1819 to 1892, and show how women are beginning to reach out. In 1892, we have a national organization and these women know definitely what they want to do. And then there was a break. I go to 1962, 1963, with Betty Freidan's *Feminine Mystique*. From then on you have real feminism. With a lot of Jews among them. And then I take from 1962 to the present day in which you're heavily involved with feminism. But it is not a history of feminism. It's a history of the woman.

∞ *And the experience of the woman?*
Yes. And it's excellent, if I say it myself. I'm very proud of it. Some documents I *had* to put in because they're historically important. Others I loved! They were unknown. They were buried in magazines. "How Women First Became Human Beings," is one I discovered. Magnificent.

This is the first woman in the world to get a Ph.D. in a German university. An American girl.

∾ *What year was that essay?*

It was 1892 or 1896, I think. "No skirts shall ever enter my laboratory," said the German professor. But she managed. She persisted.

∾ *What's your reaction to the more contemporary manifestations of women's feelings, like the women's movement?*

Well, I've had correspondence with women writers who started telling me what I should do. Nobody can tell me what to do. I point out in the history that feminists are trying to change a history that goes back at least ten thousand years, the patriarchial system. And I have a very gloomy view of that in our time.

∾ *Do you mean of the effort to change that, or of the patriarchial system?*

Whether they'll have any success. I must say that I became very sympathetic towards the women. I've always liked women, but for different reasons. I tried desperately to be fair.

∾ *We've talked before abut the problems with the use of the word "Jewess" in writing the book.*

It's used by every Jewess in my anthology.

∾ *But it's not a contemporary word. And it's fallen into disfavor because of the suffix.*

In the *Third International Dictionary* it is not a term of reproach. It's only a term of reproach in the *Random House,* bootleg dictionary.

∾ *So you still feel comfortable it?*

Oh, yes. Because it bothers me that we read any noun ending with "ess" referring to a female as unacceptable. We don't say "Negress" either. That bothers me. Because if I'm ever lucky enough to have a mistress, I'll have to say that I'm sleeping with my mister.

∾ *I think it's perceived that the ending of "ess" is diminutive. For example, when a male writes, he's a poet, but a woman who writes is a poetress, which suggests diminishing her achievement.*

Not in my opinion. My generation was never bothered by it. I looked it up in the *OED*. Incidentally, because there's been such a stink about it, I have written two and a half paragraphs, which I have here in my galleys, in the preface. In the nineteenth century, the word "Jew" was a term of contempt. But the Jewish man has turned it into a patent of nobility. Nobody's ashamed of the word "Jew" today.

ᔆ *So you value the word "Jewess" because the word "Jew" is in it?*
I'm bringing to light the majority of Jews who have always been ignored. So I'm not hiding them under a male term. We're rising through a term so that people know we're talking about females, who have been non-persons to the present day.

ᔆ *Let's move on to this question: I am wondering about your own plans to write a memoir.*
The answer is very, very simple. I have been asked that frequently. I don't think I ever will write a memoir, and I'm being very serious. I've had a very uneventful life. I've never met any of the great, number one. Number two, any of the so-called great whom I have ever met, some have been very decent people, but they've all been human beings and some have had clay feet that reached all the way to their groin, if you know what I mean.

ᔆ *So you don't want to expose anybody, is that it?*
That's it. And since I have been the recipient of many confidences, if I really wrote what I know, and I made a very interesting book, it would be a *chronique scandaleuse*. And that I refuse to write.

ᔆ *If anybody ever wanted to write a history of the American rabbinate, the story you have to tell, minus the confidences, would be significant.*
I could only write a history of the Reform rabbinate. When I joined the Central Conference of American Rabbis there were less than one hundred rabbis in the Conference, as far as I know. I'm not sure there's a complete list—the records were very inadequate in 1920 when I joined up as a rabbi. Today, there are about twelve hundred or maybe even fourteen hundred. I think I could write a history but to do a scientific job, I would want to consult a lot of bulletins. Then I would be immersed in scholarly research, quantitative research. I wouldn't want to fool with that.

ᔆ *But if you called it a memoir, that would release you . . . ?*
But it would be very difficult for me to write it because I wouldn't be

able to make any moral judgments except in a paragraph to dismiss all the pecadillos of the rabbis who've been messing around. But basically, I could sum it up in a sentence or two: Reform rabbis were the most important clergymen, most cultured clergymen, in their communities in the old days. And may still be. And they were frequently the leading clergy, not really the most cultured, but the leading clergymen in their cities. The Krauskopfs, the Emil G. Hirsches, the J. Leonard Levys, the Ed Magnins. Nobody comparable to those people in the Christian clergy. So I've said it all and you don't need any memoir.

ᐁ *Come on. You're getting off the hook too easily.*
There's another psychological reason. If you have enough strength to write a memoir, then you have enough strength to finish your scientific work. That has to be done first.

ᐁ *Isn't it possible to do a memoir as we're doing now, talking on a tape?*
No, because I have still another book over there all ready to go and for two months I haven't touched it. That's a primer, a primer for the American Jewish historian. "If I'm interested in American Jewish history, whether I'm a Jew or a Gentile, how do I work myself into the field?" I haven't got the time! I have to take a month out just to finish the primer. In the meantime, I'd have to stop the big book. I'm disturbed about it. Because at night I get tired. I'm in my eighty-fifth year. And what the French call "Kayach"—strength—I don't have after six or seven o'clock.

ᐁ *Of all the people I know, you are the one who best combines respectability and earthiness. How do you maintain that attitude of spirit?*
Well, my father had a sense of humor and was an earthy person. And I was in the Army for two years, in the first World War. And I didn't live in the city and I'm not an intellectual. I'm primarily a fact man, with a capacity to interpret the facts properly. I don't want to cut myself down. I don't ruminate. I'm not interested in philosophic abstractions. I believe, and of course this is sour grapes, a great deal of philosophic thinking is sheer verbiage. Playing with words. And as I say, I've lived in small towns all the time. And living in the Army I was associating with people where I was the only college man in the whole company of 250 people. You have to live on their level. And I've lived on their level. But, I also am an academician. When I get excited I speak like an academician and not like a common ordinary human being. Though I never, never resort to academese.

Never use gobbledygook. That annoys me. Clarity is important. If a sentence isn't absolutely clear I can't write it. I try to be absolutely exact and use no equivocation.

ᵥᵥ *You're Honorary President of the CCAR now?*
   As long as I live.

ᵥᵥ *What is the meaning of that and what is the feeling of it?*
   May I say to you that I wanted that more than anything else I ever wanted in this world as far as honors are concerned. I had to have the Ph.D. as a passport. The world that means most to me is the rabbinical world. I have no family. Out of the twelve or thirteen hundred Reform rabbis, there are a hundred that I'm very fond of. There are five or six or seven who are my intimate friends. That's my world. When I lost my family, my daughter, the only child I had, people said to me in the funeral sermons, you now have five hundred sons. *That's my world.*

ᵥᵥ *You actually pursued it?*
   Yes. It's the one thing I wanted and I asked three people, rabbis, and said "That's the honor I want." And I got it. And I've been very pleased. That meant something to me. You ask me to analyze why it means something to me. Now this is a very confidential thing, but (most of the rabbis pay no attention to it) in my opinion, it's the highest honor your colleagues can give you. Electing you for life to be their spiritual beau ideal. That meant something to me. It flattered me. In the long run, Bentham was right, all idealism or ethics are selfish, are self-concerned. I wanted that recognition. It sustains me to the present day. I still have my doubts about myself. And I say it in all seriousness. Because I know the defects in my education and the defects in my capacity for erudite thinking. Real thinking. The important thing is to do what you can with what you've got and to know your limitations. To look in that mirror and really see yourself. I can do that now.

ᵥᵥ *What's your secret of longevity?*
   My mother. My mother's genes. She lived to be over one hundred. My grandparents on her side lived to be in the nineties. You've got to pick the right mother if you want to live a long time. You want to be a rich man, you have to pick the right father.

PART II

Marcus's Essays

America

The Spiritual Center of Jewry (1916)

Editor's note:

Jacob Marcus's voluminous list of publications dates back to the year 1916. The following essay, one of his earliest articles, appeared in the Jewish Community Bulletin *of Wheeling, West Virginia in 1916.*[1] *The bulletin was edited by a young HUC alumnus: Abba Hillel Silver (1893–1963). Despite the fact that Silver had been ordained five years before Marcus, the two young men had been on campus at the same time. After ordination, Silver assumed the pulpit of Eoff Street Temple in Wheeling, West Virginia, in 1915—the very synagogue in which Jacob Marcus had been confirmed in 1909. Silver, who was himself destined to become an extraordinarily influential rabbinic figure, evidently invited Marcus—a former confirmand from his congregation—to write an essay for the community's bulletin.*

Was it merely an interesting coincidence that the twenty-year-old Jacob Marcus decided to write about Jewish life in America when he first began to publish articles? In later years, Marcus insisted that the choice was serendipitous. Still a rabbinic student when he wrote this article, the young Marcus had not even decided to pursue graduate studies in history. Six years after the appearance of this essay, he would begin his doctoral studies in Europe. After completing his doctorate, he would teach the full gamut of Jewish history at HUC, paying only scant attention to the history of the American Jew. The dramatic rise in the intensity of Nazi brutality toward the Jews in the late 1930s caused Marcus to disbelieve his own published contention that

---

1. "America: The Spiritual Center of Jewry," which appeared in the 27 April 1916 edition of the *Jewish Community Bulletin* of Wheeling, West Virginia, was not Marcus's first published article. He had, in fact, already published a historical essay two months earlier. Marcus's essay, "Mendele Mocher Seforim," which appeared in *The American Hebrew* (18 February 1916: 410), may have actually been the scholar's first publication. Joseph Jacobs, editor of *The American Hebrew,* paid Marcus the serial's "usual rate of $3. per 1,000 words" for this essay on the famous Hebrew author. See Joseph Jacobs to Jacob Marcus, 27 January 1916, Joseph Jacobs to Jacob Marcus, 27 January 1916 in Box 1, Folder 1, Jacob Rader Marcus Papers, Mss. Coll #210, The Jacob Rader Marcus Center of the American Jewish Archives, Cincinnati, Ohio (hereafter, AJA).

German Jewish life would ultimately overcome Nazi anti-Semitism.[2] *He began to contemplate what the future of world Jewry would be if its cultural centers on continental Europe disappeared. The gruesome decimation of European Jewry in the early 1940s transformed Marcus's historical orientation permanently, and he returned to a topic that had intrigued him as a young rabbinic student—a spiritual center of Jewry in North America. After World War II, United States Jewry had suddenly become the leading Jewish community in the world, and Marcus sought to provide the American Jewish community with a modern, critical reconstruction of its past. If American Jews understood the accomplishments of their predecessors, he believed they would be better prepared to positively affect the future.*

This essay, like the others that were written before he earned his doctorate, lacks the impressive breadth of knowledge that would become Marcus's trademark. Nevertheless, the article sheds light on how the writings of renowned German Jewish historian, Heinrich Graetz (1817–1891), influenced his historical thinking even at the onset of his career. While he was yet a rabbinic student in Cincinnati, Marcus devoured Graetz's eleven volume History of the Jews. *Graetz's historical conceptualizations impressed Marcus, who always referred to him as "the great master." Following Graetz, who described Jewish history as a never-ending process of growth, blossoming, and decay, Marcus similarly suggests that great centers of Jewish life have always risen and fallen in response to the waxing and waning of Jewish interest. He confidently predicts that the same will be true of United States Jewry.*[3]

How will America become a spiritual center of Jewry? Remarkably, the answer that Marcus provides presages the love of history that will characterize his career: "Oh, that we could realize . . . our debt to the past; the debt we owe of continuing the great work that has been going on for the past three

---

2. In the final chapter of his volume, *The Rise and Destiny of the German Jew* (Cincinnati: Department of Synagogue and School Extension of the Union of American Hebrew Congregations, 1934), Marcus opined that German Jewry would eventually rebound from the disabilities that the Nazi regime had imposed. He lamented this prognostication the rest of his life. Privately, he told his students that he could never forgive the German people for their role in the destruction of, as he phrased it, "six million of my people." See also, the reprint of this volume entitled *The Rise and Destiny of the German Jew with a Postmortem* (New York: Ktav Publishing House, 1973).

3. For more on Marcus's attitude toward Graetz, see Stanley F. Chyet, "Jacob Rader Marcus: A Biographical Sketch" in *Essays in American Jewish History* (Cincinnati: American Jewish Archives, 1958), 13. Graetz's own conception of Jewish history was influenced by the writings of Nachman Krochmal (1785–1840). See Michael A. Meyer, ed., *Ideas of Jewish History* (New York: Behrman House, 1974), 189ff.

thousand years . . ." More than thirty years later, in evaluating the accom-
plishments of the American Jewish Archives on the fifth anniversary of its
founding, Marcus was still recapitulating this very same theme: ". . . we are
making Jews conscious of their history in this land . . . We will consider it
an even greater achievement if we can induce some not only to reflect on
their past, but to become intelligently conscious of their future as Jews and as
Americans. This is our hope."[4]

In his later years, Marcus repeatedly maintained that future historians
would one day refer to Jewish life in the United States during the last quarter
of the twentieth century as a "golden age" in Jewish history. He survived long
enough to witness the fulfillment of a prognosis he offered in this, his first
essay on the American Jewish experience: United States Jewry had indeed
become "a fountainhead of inspiration for ourselves and for those who are
coming to us from other lands."

～

The Jew has wandered over the face of the earth, not because there is in
him an inherent wanderlust, a craving to travel over strange lands and
among strange people, but because the forces of circumstance have compelled him to roam about. So it was in the middle of the sixteenth century
that the expelled Brazilian Jews came to New Amsterdam. They came to
America as they would to a city of refuge, a spot where they might be per-
mitted to live and develop according to their inclination and aptitude.
There was in them no conscious conception of developing a cultural or religious milieu here in America, they only desired the right to live and to be
let alone. Three centuries later the Jews of Germany realized the disquiet-
ing truth that the government was not inclined to grant them unreserved
political rights, so with sad hearts they turned from their beloved "Vater-
land" and came to America: the "City of Refuge." The Germans had barely
established themselves when the terrible pogroms of 1881 broke out in
Russia. The dazed and terrified Jews of the Russian Ghettos flocked in
hundreds of thousands, as did their Portuguese and German co-
religionists before them, to the land of freedom and opportunity. It is thus
evident that the chosen people came here not to inaugurate a religious or
cultural movement but for the sole purpose of finding a home.

The time is past, however, for the Jew of America to sit back quietly
and be satisfied with the passive possession of his rights of citizenship.

---

4. *American Jewish Archives* 5, no. 1 (January 1953): 4.

The Jew must take a positive, reflective attitude toward his future career in America; the Jew must realize that for the sake of the continuity of his own specifically Jewish culture he must create in America a great intellectual and spiritual environment that will nurture not only the Jews of to-day but also the Jews of to-morrow—they who will come to him from across the seas.

In the days that Nero fiddled and Paul preached, Palestine was the religious inspiration of the Diaspora. It acquired its influence not through numbers—there were more Jews in Alexandria than in Jerusalem—but through the interest in Judaism that filled the heart of every Jew and Jewess. Judaism lived in the souls of the Palestinians; it stirred their innermost being with a fervor that knew no bounds; it was their life—their all in all. The greatest sages, rabbis, and teachers in Israel were Palestinians. It was the interest shown in Judaism by the Palestinians that made that land the arbiter of the destiny of the Jews throughout the Dispersion. After a few centuries, this interest waned and the Jewish sphere of influence was transferred to Babylonia where, after many hundreds of years, interest for things Jewish died out and the Iberian peninsula became the home of the Jewish spirit. And so the spirit followed where interest and love of Judaism lead; from Spain to France, then to Germany, and finally where it rests today, in the Russian Pale. The Russian Pale today is quivering; its penned prisoners are scattered on the roads from Kovno to Kazan; from Vilna to Vladivastok, on the banks of the Dnieper and on the plains of Siberia. They have no home, they are starving and starving people who write and moan are not concerned with culture. We cannot look to them to lead and guide us and serve as our inspiration; their spirit is broken, the rays that once scintillated from Russia have disappeared only gloom and terror is left. We cannot look to them; if aught, they must look to us. We must build a new temple in America, a temple that will radiate culture and religious inspiration throughout the land, yes, throughout the entire Diaspora. We must become a second Palestine; the Academies of Jabne and Thiberias; Sura and Pumbeditha; of Cordova and Granada of Metz and Fuerth; of Voloshin and Kovno must rise again in America. We must develop an all-consuming interesting in all things Jewish, an interest which the American youth will foster and develop.

"The American Youth," as I repeat these words slowly, I almost hear myself murmuring: "Awake, the young American Jew has no interest in things Jewish. He will not help build your Academies of Jewish learning; he has no interest and without interest and fervent devotion to the Jewish ideal, without love and labor, the goal will never be reached." And have I not a right to be pessimistic, should I not be reproached for my idle dream—a dream of a day that would come when the Jewish spirit would manifest itself in the heart and home of every Jew? What does our American youth know of the past of the Jew—his wonderful history and aspirations? What does he know of his fellow-religionists in the lands far away except that which he gleans from the Sunday magazine or a stray glance at a Jewish newspaper? Oh, yes, I know that many have gone to the Religious Schools, they went—but that was all. Now they are asking when Samuel the Second reigned. Oh, I know they have studied Hebrew; I meet many who gleefully tell me that in Hebrew "dog" is fish and that "who" is he and "he" is she. As far as the Talmud is concerned, it might be the latest type of breakfast food or a 1917 model submarine. The Mediaeval period of Jewish history, the sublimest period of all, is a blank to them; they may have received some vague impression concerning this golden age of Jewish letters and philosophy from the lips of their Rabbi, but alas, too often such casual enlightenment was productive of nothing beyond an amused smile at the outlandish sound of the name "Maimuni" or idle wonder as to the identity of Jehudah HaLevi. Their ignorance of modern Jewish thought and history is appalling. Our Christian journalists who occasionally write of the Jews are kind enough to make every prominent man a Jew, from Edison to Jack Johnson; our American Jewish youth is nonplussed, in fact, quite shocked to discover that many of the most prominent authors, scientists, and scholars of Europe and America are Jews.

If the young American Jew continues to pursue the laissez-faire policy towards Judaism, America will not only not become a living and throbbing Jewish center but, what is most to be dreaded, a stepping-stone from a half-hearted loyalty to Judaism to complete religious and cultural effacement.

The tragedy lies not altogether in the discouraging fact that America is not becoming the religious leader of international Jewry, as she should be, nor in the deplorable circumstance that the American youth knows too little of Judaism to foster Jewish ideals, but that America, which is soon to be the numerical leader of Jewry, is not prepared by any manner of means to receive the incoming thousands and to guide and lead them successfully toward all their spiritual desires.

The Jews who will come to our shores in the near future must find a regnant Jewish spirit, so powerful that it will engulf them in its current and carry them along. Thus it was when the Jews emigrated from Palestine to Babylon they found there a Jewish culture which was vigorous enough to absorb them; and so it was when the Jews came to Poland, in the end of the Middle Ages they found Academies and schools emanating a culture virile enough to supplant their own.

But what have we to offer the immigrant? What has been our experience in the past? Many immigrants, after a short struggle, have adapted themselves to religious conditions in America but many more, I fear, have not; and one does not have to go very far to find that amusing type of a fool that shows its contempt of Judaism and appreciation of Americanism by throwing peanut shells at the aged, bearded Jew as he trudges to synagog on the Day of Atonement.

The American Jew has a duty to himself and to his brother who will come to him from across the sea. The American Jew must, if he would save himself, awake and take an active, all-absorbing interest in all things Jewish that he, too, may say as a great American has already said: "Nothing Jewish is foreign to me." If America is ever to be made more than a home for the persecuted—and this can be done without superhuman effort—it must be something more positive, it must become a generator of a revived Jewish consciousness that will manifest itself in renewed Jewish activities. Study, constant study of Jews and Judaism of all times will without doubt effect the desired end.

As Americans let us apply our boast of "fair play" to our faith. We have given Christian church history a fair chance—for our Mediaeval history is after all church history—let us give Jewish history a chance; let us read more about Saadyah and less about Thomas Aquinas; let us read more about Rashi and less about Godfrey of Bouillon. Oh, that we could realize what our responsibilities are, our debt to the past; the debt we owe of continuing the great work that has been going on for the past three thousand years; and our debt to the future; the debt we owe of making America the fountainhead of inspiration for ourselves and for those who are coming to us from other lands.

As sincere Americans firmly imbued with American principles let us be fair and honest by giving our own faith a chance; let us read and study and ponder over the sublime story of our people that it may serve to guide us in the future to the end that we may do all in our power to make America the spiritual home of international Jewry.

The Jewish Soldier

(1918)

Editor's note:

Marcus interrupted his rabbinical studies at Hebrew Union College in Cincinnati to enlist in the American Expeditionary Forces in 1917. Army life was a maturative, transforming experience for the twenty-one-year-old Marcus. In a journal that he kept during this period as well as in a host of reflective letters written to his parents and friends, Marcus testifies to the challenges he (and others in the American Expeditionary Forces) faced. The army was a world apart, a culture he had never before encountered. Gone was his familiar academic context and the community of learning that he had come to love. The refinements of the intellectual world he knew so well had been supplanted by the army's crass atmosphere: "The Army today makes for brutal frankness," he wrote in a letter to his friend Morris Lazaron (1888–1979), "'if you please' is antiquated, polite terms are quite conspicuous by their absence."[1]

The army's harsh and secular atmosphere affected Marcus's view of Jewish life in America. "I have revised my conception of things Jewish a number of times since I have come over here."[2] He realized, perhaps for the first time, that the ideological assumptions he had adopted from his studies at HUC were parochial and, more importantly, irrelevant to a large number of his fellow Jews in the A.E.F. He encountered scores of Jewish soldiers who "owe allegiance to Judaism by the accident of birth" alone. It began to dawn on him that the intellectualized Judaism that his teachers at HUC propounded was not going to win the Jewish souls he encountered in the armed forces! American Judaism would need more than "mental acquiescence" if it was to be "saved."[3]

These reflections prompted Marcus to consider practical ways to address the needs of a rapidly acculturating American Jewry. In the following essay—which appeared first in the pages of the College's student newspaper,

1. Jacob Rader Marcus to Morris Lazaron, 20 December, 1917, Box 7, Folder 7, Jacob Rader Marcus Papers, AJA, Cincinnati, Ohio.
2. Jacob Rader Marcus to Morris Lazaron, 22 January, 1919, Box 7, Folder 7, Jacob Rader Marcus Papers, AJA, Cincinnati, Ohio.
3. Ibid.

the Hebrew Union College Monthly, *he argues that the rabbi/Jewish chaplain must develop new ways to keep Jewish soldiers involved in Jewish life. Religious services alone will not suffice. He calls for rabbis, social workers, and social centers that will bring Jews together in community.*

This article is unique among his other early writings in that it sheds light on how concerned he was about the ravages of assimilation. Some Jewish servicemen may have believed that they would be able to assimilate within the general culture of army life. Marcus demurs. "Even where the Jew desires to be assimilated he cannot." It is important, he writes, for Jews to "mingle with one's own." American boys of every religious tradition may wear "the khaki," he concluded, but "they are still Catholics, and Protestants, and Jews." This commitment to the distinctiveness of the American Jewish experience prompted Marcus to make this appeal for support for the American Jewish soldier. If a Jew wishes to retain his link with the community while serving in the U.S. Army, he must form a community within the military establishment that provides a social context for Jewish interaction.

Throughout the course of his long career, Marcus clung to the idea that the acculturated American Jew still needed to maintain his Jewish distinctiveness. Decades later, this same line of reasoning would enable him to advocate for the preservation of the American Jewish experience. The American Jew needed his own history, he believed, and the preservation of that distinct legacy would strengthen Jewish identity.

$\sim$

The Jew is essentially a problem, if not to himself at least to others. What a calamity it would be for budding journalists and gray-haired pendants, if they had not the ever-present Jew to dissect and descant upon—authoritatively. True to tradition, the Jew at war becomes a problem, in this instance to himself.

To crystallize into conviction the sympathies of practicing Jews and to develop an interest for Judaism among non-practicing Jews is the problem of American Jewry. The efforts to retain Jews within the religious periphery, and to cause to function any latent Jewish sympathies, are guarded primarily by the desire to advance the men themselves. Yet there is the other motive, unconscious though it may be, on the part of its thinkers, to protect and enhance the name of Jewry. The Jew, manifestly, even in the army, stands out as a distinct group, and to the American nation as a whole becomes the representative *par excellence* of American Jewry, whether they will or no. A Jewish deserter, a Jewish coward, a

Jewish scoundrel reflects not only upon himself but upon the entire Jewish following. Jews are constantly under fire; to deny this would be foolish; consequently, it is incumbent upon the group to help every individual member thereof to attain a high degree of moral pride.

The ideal which it is desired to inculcate is that of "Jewishness." The realization that every Jew is to play the part of a sympathetic brother toward his fellow-Jew; the consciousness that Judaism has a wonderful past that should be a stimulative force in the actions of every member of the group; the conviction that Judaism is the greatest, the only religion for the Jew; an attitude toward life that makes for a thorough sympathy toward all men; a discipline that demands of every Jew that he be representative of all that is true and good; living together with Gentiles, yet on a moral plane of one's own—all this means to be Jewish. This is what we would ask of our fellow-Jews in the ranks.

The business of making Jews Jewish is interesting. There are no precedents by which one might be guided. The amount of work done in the past along these lines is negligible, insufficient to suggest any future *modus operandi*. Work among any class must be guided by a knowledge of its past education, environs, and sympathies. I cannot speak with any degree of authority of the men in the national army cantonments; my own experiences since spring have been confined for the most part to observations among national guardsmen—the volunteers. Jewish guardsmen, practically to a man, are of Orthodox extraction. This fact, however, must not warrant the assumption that they have even a passable acquaintance with Jewish home ceremonial and synagogue customs. It is quite true they have come from homes where the dietary laws were observed and Judaism functioned in its abundance of ceremonial, yet the men themselves have no systematic Jewish education. Very few read Hebrew or have even the slightest conception of Jewish life as such. They come for the most part from the humbler walks of life; very many are artisans and the number of amateur and professional pugilists is relatively large.

Their attitude toward religion is characteristic not only of their own group but of all their associates; their outlook on life differs but little from that of the non-Jew. Theirs is no real hostility toward organized religion; mere indifference. Preachers and confirmed church-goers are looked at askance, as one would at effeminate, weak-minded namby-pambies. The national guardsman's ideal in the service is a "man's man"—a red-blooded fellow who can "hit 'er up" with the wildest, yet one who "plays the game square" and never "goes back on a pal." The boys seem to think, though only in a dim way, that the church as an institution has always stood for peace and harmony; that war is a rough, brutal business, and that preachers and their like have no place in the army. The thought is common that the minister is out of place; that he is only to be tolerated, for quite often he is a "good fellow." This fact is also subconsciously realized and acted upon by the authorities, for the chaplain at a post or in the field devotes much of his time to military duties of a non-religious nature. The type of the men among whom work must be done is common and distinct, men without any particular Jewish sympathies, men who are indifferent, quite often hostile, toward the church.

The nature of my experience at regimental and division headquarters has given me many opportunities of learning methods of approach to the men. Any attempt to make friendship among them that the "gospel" may be spread in their midst is doomed to failure. They must be met and studied and loved, not as possible brands to be plucked from the burning, but because of their own intrinsic merit. It is only when the men learn to know you and respect you for what you are as a man that they will consent to listen to what you have to suggest. They will listen sympathetically to you because it is you, and not because it is Judaism that you have to offer. Intensive, tireless work is necessary even to acquire a moderate success. Organized religion with its attendant apparatus is looked upon with some degree of questioning. Representatives of the rabbinate may be admired, respected; yet they can never enter into the souls of the men and make real conquests. If a cleric be civilian, he cannot acquire the intimate knowledge of military conditions necessary for a thorough understanding of the men; if he be a chaplain, he is an officer, and hence on a different plane, of a status that will not admit of intimate personal contact and confidence. Soldierly habits inculcated in the men discipline them to come to services regularly once they have made a start. Once allegiance is pledged to a service group, loyalty is unquestioned; yet if the group is disturbed by the transfer of a number of its men or their removal to another station, its equilibrium is disturbed and the attendance is affected. Men who have been trained to attend camp services do not feel at home at, and have little sympathy for, synagogal services. Possibly the most gratifying aspect of camp work is the evident loyalty of the men and the unique methods which they adopt to express themselves. In one of the regiments with which I was associated there was but one refractory member—one lost soul who would not come. He was besought by every other Jew in camp to attend, and when their solicitations failed, they held caucus and determined to "kangaroo" him. It took a half hour's pleading on the part of some tender souls to save the recalcitrant. The men were so proud of their services that one or another, every Friday night, brought his Gentile chum along. Sacrifices of "passes" and "evenings off" were made to attend, and it was not uncommon to hear one faithful son roundly curse another for laxity in attendance. It was most amusing to discover the larger number of Gentiles who suddenly found they had Jewish blood in their veins and insisted on celebrating the high holidays and securing the necessary pass therefore. One boy I knew had attended mass regularly every Sunday morning, yet came for his furlough. An investigation disclosed the fact that he was the son of Orthodox Jewish parents and had wanted his pass every Sunday, not to go to mass, but to go home for some of his mother's tasty cooking. I have found that he who would speak theologically to the men must speak in the "language of man." Theological phrases which we use with so much gusto are to them as gibberish. Theologically expressed religion is odious to them; hortatory preaching is disregarded. One must learn to think as the men think and talk as the men talk. When this is done, then a respectful hearing will be accorded.

For a more thorough understanding of ways of appeal to the spiritual nature of the men, it is necessary not only to study their sympathies and the work that has been done among them in the past but to note carefully the media through which other religious organizations attempt the solution of their own problems. Foremost of all is the Y.M.C.A., next to the army itself the greatest organization that the present crisis has developed. The success of the Young Men's Christian Association, however, is chiefly along social lines. Men come to the "Y" shacks in huge numbers to meet the "boys," to write letters, to find a comfortable lounging room, to see a free show, to hear a "live wire" talk. The religious work is not so conspicuous a feature. Yet the "Y" is, to a certain degree, doing good religious work. The direct attempt to make the men religious is a failure, but the indirect method of approach is a success. The business of writing letters home and chatting quietly with one's friends in a "Y" shack is a religious exercise that is not to be despised. If a number of the men in the camp have been attracted to the religious side of the work, it is due primarily to the social consciousness that has been stirred.

"Why, then, any specific Jewish activities?" some may ask. "None is necessary," answer Jews who contribute to "Y" funds and decline to assist the Jewish organizations in doing soldiers' welfare work.

The "Y" cannot function properly for the Jew who would develop not only a Jewish social but a Jewish religious consciousness. The Catholics, who have the clear-sightedness and courage to realize that compromises are unavailing, are building Knights of Columbus hall in the cantonments that their young men may develop themselves along Catholic lines. The objection to the many fraternal organizations that flourish in the cities near the cantonments is that they appeal only to a few—they are neither Jewish nor democratic. An organization must be free and open to Jewry as a whole before it can be accepted. Exclusive groups perfumed with secret mummery are an abomination to the true Jewish spirit.

The problem of the Jewish soldier presents a simple solution. The methods to be pursued that Jews may remain Jewish and that the indifference may be aroused are evident.

The *sine quo non* for efficient work is plenty of money. Jewry of America, as on most occasions, is unmindful of its opportunities and its duties—as Jews. Next to that of affording relief to Jews in the war-stricken lands, there is no need more vital to the future of American Jewry than the necessary salutary provisions for the thousands of young American Jews in the army. It is unpleasant to reflect that it will be necessary to wait for the appearance of Jewish "bad men" in the army before their fellow-Jews realize the necessity for action. The statement that there is no money to be secured is nonsensical. Young capable Jewish business men are on Y.M.C.A. teams and are accomplishing wonders—for the Y.M.C.A.—along financial lines. It is almost pathetic to note the feverish interest in the Christian organization and the smug complacency of the Jewish citizens. Effective work can only be accomplished when ample funds are available.

With sufficient funds on hand, a body of workers can be secured and organized. Thus far the major part of the work at army cantonments and at ports of embarkation has been done by the rabbis of the neighboring towns. Their efforts have been herculean, their accomplishments many.

Little dependence can therefore be placed on the neighboring Jewish communities, for, even though they would have the desire to do constructive work, they lack the training and traditions fundamental for active, successful Jewish communities. A trained body of workers is necessary in every camp. These men should not, like the "Y" workers, be civilians, but must be soldiers, men actually in the ranks, preferably non-commissioned officers. Civilians are never fully trusted by the soldier. The man in the ranks respects and believes in the man in the ranks, and, above all, the man with chevrons on his sleeves—the "non-com," the man with whom he comes in contact, the man he admires and often worships.

In this scheme of things the Jewish chaplain will function as a rabbi and a "social-work" director. It will be his duty to go from regiment to regiment, make acquaintances of the best, the most intelligent Jewish non-com, get them together and secure their active and sympathetic co-operation. Enlisted men with some theological training would be best fitted for this task. Students at rabbinical seminaries and Jewish schools, who wish to work actively for the cause, can do nothing better than to enlist and perform their work among the men of the organizations of which they are a part. Under the guiding hand of the chaplain, the Jewish soldier-leader could organize individual Friday evening and holiday services in every regiment. This method is bound to be successful. The men will be gratified and willing to attend the services rendered by personal friends; personal loyalty and regimental pride will bring every Jew to the meetings. This is not an a priori inference, but a proven fact. I led a service-group made up of the different companies of one regiment, held services every Friday night and every holiday, and averaged an attendance of 95 percent. The fact that these services will of necessity be simple and short will be considered a virtue by the men, not a fault. The officers of the regiments will not only provide the necessary facilities but will cooperate actively with the Jewish workers. Army officers to a man are always willing to assist the enlisted personnel of their commands in their religious exercises.

This method of regimental, battalion, or train services will necessitate no financial expenditures. The objection to a central consolidated service is evident. The camp is too vast. No man, unless he has *Jahrzeit* or wishes to collect a debt, will walk, let us say, from one end of the artillery brigade to the last infantry brigade, or even to division headquarters, especially after the grind of eight hours' intensive training, no matter how intense his Judaism.

The nature of the work which I suggest would require the chaplain that he be a camp *director* of Jewish religious work; others will do the work for him—he to be the organizer, the supervisor. The genesis of this type of an organization is not as difficult as it may appear from first glance. A capable, honest-thinking rabbi could secure the co-operation of the requisite number of men within a short time. It would require hard work on his part to gain the first few real "converts," but as soon as he did, his success would be immediate and highly gratifying.

To complement the work of the individual religious workers in the different regiments there must be a central building—call it a Y.M.H.A. hut, a Soldiers' Settlement, a Talmud shack, what you will. The Y.M.C.A. has demonstrated that the best way to approach the enlisted man is by appealing to his social nature. This is the great truth that the "Y's" have confirmed. A Jewish shack is needed where Jews may congregate, feel at home, develop themselves along social lines. Jewish *social development* will mean *Jewish religious development*—the two are interwoven and inseparable, even as the Jewish racial and religious consciousness. In this central building Jewish forums and classes might be organized that would appeal to the different types of Jew in the camp. On the proper occasion services should be held here, but only for those present or quartered in its immediate vicinity—not as a central service, since to attempt such a proceeding would be but to invite failure.

To co-operate with and supplement the work of the camp shack there should be a central congregating place within the city proper. Even the Y.M.C.A. people, who are unusually keen in ferreting out means of taking care of the men, have not yet adequately grasped the significance of this need. In all national guard and national army camps the men are engaged in intensive drill, which demands the exercise of all their faculties. At night they want to get away from the camp; a natural reaction sets in; they wish to forget the rifle and the uniform for a time. After retreat, thousands flock into the towns, if only to parade the street. The urban "Y's" have made some provisions for these men; the different fraternal organizations have made some; the Jews, little or none. The vestry rooms of the different synagogues might with advantage be suitably equipped for them; better, much better, would be a large suite of rooms, or a hall, on one of the principal streets, with shower baths and reading rooms for the men. This meeting place within the town proper is a necessity; the sooner it is established the better. It would certainly not be asking too much of the local Jewish community to support this center.

To the charge that all this is non-religious, the answer is that nothing in Jewish life which claims to be social can remain detached from the religious phase. Through the method herein suggested, the Jewish soldier, no matter how indifferent to Jewish duty, must inevitably acquire a conception of Jewish *noblesse oblige*. True, we would all be pleased to work among men purely along religious lines, but to do so would only defeat the purpose of our labors. The nature of the great mass of the men is such that certain methods are required—the methods set forth in this writing.

One might go further and petulantly demand the reason for all this emphasis on Jewish propaganda, declaring that the activities of Catholics and Protestants are not sufficient justification for our own efforts. It would certainly be splendid, ideal, if all the soldiers, united by the knowledge of a common cause, inspired by the glory of ultimate victory, would gather together in a common meeting place and serenely discuss the vital social and religious problems of the day. So the story book has it. But, despite the fact that the men have a common aim in the war, despite the fact that all wear the khaki, they are still Catholics and Protestants and Jews, yes, Baptists and Presbyterians and Methodists, North and South. Miracles as yet have not happened. The idiosyncrasies and peculiarities of temperament which have characterized the different religious groups in peace times have not disappeared.

A keen observer is almost shocked with delight to find in the most hardened "reprobate" a real desire to associate with fellow-Jews, to secure a simple, satisfying religious training, to mingle with one's own. You must build Jewish shacks because the men in the ranks want them. Tell them that their request is horribly out of place, that it is un-American, that it smacks of separativeness, and they will look at you in unfeigned astonishment, in disgust. In view of this attitude on the part of men who have no Jewish training, who have not been fed on modern theories of "group rights," there should be no hesitation in satisfying their normal, legitimate, healthy desires.

Those in American Jewry who aspire to lead would do well to make strenuous efforts to reach the soldiers. They are a prize worthwhile. The men in the ranks, almost to a man, are splendid characters, men who might do much for American Jewry after they have gone through the crucible of the trenches. To leave them drift without a real struggle would be a little less than criminal. The Jewish problem in the American army cantonments is of much easier accomplishment than a hasty thought might offer. The group is an intimate one; its sympathies are common; and, finally there is the ironic truth that even where the Jew desires to be assimilated he cannot. He is always a Jew, whether he will or no. Organization, co-operation, real interest, hard work, can do much toward solving the Jewish soldier problem.

Lost

Judaism in the A. E. F. (1919)
The Urgent Need for Welfare Workers

Editor's note:

At the conclusion of World War I, Lieutenant Jacob R. Marcus returned to Cincinnati to complete his rabbinical course of study. He carried home with him a conviction that American Jewry was missing a precious opportunity to instill Jewish loyalty within the ranks of his own generation—the Jewish men who had served by his side in the American Expeditionary Forces. Thousands of his co-religionists had served in the nation's armed forces, and their Jewish needs were very great. In Marcus's opinion, American Jewry failed to provide the Jewish soldiers in the A. E. F. with a host of basic resources that they needed and craved.

Though the war had ended, Marcus pointed out that the needs of the Jewish soldier remained most urgent. First, the process of demobilization would take a considerable amount of time to complete. The Jewish community needed to attend to the needs of Jewish soldiers who were still serving in the armed forces during this process of demobilization. Second, an Army of Occupation was in the process of being established and Jewish soldiers would be in its ranks. There was still time to help the Jewish soldier, and Marcus was determined to arouse concern for the Jewish soldier on the home front.

The Jewish soldiers needed leadership and basic resources. They needed men (Marcus estimates the need for approximately one hundred men) with organizational ability and Jewish commitment that would enable them to "come in personal contact" with Jewish soldiers and help them "to coordinate [the Jewish soldier's] efforts and to provide the physical means to permit them to function as a religious group."

As in the previous essay, Marcus's advocacy on behalf of the Jewish soldier illuminates the depth of his concern for what today is frequently referred to as "Jewish continuity." Marcus was dedicated to the survival of Jewish communal existence. The American Jewish community, he observed many years later, has been forged by "an unusually strong sense of kinship." This essay, concentrating as it does on the pressing needs of America's Jewish soldiers, called for the recruitment of Jewish communal workers who would simply "come in personal contact with the men in his diocese [and] influence them along religious lines." The article sheds light on the dawning recognition among American Jews during this period that Jewish soldiers were gravely lacking in the resources they needed to reinforce their participation in Jewish life.

Marcus's concern for the future of the Jewish soldier also betokened an idea, still inchoate, that would eventually inform his historical methodology. The history of American Jewry was for him the story of a "tightly-knit fellowship." Jews have always "shared common experiences," Marcus the historian wrote, "and the totality of these [experiences] makes up American Jewish history."[1]

~

For the benefit of those Jews in the United States who are honestly interested in the social and religious welfare of Jewry in the American Expeditionary Forces, I write what I have seen and heard and what I know to be true.

Transportation of troops and auxiliary units from the United States to England and France began in the spring of 1917; but it was not until a year later, spring and summer of 1918, that these troop movements assumed enormous proportions. Debarkations were made at English and French base ports. By the spring of 1918, the National Guard and National Army troops were being landed, division after division. The average National Guard division had about 2 percent Jews; the National Army, a larger percentage. There was no "outfit," however remote its type or the nature of its work, that did not contain some members of the faith.

Base ports were always a disappointment to the Jew who sought some form of Jewish social and religious life. One did not expect anything of French Jewry—there is but a handful of Jews in France; many of their Rabbis are at the front—have been there since August 1914—and they are doing splendid work among their compatriots. One expected more at the English base ports—especially those adjacent to some of the most prominent English cities—but, as far as I could ascertain, English Jewry did not find it possible to meet the problem of providing for the welfare of their incoming American coreligionists.

1. Jacob Rader Marcus, *The Colonial American Jew,* vol. I (Detroit: Wayne State University Press, 1970), xxiii.

In the Training Areas

After a rest of a few days at or near the base port, troops were sent to the training areas where they usually remained for a month before being sent to their initial sector. Although these areas are not as consolidated as rest camps near ports of debarkation, yet an entire division (about 28,000 men) is grouped in an area about the size of a small American county. A worker would have had no trouble covering the ground on a bicycle.

This is the most susceptible and momentuous period in the Jewish soldier's life. Despite the submarine danger, the voyage across the Atlantic is one of absorbing interest; the landing on French or British soil is fascinating; the trip across the country is a joy outing. But in the training area all levity disappears. It is vigorous, intensive, disciplinary drill, hour after hour. At night, in the billets or barracks, they can often hear the distant booming of the guns on the firing line. Men become sedate, thoughtful, and though they may not realize it they yearn for and are very susceptible to religious influences. They realize, consciously or unconsciously, that they are about to engage in a piece of work from which there is no turning back; in which there is no equivocation, in work the like of which they never dreamed in their younger years. This desire for religious expression; the yearning to "square up all accounts," to be mindful of one's Judaism right at the firing line, often culminates in spontaneous religious services. They had no "workers." They got together, and had a *minyon,* and that was all there was to it. Their action was quite objective and not at all introspective.

I have attended just such services a week or two before the end of the training period, and I found the men serious and sedate. The service was so full of quiet and dignity that it was an inspiration merely to stand and watch. Individual soldiers, themselves, no matter how interested they might be, could do no more than organize a *minyon* in a regimental area; and even this was done at a sacrifice, inasmuch as battalions were often five and six kilometers apart and men had to walk long distances in order to participate, and after a day of hard drilling, too. It needed active workers to provide for the care of an entire division scattered over the hills for miles.

What Jewish Soldiers Expected

It was inevitable that the Jew should compare the feverish activity of the Salvation Army, the Red Cross, with the *oeuvres* of his own people. Not that the Jew over here expected American Jewry to build huts and to pro-

vide a trained, interested personnel that would compete with other associations. Not at all. The "Y" affords all that any soldier can ever expect in
the way of amusement and material comfort; but the "Y" could not and
did not give the Jew religious inspiration. It was stimulating to enter the
quiet, darkened chapel of a Champagne hut and reverently listen to a
powerful prayer—but the common link of participation was quickly
snapped asunder by the inevitable: "We ask it in thy name . . . Jesus Christ
our Lord and Savior. . . ."

It is practically a physical impossibility to hold services in the trenches.
Even so small a unit as a platoon, about sixty men, is often scattered along
a front of a kilometer. Distances are so large and the nature of the front-
line work is so urgent that services are impracticable, though individual
activities of a worker are possible and are highly advisable. However, the
actual tour of duty in the trenches is normally very short, rarely exceed-
ing two weeks. In support and especially in reserve positions, the men are
often in barracks and are accessible for services. Services organized by the
men themselves are sometimes held, though never to include a unit larger
than a battalion, seldom as large as that. The men actually desire and
crave for religion as expressed in the *minyon,* the assembly, and they organize their *minyonim,* especially when one or another has *Yahrzeit.*

What They Received

Rosh Hashonah was observed on the front by the Jews in groups here and
there. Out of the very many divisions on the lines, I question whether
more than four or five had organized services, emanating from Division
Headquarters. There were, however, I understand, in many divisions, services, springing up here and there, composed of a handful of enthusiasts
who would not be balked by lack of organization or prayer books.

The military authorities invariably offered the men the opportunity to
celebrate the day except, of course, where the exigencies of the services so
forbade. Jewish officers were too busy to undertake religious work and
too often lacked the inclination to do so. The senior chaplain of the division, either Protestant or Catholic, in some units made strong efforts, and
in two divisions that I know of, a very successful effort, to establish Jewish
services. Senior chaplains found it difficult to secure the Jewish representatives with whom to co-operate. The officers, as I have stated, were not
available; non-commissioned officers were too busy; the men did not
have the opportunity nor the ability in many instances.

Jewish Work in A. E. F. Practically Nil

Summing up, I do not think that it would be unjust to say that the Jewish social and religious work in the A. E. F., because of the paucity of workers, up to the signing of the armistice, was practically nil. Although the percentage of Jews is but a fraction compared with the number of non-Jews, yet, by virtue of the fact that Jews are scattered and are found in practically all organizations in greater or less degree, the necessity for a large number of workers was pressing. Yet division after division went over the top without any religious inspiration for its Jewish men.

It was not an uncommon sight to see hundreds of Catholic soldiers on their knees praying before battle. It was a touching picture. The prayer service was an inspiration to the Catholic. The Jew had nothing like it.

Until very recently, to cope with the Jewish religious problem affecting men of the American Expeditionary Forces who were stationed in England, Scotland, France, Northern Italy, Belgium, and the Murman Coast, we had, I believe, as many workers as could be counted on the fingers and thumbs of one's hands. And even though their efforts might be heroic they would be but a drop in this vast ocean of men.

In spite of a strong active sympathy on the part of the military authorities; in spite of a strong predilection on the part of the men to things Jewish, American Jewry accomplished very little.

What American Judaism Lost

Here is what American Judaism has lost: the picked men of American Jewry; the pride of the race, thousands upon thousands of them, are let loose on the fair fields of France to find their own spiritual pastures. Some have. Others have not.

Do not fancy for a moment that they could find Jewish life here. There is no French Jewish communal life available for the soldier. Soldiers are invariably stationed in the towns and hamlets, and the small Jewish communities that may have once inhabited the towns have moved away. If there is a Jewish family or two there, their sole relation to Judaism is the fortune of birth. That is all.

Young American Jewry therefore was practically banished from Judaism since its debarkation overseas. American Judaism has lost an irretrievable opportunity to step into the lives of myriads of Jews; to mold these men; to fashion them as they would have desired and to have returned them a catholic group; a group sympathetic to the general principles of a broad Judaism, if not to the details of Reform or Orthodoxy.

American Jewry was possessed of a deplorable apathy in dealing with the overseas situation. When a hundred men were necessary, five were sent. There was no Jew to welcome the men at the ports; at the rest camps behind the lines. The Jews were left to shift for themselves, and some querulous rabbis and social workers will be indifferent to its advances back in the States.

Soldier's Prayer Book Is a Nightmare

A primary error that was made was the adoption of the recognized prayer book for Jewish soldiers. I cannot see how the organization which brought that book into being could honestly put their seal of approval on it. It is a nightmare.

To one accustomed to the lofty diction and inspired pages of the Union Prayer Book, the English translation is unintelligent at places; cacophonous and disconcertingly literal. To the Orthodox Jew the lopped prayers; the fractional *Shemonah Esra* is an object of dismay.

This prayer book is a serious error. You would feel quite dejected if you saw a group of American soldiers trying to conduct a religious service with a set of them. The young man who has been accustomed to pray with the aid of the Reform Liturgy finds it bewildering, and after aimlessly turning a page or two, stops reading altogether. The Orthodox boy takes a look at it, reads whatever there is of the Hebrew prayers and supplies the remainder from memory. More common is the sight of five or six buck privates straining their necks over the shoulders of the fortunate possessor of an orthodox *Siddur*. One cannot obtain *Siddurim* in all Gaul.

The error of the soldier's prayer book is a far more serious one than might appear at first glance. The Jews of today are a "people of the Book"—not the Bible, the Prayer Book. Judaism is a liturgical religion, altogether different from most Protestant sects. Give ten Jews prayer books and you have a congregation. No rabbi is necessary. Any one who can read can lead. I am convinced that if fighting Jewry had the proper prayer books it would be much more of a praying Jewry.

Leaders among Jewish groups should rid themselves of the false notion that they can legislate Judaism for the Jew. The mere fact that the representatives of all the important Jewish groups determined on a literary error does not mean that the Jewish soldier will bow in reverence to it. American Jewry "in committee assembled" can never induce Isidore Goldstein to pray out of anything but a *Siddur* despite all the resolutions unanimously adopted. American Jewry soldiery is such a broad institution that no policy that attempts to prescribe detailed action and attitude can ever hope for success. American Jewry should provide means and men for the work, but should not prescribe the method.

Suggestions for Future Action

I have tried to indicate in the foregoing paragraphs what has not been done and shall now attempt to formulate (on the basis of seven months' experience in France as a soldier and as an independent Jewish worker) the general principle of future action in the A. E. F.

The Army of Occupation is still in the process of organization. It will ultimately have anywhere from one-quarter of, to half a million troops with their normal percentage of Jews.

The stay of this army, which will constantly change its personnel, is indefinite. A Jewish worker will be needed for every division. He must be provided with a motor car in order to reach all units of his division. The problem of working among the Jews in the Army of Occupation, which will probably occupy Luxembourg and the Coblenz region, should be relatively easy, for the regiments will probably be consolidated in barracks in town and cities, and will not be scattered over the wide area which characterized group arrangement during combat periods.

It is obvious that there will not be any religious activity on the part of the inhabitants of the occupied territory. If American Jewry wishes to influence Jewishly the relatively large number of Jews who will remain in the Army of Occupation, they must take the necessary means to provide a chaplain and the necessary transportation in each division or other large tactical, technical, or supply unit. The number of all these units in the Army of Occupation is relatively small; not more than ten, I should judge. American Jewry should provide workers for the Jews here, not so much because American Jewry wishes to evidence to an admiring world that it "takes care of its own," but because the men actually want Jewish representatives. No, the men will not flock in hundreds to the services, break down the doors of the hut to get in; but a large percentage of Jews in every unit will co-operate gladly with an honest worker.

For many months to come activity must be directed not only toward the Army of Occupation but also toward the immense number of troops in France proper. The demobilization of the A. E. F. will be of necessity a slow process. It is manifestly impossible to send troops home in large numbers, in as much as the terms of peace have not been formulated. There are immense stores and works, foundries and factories, depots and railroad yards which will require the work and presence of the authorities here for many months. America should not expect that the feverish cumulative efforts of eighteen months be dissipated in as many weeks.

Headquarters Should Not Be in Paris

In order that the men in all France be reached all activity should emanate, I believe, from General Headquarters and not, as has been the custom, from Paris. General Headquarters, in the Department of Haute-Marne, is far more centrally located for troops in the A. E. F., especially with reference to the Army of Occupation. The objection to Paris as a center of all religious activity is that it is closed as a leave area to enlisted men, and the only soldiers found there are those who are assigned in that area or go there surrepitiously. At General Headquarters there may not be so many opportunities of finding means of entertainment for the men in that immediate vicinity, yet one may there feel the pulse of the whole Expeditionary Force and may there be able to better gauge all projected work.

Starting with the Army of Occupation and going backward to the sea, there are advance areas, intermediate areas, and base areas with the concomitant depots, enormous base hospitals, school areas, and regulating stations. All have hundreds and thousands of troops, and all need Jewish workers. The order of the day requires the construction of immense camps at the ports of embarkation for America. Some of them will hold 100,000 men. Here the men will rest until they secure the necessary overseas transportation. The need of trained workers here is palpable.

The A. E. F. today has urgent need of workers. There must be a corps of workers here who will fit in the admirable organization of the A. E. F., from base port to Coblenz, just as the Roman Church fitted itself into the shell of the Roman Empire. These workers should be men who can command the absolute respect of soldiers and officers by their personal dignity and academic training. They must be of such a type that they will have access to the military authorities at all times, yet this freedom of approach should not be secured by a negation of religious character.

I have designedly used the term "worker." It is not altogether necessary to have rabbis or chaplains. The need is for a group of intelligent, sympathetic, honest-conscienced Jews with an unlimited fund of idealism and good common-sense. Men who are broad enough to understand the psychology of the individual Jew who will do everything countenanced or discountenanced three hundred and sixty-four days in the year, but will be rigidly orthodox on the three hundred and sixty-fifth; to appreciate the character of the man who has an aversion for anything that smacks of Orthodoxy.

There are as many types of Judaism in the A. E. F. as there are Jews, and the man who undertakes to handle these men must be capable. He must not be bound by one prayer book or by the teachings of his particular school of Judaism. He must give himself to and co-operate with the men as they dictate. He must realize that he is there only to co-ordinate their efforts and to provide the physical means to permit them to function as a religious group. No worker should feel for a second that he represents the Jewish Theological Seminary, or the Hebrew Union College, or the Orthodox Rabbinical Seminary, or Zionism. He should feel that he has not come over here to represent anything but the Judaism of the men with whom he comes in contact at a particular place. All that he will need will be prayer books—the unabridged Hebrew prayer book and the Union prayer book.

The function of the worker here is religious—whereby I connote religious services, religious influence through personal contact and class work, the latter wherever practicable. There should not be the slightest attempt to compete with the "Y." There is no necessity for it. The "Y" is well taking care of the social, the amusement interest of the individual soldier. All that is expected of the Jewish worker is that he come in personal contact with the men in his diocese; that he influence them along religious lines; that he be something of a circuit rider.

There is a need for at least one hundred active men adequately to answer the needs of the American soldiery of the Jewish faith in this expedition. The game is worth the candle.

Zionism and the American Jew

(1933)

Editor's note:

Marcus's analysis of Zionism and its significance to the American Jew is among his most important and oft-cited essays. The article appeared in the second volume of Phi Beta Kappa's recently inaugurated literary journal, The American Scholar. *It seems to have been the only time in Marcus's long career that he published an essay in an academic periodical of this genre. Published in 1933 as the full force of the Nazi calamity was just beginning to unfold, the essay provides the reader with a general description of the Zionist landscape as it developed up to that point in time. In addition to identifying the various Jewish groups that support and oppose Zionism, Marcus seeks to explain why so many American Jews had been attracted to the movement.*

It is interesting to contemplate what may have prompted Marcus to write an analytical essay on Zionism for an intellectual journal like The American Scholar. *He composed this essay at a time when American Reform Judaism was in the midst of an ideological transformation vis-à-vis the Zionist movement. After the promulgation of the Pittsburgh Platform in 1885, many American Jews had come to believe that Reform Judaism and Zionism were mutually exclusive ideologies. This proposition reached its apogee when Kaufmann Kohler was at the helm of the Hebrew Union College. An outspoken anti-Zionist, Kohler's strong views on the subject influenced the thinking of HUC students and faculty alike. Still, Kohler's ideas on Zionism did not go unchallenged. Some of Marcus's fellow rabbinic students, men like Abba Hillel Silver and James G. Heller for example, were dedicated Zionist advocates, as was his teacher, David Neumark. By the 1930s, the number of Reform rabbis who were positively disposed toward Zionism or, at minimum, neutral on the subject had increased to the point that many in the Central Conference of American Rabbis began to suggest the adoption of a new statement of principles that would supercede the manifestly anti-Zionist Pittsburgh Platform.*

Marcus lived through these changes. He had friends on both sides of the issue. Furthermore, Marcus visited Palestine in 1926 where he had an opportunity to spend three months exploring the Yishuv for himself.[1] This

---

1. Chyet, "Jacob Rader Marcus," 12.

analysis reflects an objective scholarly appraisal in which Marcus attempts to describe the Zionist landscape accurately and fairly. Though Marcus did not consider himself a Zionist per se (he never joined a Zionist organization), his analysis emphasizes Zionism's growing significance as a mass movement among Jews in every part of the world. The author is also fully aware of the fact that Zionism enjoyed broad support in the American Jewish community.

Interestingly, Marcus is one of the first to recognize the fact that American Jews had embraced a rather unique form of Zionism. Like Zionists around the world, American Zionists believed that the establishment of a national homeland would serve as a much needed refuge for "hundreds and thousands" of "physically downtrodden" Jews. Similarly, the establishment of a Jewish national homeland would make Jews a people like all other peoples of the earth. At the same time, Marcus stresses, most American Zionists do not consider themselves to be personally in need of a safe-haven or national homeland. Working for the Zionist cause, then, provides many American Jews with a venue for expressing their Jewish loyalties in the American political arena and not exclusively in the American synagogue. "The truth is" Marcus wrote, "the 'secular' Jew, who threatens to outnumber the 'religious' Jew, needs a sphere of activity in which he can express his Jewish affiliation."

Ultimately, Marcus returns again to a question that arises in many of the essays in this volume: What is it that transforms an ordinary Jewish community into a Jewish spiritual center? Marcus insists that to become a true spiritual center, a Jewish community must be a greenhouse for the flowering of Jewish culture, Jewish learning, and Jewish values. As he had done since 1916, Marcus would continue to urge American Jewry to make itself into a Jewish "spiritual center." The historian concludes his analysis by pointing out that American Zionists expect that a Jewish homeland in Palestine would also become a Jewish "spiritual center that will give birth to new ethical and scientific gospels."

~

What does Zionism mean to the American Jew? What can be his relation to this movement centered as it is on a tiny, barren country far from his own fertile shores? Does he pour effort and hope into it or does he fear and discourage it? How is it that Zionism has come to be such a potent force in Jewish life in this country today?

Modern political Zionism, created by the Viennese journalist Theodor Herzl, was a distinct reaction to the Dreyfus case of 1894. Hermann Bahr, the Austrian dramatist, who had often discussed the subject with Herzl, gives this account of the origin of Herzl's Jewish nationalism:

> He was an eye-witness of the cruel and historic ceremony when Captain Dreyfus was stripped of his insignia, and degraded from his rank, prior to his deportation to Devil's Island. The majority of the public was convinced that Dreyfus was guilty; and Herzl was convinced among others. And yet the brutality of the ceremony made a strange impression on him. . . . When the performance was over, when the traitor had been led away, and while the faces of the dispersing throng still glowed with happy excitement, Herzl turned . . . to one of his colleagues of the press. "Why are they so delighted? The traitor deserved his fate, and he received no more punishment than he merited. But how can they find such intense joy in the suffering of a human being? Granted he is a traitor—but a traitor is still a man." His colleague replied: "No, the French do not feel that he is a man. They see him not as a human being but as a Jew. Christian compassion ends before it reaches the Jew. It is unjust—but we cannot change it. It has always been so, and it will be so for ever." It was at this moment that Herzl's Zionism was born.

He probably reasoned that if the French people, one of the most cultured and liberal of Europe, the first people to emancipate Jewry, would not accept the Jew into their spiritual fraternity of citizenship there was little bone for the Jew in any land. Moved, therefore, by the conviction that the Jew was rejected by his environment, he appealed in 1896 to world Jewry in the pamphlet, the *Jewish State*, to rally around him and to create a national home.

His call found his people in a receptive mood. Western European Jewry had now been trying for three generations, since the beginning of its emancipation, to adjust itself in every respect to the cultural pattern of its native lands. In its feverish enthusiasm, its political devotion often assumed a chauvinistic hue. Because it recognized no higher loyalty than devotion to that state which had brought it freedom from the old restrictions, nationalism became almost an instinct. Yet the rising anti-Semitic movement questioned the sincerity of the Jew, in spite of the fact that he had sacrificed practices for which his fathers, only a century or two earlier, had gone to the stake. On the one side of the Rhine, in Germany, Ahlwardt was accusing the Jewish munition manufacturers of betraying Germany to the French, while on the other side, in France, Drumont was denouncing the un-Jewish Dreyfus as a Jewish traitor who had betrayed the army to the Germans. Many Western European Jews were completely identified with the nationalism of their land of birth, yet they were dismayed by the consciousness that their country would never forgive them for having been born Jews. In Eastern Europe, Jewish nationalism was nothing new; in the Russian Pale of Settlement the penned-in masses had always been granted national or "minority rights," a hang-over from the medieval class-state. The increasing severity of the political and economic disabilities imposed by the Russian bureaucracy, and finally the wholesale massacres beginning in the 80's, merely served to bring to a climax the hopes of the religiously minded masses for a way out, for a Messianic revelation, as it were. It was nothing new for Jews to cherish such expectations. They had listened to scores of "redeemers" since Jesus had preached in the days of the iron-fisted procurators.

It was at that moment, when Russian Jewry was distraught and when Western European Jewry was spiritually dejected, that Herzl published his *Jewish State*. It was not a great book, but it fired the imagination of thousands and rallied a band of devoted followers around this fascinating man. The first Zionist Congress soon assembled in Basel, and there in August 1897 formulated its political program: "Zionism aims at establishing a publicly and legally assured home in Palestine for the Jewish people."

Up to the World War, Zionists had accomplished little in Palestine; in the Diaspora they carried on a vigorous propaganda. Then, early in November 1917, when the Allied cause looked hopeless, the British, in a very ambiguous statement, announced that they viewed "with favor the establishment in Palestine of a national home for the Jewish people." This was the Balfour Declaration. It was motivated by a curious jumble of traditional English interest in the "seed of the Messiah," by a sense of justice, and above all by political expediency. The British government practically offered a land which it did not yet possess in exchange for international Jewish support—which never existed. Later the land was won and the League of Nations gave world sanction to the creation of a Jewish homeland under the supervision of the British government. In August 1929, the World Zionist Organization, which until then had been the recognized agency for the creation of a Jewish homeland in Palestine, was "extended" to include many non-Zionist Jews all over the world. But the Jewish Agency as a world union of Zionists and non-Zionists has been a failure; the Zionists within it, almost exclusively, have been responsible for the enthusiasm and the work.

America and the American Jew have done a great deal to further the Zionist cause. Woodrow Wilson, on the advice of his Jewish friends, encouraged the issuance of the Balfour Declaration, and Congress, in May to June 1922, passed resolutions expressing its approval of the establishment of a national home for the Jewish people in Palestine. American Jewry has supplied the bulk of the monies for the building up of the land, and has sent over technicians, experts, and a few leaders. Nevertheless, it is by no means indispensable to the movement, and though it is the largest Jewish group in the world its defection would not be calamitous.

There are many in the United States, however, who believe that Zionism is indispensable to the American Jew. Many, but certainly not all. For the sake of convenience, Jews in this land may be divided into two groups: the so-called Germans, for the most part immigrants from the Germanic lands, who came to these shores from 1830 to 1870; and the Eastern Europeans, who came here from 1870 until 1924 when the Johnson-Lodge immigration bill went into force. The Germans—many of whom are natives of the third generation—are on the whole, and for varied reasons, definitely opposed to Zionism. They assert its impracticability, pointing out the known poverty of Palestine, its almost complete lack of natural resources, and its occupation by an overwhelming majority of nationally and religiously conscious Moslem Arabs. They point to the tacit threat of the great sea of Moslems in the hinterland which stretches from Turkey, through Asia Minor and Egypt, on east into India, and even farther. And, because of religious reasons, they look with disfavor on the movement, for many of the older settlers, followers of the Reform movement in Judaism, emphasize the universalistic aspect of their creed. Nationalism, they believe, is a step backward, a flouting of the highest humanitarian ideals of the prophets of Israel. Because of its secular tendencies and because it refuses to ally itself with any one party in Judaism, they have been quick to reject it. They believe that there is no religious future for Jewry in that little pocket of valleys and hills on the fringe of the great Arabian desert. On the contrary, they feel strongly that the world at large is Israel's field wherein it may spiritualize itself and impress the prophetic truths on the nations of the earth.

Zionists, for over a generation, have poked fun at this Reform Jewish "mission" theory of Israel's destiny—and unjustly. For not only is this concept as old as the Diaspora and its Hellenistic apologetic literature, but, in slightly different form, it is found in the teachings of Asher Ginzberg, the founder of cultural Zionism, and in the writings of some of the more notable Zionist ideologists, who look upon Jewish nationalism not as an end in itself but as an opportunity to evolve the highest possible expression of a socialized, ethical living-together. Yet in practical Zionism the motif of influencing the world by example is subordinated to the immediate problems of distressed Jewry. The stand of the Reform Jew who objects to Zionism because it must needs stress nationalism is indeed most valid, and raises the controversy to a very high plane. It is all the more regrettable, therefore, that this high stand is somewhat vitiated by the fact that many American Jews who most earnestly deprecate Jewish nationalism because it is nationalism, most earnestly advocate a type of American patriotism that falls little short of chauvinism.

There are others, too, who reject Zionism because they think it lays them open to the charge of "dual loyalty." No Jew, they believe, can be an American citizen and at the same time work for the creation of a Jewish state. They readily admit that a man may be a loyal Irish-American, and yet work for the furtherance of the Irish Free State, but they refuse to apply this analogy to the Jew. The reasons for their dread of the accusation of a divided loyalty are, I believe, not difficult to analyze. Civil and political liberties have been granted to Central European Jews only since the '60s and '70s of the last century. Many of the German immigrants, therefore, had their first taste of civil liberties in this land. Many of them who were attracted to the shores of America to enjoy these liberties have never forgotten that in Europe they had been treated as aliens whose devotion to the state was questioned by the conservative press. The consciousness of gratitude to America for the freedom it gave them, added to the haunting dread of the reproach of being aliens, has made them very sensitive about their American political loyalties, and quick to resent the imputation—never made here—that their political loyalties are somewhere else.

Furthermore many of the older settlers look askance at Zionism because it is not yet socially "respectable." It is for the most part the movement of the later, the Eastern European migration, of the Jewish proletariat and the petty shopkeepers, many of whom have not yet become adept in American manners and mannerisms. Of course there are Brandeis, Felix Frankfurter, Julian Mack, the Strausses of New York, and a number of leading Reform rabbis who are Zionists, but they are notable exceptions. The indifference, even hostility, of the older settlers is regrettable. Reform Jewry would certainly benefit from the intense Jewish enthusiasm that Zionism engenders; Zionism on the other hand is sadly in need of the support of this sturdy, clear-sighted, and responsible group in American life, a group that in its own quiet way is devoted to Jewish ideals and has done a great deal to bear the financial load of Jewish institutions down to the present day.

Likewise quite a number of the Eastern European orthodox object to Zionism, but solely on religious grounds. They are opposed to political Zionism because they believe that when God wishes to restore Israel He will do so in His own way; His hand need not be forced. Thus they cannot accept a program of Jewish life that is not avowedly pledged to the principles of traditional orthodoxy.

Not all the observant orthodox here have had the courage to maintain this attitude of intransigence. Their love for Palestine is too intense, too real. They have thrown themselves heart and soul into the struggle for the rebuilding of the Holy Land, but are attempting to counteract the modernistic secular tendencies of the Zionist organization by creating, for one thing, a system of parochial schools, in which orthodoxy prevails. They have consistently set themselves against the secular tendencies of Jewish nationalism and hope to impress their conservative religious spirit on all the social and political institutions in the new State. They call themselves the *Mizrahi,* those who look "eastward" to a "spiritual center" where a new Jewish life will arise on the old foundations of rabbinic law and authority.

The Jewish working-class, concentrated almost solely in the large cities of the Atlantic coast, particularly in New York, are for the most part out of sympathy with Zionism. They are completely dominated by concepts of socialism, have no religious interests, and look upon this new Jewish activity as a form of political reaction. In their opposition to its stress on nationalism they are at one with the older Jewish settlers, who have rejected the movement on political and religious grounds. Their urge for idealistic expression spends itself in the struggle of the liberal and radical political parties for recognition in American life. But like the orthodox, many of the trade unionists also, the *Poale Zion* (Workers of Zion), have been unable to resist the romantic appeal of the Holy Land, and have created a synthesis of nationalism and internationalism, thus effecting a harmony between Zionism and socialism. They seek to create an ideal socialistic state in Palestine on a national background, a state that will, through its exemplary form, exert an influence on the capitalistic lands of the West.

Though it is difficult to speak with accuracy, it is nevertheless fair to assume that most of the new immigrants in this land are heartily in sympathy with the ideal of the restoration of the Jewish state. They may not support it actively—the actual paying membership of the Zionist Organization of America does not exceed 65,000—but they are definitely in sympathy with the cause, and the ideal itself exercises a strong influence on their lives. The emotional and intellectual power of this movement of national renascence cannot be measured by the number of its contributing members. Of the three forces which have indelibly impressed themselves on American Jewish life during the last generation—religious change, political and economic liberalism, and Jewish nationalism—the last is by far the most potent.

Why should a movement to create a "politically and legally assured home in Palestine" be popular with hundreds and thousands of Jewish citizens in this free land, members of a group to which Washington in 1790 could write:

> The citizens of the United States of America have a right to applaud themselves for having given to mankind examples of an enlarged and liberal policy: a policy worthy of imitation. All possess alike liberty of conscience and immunities of citizenship. It is now no more that toleration is spoken of, as if it was by the indulgence of one class of people, that another enjoyed the exercise of their inherent natural rights. For happily the Government of the United States, which gives to bigotry no sanction, to persecution no assistance, requires only that they who live under its protection should demean themselves as good citizens, in giving it on all occasions their effectual support.

With such a character of liberties why should any people even think of rebuilding its old homeland? As a matter of fact, the average Zionist, in this land at least, has no desire to return to the land of his fathers. Even if the masses here wished to go they could not. Palestine, this side of the Jordan, even under the most favorable circumstances, could never support more than a million and a half or two million people; there are already over a million Arabs and Jews there now, and there are over four million Jews alone in this land. But Palestine can serve as a place of refuge for hundreds and thousands who sorely need it, argues the Zionist. There is obviously a Jewish Problem, the problem of finding a home for those Jews in all lands who are "unassorted," who are nationally maladjusted, who are physically downtrodden, who have not had the opportunity to "exercise their inherent natural rights," as Washington was pleased to put it. There is a need for such a home in this year of grace and the American Zionist has set out to do what lies in his power to open Palestine for settlement to the Jew. There is no other land open to him throughout the world today except Biro-Bidjan, communistic Siberia. The following captions, picked at random from the various issues of *The Jewish Daily Bulletin* of the month of January 1933, may indicate why many American Jews still think it necessary to create a state somewhere where Jews will be admitted "as of right":

Jan. 6. Harbin, China. White Russians suspected of murder of Jewish president of Jewish community of Harbin.

Jan. 6. Berlin. The blood ritual murder accusation levelled against the Jews of Rastenberg by a Nazi organ took a further turn today with the arrest of a Christian butcher, Popp, who was charged with the murder of an eight-year-old Christian child, Benno Haffke.

Jan. 13. Bucharest. Deputy Michael Landau, Jewish representative of the Roumanian parliament, yesterday announced that he will again press for parliamentary investigation into the shooting on January 8, 1932, of five young Jews, two of them girls, by Roumanian frontier guards at Soroca.

Jan. 14. Warsaw. Warsaw anatomic institute closed; fear troubles as Jewish students barred by authorities.

Jan. 18. London. An American Jewish sailor, Abraham Epstein, as a result of the Jew-baiting and persecution to which he had been subjected by his shipmates, jumped overboard from an American ship on which he served.

Jan. 20. Berlin. Nazis demand Prussian Diet enact *numerus clausus* law limiting Jewish lawyers. Would permit one Jew to practice for 100 non-Jewish [lawyers?].

Jan. 20. Salonica. Vassil Missolonghitis, one of the publishers of *Makedonika Nea,* gets 30 days for anti-Semitic series. . . . The Minister of War, General Kondylis, is reported to be the paper's owner.

And January 1933 was a relatively quiet month.

But the American Jew is interested in Palestine not only for what it can do for others, but for what it can do for him. Thus there is a considerable proportion of Zionists who, in spite of their devotion to American political institutions, wish to see Jewry become a people "like all the nations." They want all the paraphernalia of a nation simply in order to have the inner satisfaction of "belonging" in the world which they conceive of as a commonwealth of nations. Nationalism betokens respectable conformity, normalcy. They believe, too, that with a Jewish state behind them they will for the first time be accepted completely as citizens, without the mental and emotional reservations of which they often suspect their fellow

Americans. If the Jews had a common land, they think, Jewish citizens in their respective lands would never again be suspected of being aliens.

Another reason for seeking a Jewish state abroad is that the existence of such a state, even though remote, helps one become adapted to a not altogether friendly environment. Identification with Palestine invites one with the dignity and pride needed to cope with the discrimination one occasionally experiences in this country, for it is a fact that social and economic disabilities have played their part in predisposing many Jews to a Jewish nationalism. Although there are many individuals who deny that they have ever suffered as Jews, they do not represent the entire Jewish experience. The need for a series of Jewish defensive leagues since 1859, and the details of generous annual reports, will lead the historian to believe that the Jewish status in this land is not yet ideal. It is fairly obvious that there is something of a Jewish problem in this country, also, for foreign publicists are agreed that social discrimination is probably stronger here than in some of the anti-Semitic lands of Europe. Many hotels, clubs, schools, apartment houses, and residential sections are closed to Jews. Social discrimination is an old story here; it became notorious in 1877 when Judge Hilton closed the Grand Union Hotel in Saratoga Springs to Joseph Seligman, the banker who once declined the post of secretary of the treasury in the Grant Administration. Since the War and the present economic depression, a definitely increasing prejudice against the employment of Jews has expressed itself in a variety of ways. Even more so than in the past, it is believed that now banks, insurance companies, railroads, public service corporations, and basic industries refuse to employ Jews. There is a growing discrimination against the employment of Jews as clerical assistants. In the smaller towns Jewish men and women are unduly limited in the teaching profession in the primary and secondary schools, and even in the state and municipal colleges and in the larger semi-public, nationally known universities the percentage of Jewish instructors is effectively though unobtrusively limited. It is notorious that many professional schools, particularly medical colleges, will admit only a certain percentage of Jews. Hundreds of rejected candidates, Americans, have been compelled to go to Germany, Scotland, and Switzerland, and in some of these places, too, they are experiencing difficulties because they are Jews. Dean Shaler of Harvard in his essay on the "Hebrew Problem" in *The Neighbor* was already concerned about the social discrimination against Jewish students. This was in 1904. Eighteen years later the Jews had become such a problem to this university that President

Lowell went so far as to suggest that "if every college in the country would take a limited proportion of Jews, I suspect we should go a long way toward eliminating race feeling among the students, and, as these students passed out into the world, eliminating it in a community." His suggestion, no doubt, was kindly meant, but it came as a terrific shock to every American Jew. The details of discrimination in commercial, industrial, and professional life today may be found in Heywood Broun's and George Britt's *Christians Only*. It is not pleasant reading. One wonders how much truth there is in the statement (page 231) that "in general office work, about 90 percent of the jobs available in New York are barred to Jews." The Jew has learned during his two thousand years in the Diaspora that he can survive *pogroms*, but not unemployment.

There is a distinct relation between this silent, effective, pervasive discrimination against the Jew and the turning of many to Zionism. It is true that some Jews, under the impact of prejudice, have gone over completely to the contemporary Gentile culture by denying their Jewish origin and by assuming Christian names. Far more, however, under the influence of Zionism, with a knowledge of the history of their past, have accepted with patient dignity the added disabilities of a difficult period. Zionism has prevented the morale of many from completely collapsing. It has bolstered up a pride that cannot easily be broken down by prejudice; the consciousness of their own worth is, to some, ample compensation for the aloofness and bland disregard of their fellow Americans. Zionism brings them comfort; it instils new hope in them by emphasizing the fact that they belong spiritually, at least, to a group with whom they share the tradition of a courageous past and the hope for a better future.

In a more positive sense—and this is particularly true of the immigrant masses and their children who came here with high hopes—Zionism fills the void in the heart of many an American who still hungers for spiritual fulfillment. It was not merely the prospect of a better living that brought them, for if that was all they wanted, they could have remained in old Russia or the Balkans where there was always an opportunity for a career for the man who was willing to forswear his faith. "It was the faith in America and not the occasional criticisms that touched me most," said Grace Abbott in a study of southern and eastern European immigrants. "I felt them, and I have felt many times when I have met some newcomer who has expected a literal fulfillment of our democratic ideals, that fortunately for America we had great numbers who were coming to remind us of the 'promise of American life,' and insisting that it should not be forgotten." (In Mary Antin's *They Who Knock at Our Gates*, p. 140.) If America were truly liberal and democratic—as the immigrants interpret those terms—if it treated every Jew on his individual merits and did not think of him as a "Jew," if there were a reasonable hope that here a high idealism would find a response in the hearts of America's millions, then in all probability Zionism would not have the sort of hold it now exercises on the Jewish masses of this land. There may be a touch of intellectual and spiritual arrogance in this attitude of the Jew, although he is not consciously aware of it. There is something ironical in the fact that some of the leaders of Zionism, powers in local politics, bulwarks of our great conservative political parties, are devoted—sincerely, too—to a social and economic program in Palestine that is diametrically opposed to everything to which they are committed in this country! Is Palestine a spiritual escape, a projection of the political ideals which they feel cannot be realized here?

It is interesting to reflect that the prime reason assigned by many for the need of Zionism here is that it will save American Jewry from assimilation, assimilation being understood in the sense of a complete surrender of religion and folk-ways, and the ultimate disappearance of the Jewish group through intermarriage with the Gentile majority. This appeal for the need of Zionism, the most popular one advanced, is interesting and dramatic, but unnecessary. Jewry in America is not disappearing; it is not disappearing anywhere except in Russia. On the contrary, world Jewry has grown at least 50 percent during the last generation. The truth is that the "secular" Jew, who threatens to outnumber the "religious" Jew, needs a sphere of activity in which he can express his Jewish affiliation. The industrial revolution and the factory system have made Jewish distinctiveness in dress and food and religious observances almost impossible; the modern uni-national state with its cultural institutions has swept away the autonomous Jewish cultural group of preemancipation times; modern science has undermined orthodoxy and put religion itself on the defensive; and the desire for conformity and standardization in things of the flesh and the spirit has completed the process of secularization. It is these secularized Jews, whose numbers are growing, who are left without a spiritual haven. They cannot assimilate: they wish to remain in the ambit of Jewry, they have no desire to efface themselves, and even if they had, they would probably find that the world about them would not readily accept them. It is men of this type who frequently find rest in the bosom of Zionism, for here they may be good Jews in spite of their refusal to identify themselves with any particular Jewish religious group.

There is one aspect of Zionism that appeals to all groups in Jewry, even to non-Zionists—the cultural aspect. For at least two thousand years the Jews have maintained a tradition of learning. Their common bond was not so much race or language or land of origin as it was a common literature, religion, and way of life. The pursuit and study of biblical and rabbinical lore was not merely a perfunctory academic exercise. It was marked by the most intense application and devotion, for rabbinic study was a mode of worship and, what is just as significant, rabbinic teachings were valid law in the Middle Ages for the Jewish community which operated under charters granting it wide powers in matters of internal organization and civil jurisdiction. From the thirteenth to the nineteenth centuries rabbinic studies practically monopolized intellectual activities. The social exclusiveness of the medieval state, the domination in the Jewish community of a hierarchy which found its authority in the Talmud and its commentaries, intensified this occupation with literary materials. The opening of the professions to the Jews in the nineteenth century gave them a chance to maintain this intellectual and academic bias; Jewry in the modern world began to produce men of distinction in every field of science and thought. Gradually the belief spread that in Palestine, amidst the most favorable surroundings, the Jewish intellectual genius would find its finest expression and its greatest opportunity. Many distinguished American Jews are convinced that such a cultural center in Palestine is most desirable and that the hope of making a distinct contribution to thought and culture in the modern world is adequate justification for the effort to create it.

It may be that Zion's appeal to the American Jew lies in its incitation to purposeful activity. It offers a rounded-out, well-integrated national ideal. The fathers who were religious Messianists since Chaldean days were content for the most part to wait patiently for the Kingdom of Heaven; the sons have attempted to force the hand of God. They have shifted the Messianism of the prophets and sages from the religious to the social scene and have gone to work. The Jew is tired of waiting for his Messiah; he has determined to create him—in Palestine. He is thrilled by the feeling of participation in creation. In the many-sided life of Palestine every Jew can find the opportunity to help rear anew, and better, that which appeals to him. The humble cloak-presser furthers the General Federation of Jewish Labor, Einstein interests himself in the Institute of Mathematics of the Hebrew University. In the short period since the war the Zionists have fashioned beautiful modern towns and villages, settled thousands of colonists, drained swamps, built roads, set up model farms.

They have erected a great power plant, introduced modern machinery, established new industries, and gone far to introduce Western standards and ways of living to a primitive land. They have built hospitals and clinics, have laid the foundations of a great university, have already assembled the largest library in the Near and Middle East, and have established a modern Westernized school system with Hebrew as the language of instruction. They have stimulated a linguistic and literary renascence, brought to birth a romantic nationalism, and inspired a network of enthusiastic groups and followers in almost every country of the world.

The historian who would rise above the passion and controversy about him cannot ignore the somber background of the Palestinian scene. He is conscious of the fact that the British colonial administration does not look with any particular favor on the whole experiment. Three riots of major proportions are ample index of the bitter and uncompromising hostility of the Arabs, who outnumber the Jews four to one and who resent the penetration of their land. If he retains his perspective he will note that everything is being done in miniature. The total area in possession of the Jews does not exceed 325,000 acres, there are not 50,000 Jews on the soil, and actually fewer Jews in all of Palestine than in the state of Massachusetts. Yet he cannot but be moved by this attempt of a people to recreate a new national and spiritual life for itself. Unless his emotions have been dulled by an age in which the exceptional occurs too frequently to startle, he will not find it difficult to understand how the new Palestine has caught the imagination of many an American. Everything there pulsates with the freshness of experimentation, creativity, youth, and idealism. Black-eyed Bokharan and blue-eyed German-Jewish children sing the same Hebrew nursery rhymes. A huge American tractor plows through the fields where once Assyrian, Greek, Arab, and Crusade troops fought, and when the day's work is done husky pioneers in their low roofed barracks read Oscar Wilde's *Picture of Dorian Gray* or Windelband's *Geschichte der Philosophie*—in Hebrew.

It is undeniable that the apologetic of Zionism has exercised a strong fascination on many here. Palestine is an ideal in which, the Zionist believes, he can justly glory. He is proud of his institutions that provide for the sick and the unfortunate. He boasts that there is no child labor, no exploitation of women workers, no speculation in land, for all Zionist-owned farms have been nationalized. He is proud of his communistic and cooperative enterprises, of his innovations in the Near East, in agriculture, housing, hygiene, and city building. He glories in the schools he has built, in the example he sets of respect for women, in the cultural values he upholds. Of course he is not unaware that Jewish nationalism has been of great service to him as an individual in aiding him to find himself in his own environment, that it has given him an appreciation of the historic ideals of ancient and medieval Jewry, that it has taught him the beauty of Jewish folk-life and strengthened him in his sense of Jewish self-respect. It is a source of satisfaction to him that through the fraternity of a common venture in idealism there is being forged a new bond of unity that will serve materially to retard the many forces working toward a disruption of world Jewish unity. But it is his fondest hope that through the social experimentation in which he is now engaged in his old homeland his own spiritual heritage will flower again. He trusts that there a new social order will evolve, an order which will point the way for other peoples. He is confident that the soil that nourished prophetic thought may again become a spiritual center that will give birth to new ethical and scientific gospels.

Mass Migrations of Jews and Their Effects on Jewish Life

(1940)

Editor's note:

In this essay, Marcus examines the vicissitudes of the Jew in the Diaspora and its effects on the ebb and flow of Jewish culture. Significantly, Marcus's analysis of the impact of migration on Jewish history appeared long before other American historians began to fully appreciate the importance of this phenomenon.[1] Marcus notes that true "mass migrations" have been a very rare event in Jewish history. Still, throughout the course of Jewish history, peregrinations from one place to the other have caused the populations of Jewish communities to wax and wane. As a rule, Jews are loyal to the land of their nativity; they abandon their homeland only when they are literally compelled to do so.

Marcus has identified a number of broad lessons that the study of the history of Jewish migrations teach. First, he notes that there is not necessarily a direct correlation between the size of a given Jewish community and the level of cultural dynamism that community exudes. "Jewish centers" he writes, "do not emerge in mechanical succession through the automatic transference of populations and cultural values from one part of the world to the other." This observation led him to identify a principle he repeatedly emphasized in his teaching: Numbers do not, in and of themselves, create an influential Jewish center. Marcus validates this generalization by pointing to the large Jewish population that settled in Poland during the sixteenth and seventeenth centuries after being run out of England, France, Spain, and the Germanies. Though numerically significant, the Jews of Poland had little or no cultural exchange with the wider culture that surrounded them. The community became ingrown and parochial. Conversely, a numerically small Jewry, such as the Jews who lived in Palestine, continued to impact the totality of Jewish life

---

1. Oscar Handlin (1915–), a pioneering scholar of immigration and its effects on the American nation, published his study on Boston's immigrants in 1941 (*Boston's Immigrants: A Study in Acculturation* [Cambridge: Harvard University Press]). Handlin's best known publication, *The Uprooted: The Epic Story of the Great Migrations that Made the American People* (New York: Grosset and Dunlap) appeared in 1951.

both spiritually and culturally. Marcus argues that a dynamic Jewry is one that fosters "great nurseries of Jewish learning" that provide Jewish life with "the strongest fortifications of the spirit." Following the teachings of Heinrich Graetz, Marcus understood Jewish history as being "predominantly a history of culture." The historical reconstruction of Jewish migration patterns illuminates how this cyclical process of cultural evolution unfolded.[2]

Marcus identifies a second vital lesson that the history of Jewish migrations teaches. Whenever Jewish centers declined, many Jews (though perhaps not the majority) managed to emigrate and strike roots in nearby or distant locations. This trait projected Jews to settlements around the globe, and the very existence of numerous Jewish centers of life has proved to be the "ultimate salvation" of the Jewish people. Marcus coined his own term to refer to this phenomenon: "omniterritoriality." The coexistence of numerous Jewish communities in all corners of the globe has been a critical factor in Judaism's remarkable durability, according to Marcus.

These lessons from the study of Jewish migrations bring Marcus back to his own epoch. Ever since the middle of the seventeenth century, Jews have moved eastward in pursuit of a spiritual sanctuary and, simultaneously, westward in search of physical security. By the dawn of the twentieth century, this bifurcated migration pattern found its destination in two great Jewish centers of the East and West respectively: Palestine and America. Jewish culture, that is, the intellectual and artistic life of the Jewish people, will issue forth from these two communities. In affirming the vital significance of both the American Diaspora and Palestine, Marcus identifies himself with the teachings of the Hebrew essayist Ahad Ha'am (1856–1927), and his friend the Jewish historian Simon Dubnow (1861–1941), both of whom argued that Jewish survival ordained the need for an enduring symbiotic relationship between the ancient homeland and Diaspora Jewry.[3] *"There is no longer to be a choice of Palestine or the diaspora," Marcus writes, ". . . we must be prepared to accept both Palestine and the diaspora. The two are not mutually exclusive."*

2. For more on how Graetz influenced Marcus, see the introduction (pages xi–xxix and the editor's note to Marcus's essay, "America: The Spiritual Center of Jewry," especially note 3 (page 38). On Graetz's conceptualization of Jewish history, see Meyer, *Ideas of Jewish History*, 217–44.

3. Ahad Ha'am argued that the relationship between the Land of Israel and the Diaspora of Israel could be understood by the image of a center (i.e., the Land of Israel) and a circumference (the Diaspora). Dubnow posited a different concept. On Ahad Ha'am and Simon Dubnow's theories regarding the national-cultural identity of the Jews, see Gideon Shimoni, *The Zionist Ideology* (London: Brandeis University Press, 1995), 104–12. For a

How will these two centers exert a powerful influence on Jewish life? Palestine, the non-Zionist Marcus avers, must become more than a "catchbasin for desperate refugees." It must aspire to be "Zion"—a community that successfully fosters "ancestral ideals and traditions, the search for prophetic conviction and practice, the spread of Hebrew language as a medium for Jewish expression, and the furtherance of Jewish solidarity." Similarly, American Jewry in the West will merit the appellation of a great spiritual center of the Jewish people if it can "initiate for world Jewry a new Golden Age of learning, inspired by the finest in the civilization of this generation."

This essay is very rich. It not only illustrates the astonishing breadth of Marcus's historical knowledge, but it also showcases his impressive ability to identify, summarize, and interpret broad historical trends. In doing so, Marcus demonstrates how a historian may convert the past into a useful lesson for the present as well as a worthy compass that can guide us into the future.

~

Two hundred years ago, when Parliament passed the Naturalization Act of 1740, the population of the American colonies included scarcely 500 Jews. In 1877 there were 250,000 Jews in the United States. Today, scattered in over 4,500 cities, villages, and country districts there are 4,831,180 of them, constituting the largest and most important Jewry in the world today. One might venture to state that we have here the greatest and most significant aggregation of Jews the world has yet seen. This tremendous community functions through at least 10,000 Jewish organizations which touch every phase of cultural, social, religious, and economic life.

The American Jew is distinguished for the part he plays in the political life of the land. His presence in the national cabinet, in the halls of Congress, in the gubernatorial chairs, in the Supreme Court attest the extent of his services to America. In the professions, in the universities, in the scientific laboratories, one finds an appreciable number of cele-

---

summary of Dubnow's historical perspective on this subject, see also, Meyer, *Ideas of Jewish History*, 247–69. It is also quite possible that Marcus was familiar with the work of Simon Rawidowicz (1897–1957), who characterized the relationship between the Land of Israel and the Diaspora of Israel as an ellipse with two foci. Rawidowicz was a disciple of both Krochmal and Dubnow. See Rawidowicz's essays "Two That are One," "Israel: The People, the State," and "Jerusalem and Babylon," in *State of Israel, Diaspora, and Jewish Continuity* (London: Brandeis University Press, 1998), 147–61, 182–93, and 229–39.

brated Jews. Three Nobel prize winners of Jewish origin have worked or lived on these shores. In two fields of economic endeavor, merchandizing and cinema, Jewish efforts have been particularly fruitful. Both of these industries owe much to the energy, vision, and courage of Jewish entrepreneurs.

A number of individuals have taken advantage of the opportunities in this land to amass great wealth. This good fortune has generated a feeling of gratitude which has promoted philanthropic gifts of a far-reaching social character. Julius Rosenwald, for example, has helped, through the Rosenwald Foundation, to build over five thousand Negro schools. The Guggenheims, to cite another prominent Jewish family of philanthropists, through the John Simon Guggenheim Memorial Foundation, has sent hundreds of brilliant American scientists, artists, and writers all over the world to study and to bring back to these shores the fruits of their investigation and inspiration.

The larger achievements of American Jewry date back to the arrival of the German Jews in the United States in the middle of the 19th century and especially to the subsequent appearance in 1881 and thereafter of large numbers of Eastern European immigrants. These Russian and Polish masses of the so-called Slavic wave of immigration effected a profound change in the pattern of our communal life. They found, upon their arrival, a small, provincial Jewry, liberal in religious outlook, Germanic in background, and bourgeois in social composition. But today American Jewry, being overwhelmingly Eastern European in origin, has another complexion altogether. It is a numerically large metropolitan group, conservative in its religious sympathies, largely proletarian in its social position, and fiercely zealous in its Jewish loyalties. From its Yiddish roots, nurtured in Oriental imagery and toughened with Slavic bucolic traditions, it continues to draw refreshing vitality and cultural sustenance. We have here an excellent example of the way in which an older pattern of Jewish life is altered due to the impact of a new wave of immigration.

To the Jews of Eastern Europe, America was the open sesame to new cultural and spiritual treasures. It marked a great step forward in their intellectual and social advance, for they were leaving backward lands to settle in a realm of culture, freedom, and democracy. Indeed, one of the most interesting social phenomena associated with this migration is the fact that within the span of a mere generation so large a segment of world Jewry was transported from benighted to enlightened areas. And in this new land of technical progress and cultural receptivity, the Jew was to live in the very heart of enlightenment, in the large metropolitan centers.[4]

In these large metropolitan centers the new immigrants created a virile communal life with a host of institutions to express every nuance of activity and aspiration. Here the masses became politically, economically, and culturally articulate. Mindful of the horrible conditions from which they had fled, they struggled vigorously to provide relief for those who were left behind and to transfer the spirit of orderly, democratic, free American institutions to the ghettos of Poland. They salvaged what they could of the old communities. To those who could not immediately escape the lands of persecution they sent part of their meagre savings and buoyed their hopes for a better and fuller life here on this continent at some future date. Determined also that economic exploitation should not blight their own lives here and reduce them to a slave-like existence, they furthered the cause of trade-unionism in the garment industry, initiated permanent arbitration machinery for labor disputes, fought for good municipal government, and became conspicuous in the front ranks of political liberalism. If there is a clean government in New York City today, it is due in no small measure to the efforts and cooperation of the Jewish proletariat which rallied around the banner of the American Labor Party and the progressive wings of the two major parties and which finally succeeded in ousting the corrupt Tammany machine from power.

Yet for all its economic and cultural advantages, life in the large metropolitan centers was very trying for these Russian masses. It was difficult for the Orthodox-minded among them to maintain their village-bred traditions in an urban industrial environment. Of course, the Marxist-inclined proletarians adapted themselves far more easily than did their more placid contemporaries of similar origin. Theirs was now the opportunity to throw off the shackles of a pietistic way of life which they associated with spiritual medievalism and economic exploitation. But their reaction was by no means exceptional, for almost all of these Jews experienced the same pull away from the old-fashioned, observant modes of living which

4. In this respect it is significant to note that nearly 80 percent of the American Jews today live in communities of more than 10,000 people, and that even before the arrival of the Slavic Jews, 40 percent of German-American Jewry was settled in New York City. This concentration in the larger cities was, however, not a unique characteristic of Jewish immigration. It was part of the general movement of all peoples from the countryside to the cities and to the industrial areas.

the attractive culture of this strange new world exerted upon them. They revelled in the new vista of science, art, and literature which suddenly unfolded itself before them in the schools, the newspapers, and the various other media of communication. They yearned for the sense of personal and spiritual security that came with belonging to the pulsating life of America, and they wished to be identified with their environment as speedily as possible.

True, not all the immigrants found it possible to be completely happy in the new world. The old traditions and taboos of the ghetto community meant little or nothing here. There was such a yawning gap between Bialystock and Boston. The old values gave way to the pressure of the American environment while new ones were not so easily established. Many a Jew, attempting the hazardous leap from the crude agrarian economy of old Russia to the complex capitalistic structure of new America, failed in the attempt. Thousands of sensitive, thoughtful individuals were broken in the effort to effect a safe transfer of their ancient cultural heritage to this land and to carve a niche for themselves in this bewildering new society. Their children, soon adrift in the teeming waters of American life, failed to understand their elders and grew up worlds apart from them. This was the background against which untold tragedies were enacted in American-Jewish family life. Jewish parents came to know the heartbreak of complete spiritual estrangement from their children. And many of these children having neither understanding nor appreciation of the sanctions and sanctities of the old world, and unable to sense the ideals of the new, grew into a generation without cultural roots, belonging nowhere. The extent of this tragedy is illustrated by the fact that some of these unfortunates are found today among the gangsters of our metropolitan communities.

The assimilation of the immigrant Jews was likewise retarded on account of the uniqueness of their cultural traditions. Their language, demeanor, their very garb, singled them out from the rest of the population. The massing of hundreds of thousands of them in the large urban centers, their concentration in specific trades and professions, were additional factors in accentuating their differences and arousing that curious attention which leads to prejudice. It was the "old dislike of the unlike" appearing in a new guise. Soon enough, after the '80's, the new anti-Semitic literature turned its attention from fulminating against the German-Jewish "criminals" of the East side to attacking the real and imaginary vices of the "alien Slavic-Jewish hordes."

This attack upon their poor Slavic relatives frightened the old-line German-Jewish settlers who forgot that they had proudly survived the same type of assault a few generations back. They hastened to establish institutions for the Americanization of the new immigrants. Out of these efforts, initiated by the methodical and systematic Germans, came the farm movement in the country which has been responsible for the settlement of 100,000 Jews on the soil, and the philanthropic institutions which have made American Jewish social service exemplary. Out of the welter of this activity there emerged also the skills that later made possible the organization of post-war overseas agencies which have prudently and sympathetically salvaged European Jewry through the expenditure of $100,000,000 for rehabilitation and relief work abroad. The co-operation of native and immigrant Jewry in this gigantic humanitarian task has furthermore stimulated a sense of Jewish solidarity in this country and fostered the development of a united communal spirit which is gradually overcoming the differences existing among the various sections of American Jewry. Through this common experience and growing solidarity, the way has also been paved for the founding of a world Jewish organization to cope with the terrifying and stupendous problems of the Second World War.

In our own day the relentless attack upon German Jewry by the National-Socialistic administration has produced a new migration of Jews to America in a search for peace and freedom. The present experience of the recent German emigrés in effecting their adjustment offers a striking contrast to that of their Russian predecessors of the '80's. It should, however, be noted at the outset that it is doubtful whether these German Jews will profoundly alter the complexion of American Jewry. The most we can expect is that hundreds of scholars and scientists who have found a refuge in the laboratories and schools of America will indeed leave the impress of their learning and research upon our intellectual life. Without doubt, they will stimulate American activity in the natural and social sciences. But the immigration as a whole is too insignificant a total to exert an appreciable influence on American or even on American-Jewish life. This fact becomes the more patent when we realize that it comprises at the most but two percent of American Jewry. This new German *diaspora* will therefore be in no position to create a new cultural community as did the East European arrivals in the Jewries of the United States, Belgium, France, England, South America, and South Africa. German Jewry, now scattered all over the world, is gradually being atomized. With the sole exception of the settlement in Palestine, it is losing its identity as a distinct group and is slowly being absorbed by the native Jewish populations among which circumstance has caused it to take refuge.

The East European Jews of a generation ago were in a far more advantageous position than are the present German wanderers. They had not given themselves over to the pan-Slavic culture that demanded conversion as the price of security. The East European Jews were not Russian. The German Jews, on the other hand, were German to the core. They were unquestionably more German than Jewish. That was to be expected in view of their historical background. Thus when the Germanism which was the essence of their lives was rejected by the anti-Semites, precious little was left of them. Now theirs is the compulsion in alien lands of adjusting themselves to a new nationalism, a nationalism that may be kindly and tolerant, but one that is not their own, that is not their own, that is not the marrow of their bones as was Germanism. The pain which these German migrants must suffer cuts deep.

Though, as we have intimated, the Jews of Eastern Europe were to a certain extent cultural aliens, they passionately loved the soil in which they were rooted. Why then did they leave home? They did so because everyone who could was leaving. The whole world was on the march in the nineteenth century and the Jews were merely participants in the gigantic *Völkerwanderung:* the greatest of all times. They followed the lanes of commerce which are always the roads of flight and escape from intolerable conditions, and which at this time were winding westward.

Since the dawn of the last century, fifty to sixty million people have moved from one continent to another. This shift of population involved more men and women than inhabited the entire Roman Empire. At first, the people of the more advanced lands of Central and Western Europe became mobile; then came the turn of the East Europeans to move forward. The railroads penetrating Eastern Europe gave celerity to flight, until in the decade before the last World War, one and a half million people were leaving Southern and Eastern Europe each year. It was this mass movement that the Jews joined. Of the four million Jews who had left their countries of origin since 1881, over three million came to the United States. As a result, America today boasts of 32 percent of the world Jewish population, whereas in 1815 its share was only three-tenths of one percent. The wave of immigration which transported an average of 93,000 Jews from Eastern Europe every year from 1900 to 1914 thus played an important role in shifting the center of gravity of Jewish concentration and influence from the East to the West and to America.

In seeking admission to our shores, our Russian brethren were lured on by the same enticing prospects which beckoned to the peasants of Eastern Europe. For during the slow transition from serfdom to some semblance of equality in the nineteenth and twentieth centuries, the latter groaned under the yoke of economic servility. Freedom meant the right to starve and no more. The inadequacy of the slowly evolving capitalistic structure left them hopeless and jobless. America, on the other hand, spelled opportunity. Across the seas there were to be found industrialized and underpopulated areas where millions of laborers were needed. The New World was sparsely settled; there were no immigration laws to hurdle and even the illiterate were made welcome.[5]

But the Jews had even further cause for departing from their ancestral hearths than did the land-bound peasantry. They suffered on their own account at the hands of the Czarist regime. The Russian agrarian lords, seeking a scapegoat for their exploitation of the underprivileged peasants, drove the Jews out of the rural districts of the Pale into the towns and cities. In that restricted area of settlement, since 1880 alone, about 400,000 Jews, expelled from the villages, were compelled to begin life over again elsewhere. It was not enough that they were penned within the huge ghetto; now the very walls of that ghetto began closing in on them.

Opportunities for making a livelihood in the cities of Poland and Russia were very scarce. Jewish craftsmen could not compete with the factories; the factories, few and inadequate, could not absorb both the surplus Jews and the landless peasants. Economic competition was therefore rampant, and its cruel effect upon the masses was seen in a standard of living which fell lower and lower. When the peasants became restless and impatient, the State beguiled them with the argument that the Jews were responsible for their misfortune. Anti-Semitism thus became an instrument of state policy to divert the attention of the oppressed masses from their just claims against the Romanoff regime. Thousands of anti-Jewish laws were accumulated on the statute books of Russia. While the disenfranchised Jews fought at the front to save the Fatherland, the State at home incited the Greek Orthodox masses to plunder and murder their

---

5. Indeed 35 percent of all those who came from Eastern Europe could neither read nor write.

wives and children. It was from an inferno of economic privation and physical insecurity that the Jew fled.

Thus the floodgates of the greatest of all migrations in Jewish history were opened and a gigantic shift in Jewish population took place. Though this mass movement was unique in certain respects, it had some features in common with previous similar episodes, as we shall see from a cursory and retrogressive view of Jewish migrations in the past.

Outside of his almost instinctive love for the soil that gave him birth, there was little to hold the Eastern European Jew in Poland and Russia. That center of Jewish life was slowly being extinguished. It is true, on the one hand, that it contained millions of his brethren whose religious loyalties were unquestioning and whose rabbinic scholarship had reached a high level of attainment. Yet this great Jewry had not been playing an effective leading rôle in Jewish life since the middle of the 18th century. It was rich neither in financial wealth nor in political and cultural background.

At one time in the past, Poland had indeed been the last frontier of hope, a haven of refuge, the "America" of its day. It occupied this prominent place after England, France, Spain, and the Germanies had cast out their Jews. It had long been a veritable land of opportunity, for the standard Austrian charter of 1244, adapted for their benefit, made the Jews a privileged economic group in this backward land. This was in line with medieval tradition and practice, since the Jewish immigrants were always the carriers of economic development and progress and hence enjoyed the most extensive economic privileges in the underdeveloped countries. Furthermore, the Crusades, the increasing disabilities suffered under the medieval state and the rising might of the papacy, spurred on the Central European Jews to take advantage of Poland's opportunities. Nor did the Polish kings and magnates make a mistake in welcoming and deliberately inviting Jewish merchants and financiers into that primitive country, for the latter helped to develop its crafts, farmed its estates, managed its exports, and brought to it the wealth of economic experience which had been acquired in Germanic Europe.

As a result, the Germanic-Jewish immigrants, who soon imposed their cultural forms on the early Slavic-Jewish pioneers, attained a rather satisfactory economic status. The proverbial Polish anarchy made possible a large measure of self-government, which was subjected to the jurisdiction of rabbinical law. This autonomy reached its first great administrative triumph in the last two decades of the sixteenth century in the form of the nation-wide Council of Four Lands. Thus, almost a century had elapsed after the fall of Spanish Jewry before Poland became the center of Jewish life. During this period its rise, Turkey also made a bid for cultural hegemony in Jewish life, but the vitality of the Sephardic culture there was not sufficient to break through the dead weight of Turkish despotism and administrative inertia. It must not be assumed, however, that there was a real tie between Spain and Poland. Only the remotest relations existed between the Arabic-Christian Spanish culture of the fifteenth century and the Polish Jewish life which was emerging at the other end of Europe; a common rabbinic tradition alone served to maintain a semblance of continuity between these two Jewries.

Some scholars believe that when the Golden Age of Spain and Portugal came to an end after flourishing for hundreds of years, as many as 250,000 men, women, and children braved the perils of exile. If this figure is accurate, then this migration included about 25 percent of the world Jewry of that day. Spreading throughout the basin of the Mediterranean, these refugees managed to create a new Sephardic cultural empire, whose intellectual and religious stimulus was to endure for several generations. Thoughtful reflection on their downfall and the hope for survival gave rise to a large body of historical literature, stimulated a resurgence of Kabbalah, inspired grandiose plans for the re-settlement of Palestine and the re-creation of an authoritative world Jewish governing body bound together by a common code.

Yet, in spite of the benefits conferred on Mediterranean Jewry by the admixture of these Sephardic elements following the Spanish expulsion, it would be a perversion of history to conceive of the Spanish exile of 1492 as a salutary event. It was a mortal blow to Spanish Jewry, that group which for centuries had produced so many rabbinic scholars, philosophers, poets, and scientists of unusual brilliance, and which had demonstrated how Judaism could be ennobled through the best of medieval Arabic and Christian culture. Uprooted from the soil of its development Spanish-Jewish culture withered after having dominated Jewish life for four hundred years (1100–1500).

Spain had taken over the post of leadership in world Jewish affairs from the Babylon of the Abbasids. Spanish Jewry, however, was only the *testamentary* legatee and not the *physical* heir of the schools of Babylon. There was no *mass* migration from Babylon. Spain had been preparing for centuries to assume hegemony in Jewish life when Babylon's dominant rôle came to an end. For seven hundred years Babylon had ruled

Jewish life, developing various forms of communal organization, creating the basic code of the Talmud, and gradually adjusting the old hidebound Jewry to the new Arabic culture—a culture which was destined to exert its greatest influence in Jewish life in the Spain of the eleventh and twelfth centuries. But as a result of poor government, the ebb of economic opportunities, the invasion of alien hordes, and the shifting of trade routes to the broad Mediterranean, the Tigris-Euphrates are declined as a center of Jewish life.

Babylon had, in its turn, taken over the slack reins of leadership from the lifeless hands of Palestinian Jewry in the fourth century of the Common Era. At that time, the economic breakdown of the Christian Roman Empire and its religious bigotry made it impossible for Palestinian Jewry to exercise the controlling influence in Jewish life. The Hellenistic Jewish settlements, however, still remained in existence, while the new centers established in Italy, France, and Spain continued their steady growth. These had all been built up by the voluntary migration of merchants and adventurers from impoverished Palestine and crowded Egypt. Wherever they went, these immigrants brought their ethical code, their respect for family traditions, their violent hatred of idolatry and paganistic carnality, and their Messianic hope for a better world. Indeed they were sowing the seeds whose harvest the less particularistic Christian world was to reap some day in the future.

In retrospect, we may safely say that mass migrations have been rare phenomena in Jewish life. The *diaspora* communities in pagan Rome, Babylonia, Spain, and Poland did not come into being as the result of far-sweeping changes in the distribution and concentration of the Jewish population. The only large-scale movements that can be graced with the term "mass migration" are the nineteenth century exodus from Russia and Poland; the Spanish exile of 1492; and possibly the invasion of the Hebrew tribes in the second pre-Christian millenium.

In fact, sudden shifts of population are not essential for the establishment of an influential Jewish center, although it is true that every aspiring Jewish community must have numerical strength. Migrations do not always bring about a "steady constant shift of dynamic centers" as many observers maintain. Every great Jewish community has undergone a *long* process of growth and development before achieving hegemony. On the other hand, a steady emigration does not necessarily destroy an older Jewish center. Palestine, for example, maintained itself as the source of Jewish authority for centuries, even while sending forth thousands of immigrants annually into the Mediterranean, the Nile, and the Tigris-Euphrates basins. Above all, we must bear in mind the fact that Jewish centers do not emerge in mechanical succession through the automatic transference of populations and cultural values from one part of the world to the other. New cultural communities which add links to the chain of Jewish continuity always arise independently of preceding Jewish centers. A striking illustration of this principle is afforded by the fact that it cannot be definitely established that any Spanish Jews reached Poland after the expulsion.

Whenever a Jewish center disintegrated, its Jewish masses died along with it. For the most part they did not escape to new areas of concentration which were simultaneously arising in nearby or distant lands. It is, however, true that a considerable number of individuals always managed to escape the death-grip because of the heightened mobility of the Jews as an urban and mercantile group. Large-scale movements of Jews were further facilitated because their corporate existence and autonomous status prevented them from becoming wholly assimilated to the local cultures with which they came in contact, and because nationalism was as yet not sufficiently powerful to enthrall people and to restrain their freedom of movement. Thus a *minority* could always escape the menace of extinction, for there was at all times another Jewry to which flight was possible. It is this "omniterritoriality" that has proved to be the ultimate salvation of world Jewry.

Yet it should be noted that the "tradition" of wandering and exile so intimately associated with their history did not deter them from seeking to strike deep root in the places of their sojourn. This desire came to fruition time and again, despite the profound influence of the liturgy with its almost morbid nostalgia for Palestine and with its perennial equating of the *galut* (exile) with suffering. If the Jews allowed themselves to be dislodged, it was due in the main to the pressure of external factors such as religious prejudice and the economic attacks levelled by the State or the medieval Church. If the Jews became aliens and undesirable elements of the body politic, it was largely because the State decreed such a fate for them. Never was it their own wish, never did they bid voluntary farewell to their homes. They resorted to emigration only when it became their last chance for survival. Let us bear in mind that the *galut* was a creation of the outside world, not a fiction of Jewish theology. Our people knew through grim experience that migrations always bring death and disaster in their wake. Of the Jews who left Germany and Bohemia during the

Crusades treking across the borders of Poland, many indeed never reached their desired goals but fell by the wayside as mute evidence of the fate awaiting those who *would* not leave but *must*. Furthermore, it is no consolation to the individual Jew to be informed with the smugness of undemonstrated sociological theory that these acts of stark tragedy have weeded out the weak and unfit among them and have left a remnant of select superior stock. The weak and the unfit—and it is not known that those who perished actually were the weak and unfit—were his own flesh and blood.

The Jew knew, moreover, that in the long run every expulsion resulted in the retardation of his cultural progress and in the burial of glorious traditions and significant achievement. What a world of Jewish literary and scientific accomplishment vanished when the Spanish Crusaders re-conquered their land and drove the cultured Arabs into the Mediterra-nean! The decline of Alexandria 1,800 years ago and the destruction of German Jewry in our own times are both cultural catastrophes of the first magnitude. Their losses are almost irreparable. Indeed the death of every Jewish center was accomplished only at tremendous cost both to contemporary progress and to future generations. Though new ones arose to replace them, they could never fully compensate for those that had vanished from the face of the earth.

Nor does the succession of Jewish spiritual nurseries necessarily and automatically bring about Jewish cultural progress. This is evidenced by the example of Polish Jewry which assumed hegemony in Jewish life in the late sixteenth century. From the point of view of world influence its emergence was in some respects infelicitous. For prior to this event every rising Jewish colony, whether in the Roman Empire, Perso-Islamic Baby-lonia, or Arabic Spain, was fortunate enough in coming into contact with a surrounding culture that was superior to its own, and from which it could profit in a cultural interplay. Hitherto, every migration had meant a rise in the Jewish cultural level. Poland, for the first time, however, marked a decline, a retrogression that reached tragic depths in the social revolt of the peasants in 1648.

The reign of terror unleashed by Chmelnicki furthermore marked a sudden and drastic turning point in Jewish history. Up to that moment, ever since the expulsion of Jewry from England in 1290, the trend of Jew-ish migration had been eastward. Now the terror-stricken people were confronted with the blank wall of Russia whose domain was tightly closed against Jewish penetration. The Jewish masses, fleeing from the combined wrath of the revolting peasants, Cossacks, and Tartars were compelled to turn towards the west, to Germany, and to the lands of the Hapsburgs.

The rabbinic scholars among them found homes in the great cities of Central Europe as far west as Amsterdam, Metz, and Venice. Polish talmudic scholarship brought new life and learning to the quiescent *yeshibot* (colleges) of the West, the seeds of which were to flower generations later in Germany as *die Wissenschaft des Judentums,* the Science of Judaism. As these refugees plodded westward in the middle of the seventeenth century, they stumbled into the new world of a rising capitalism, the new society that was soon to bring undreamt-of freedom to the Jewish masses everywhere. For since the discovery of America by Columbus, vast commercial opportunities had been opened up for the maritime states bordering on the Atlantic. There was consequently a gradual shift of economic opportunity, wealth, and culture from the Mediterranean to the North Atlantic. Men, money, brains, and economic daring were at a premium. The gradual rise of an extensive credit economy likewise helped to break the shackles of medieval life and gave men the precious right to change their places of residence without let or hindrance.

Many of the West-European Jews who had survived the expulsions had themselves been quick to grasp the significance of the changes that were taking place in the world. Thus some of the Marranos had already crossed the ocean to settle in the Spanish colonies of the West Indies, South America, and Mexico. Others filtered across the French borders in small groups and sought homes in the growing cities of the North Atlantic littoral, from Bayonne in the southeast to Hamburg in the northwest. A small colony even came into existence in Elizabethan England. Wherever these refugees went in the North Atlantic regions, the West Indies, or in North America, they brought their commercial experience and the superior Western culture which made them socially acceptable and paved the way for their ultimate emancipation in those slowly emerging democratic states. Cities expanded at a rapid pace as pioneering endeavors in the field of medicine opened up new possibilities for safeguarding the health of the populace. Epidemics were gradually conquered while the general mortality rate declined sharply, with the result that a Jewry which could boast of only one and a half million inhabitants in the seventeenth century increased to ten million in the nineteenth.

It is interesting to note that this movement of westward expansion which began in the seventeenth century came to the attention of one of the most distinguished Jewish leaders of his generation, Menasseh ben Israel, of Marrano stock. Like Columbus, who may have been a Jew, he too turned his thoughts to the West. He saw the Polish refugees pouring out of the East. He had also seen hundreds if not thousands of German Jews crushed in the disastrous Thirty Years' War, which ended in 1648. He wanted a home—a political refuge—for these wanderers, possibly in England, and ultimate spiritual home—somewhere else. Columbus and his Marrano friends had turned West, in the desperate days of 1492, in order to find a new road to the East. Their goal was solely political. Menasseh likewise looked towards the West, but his hopes beckoned from the East. His goal was not India; it was Messianic Palestine. He not only wanted to open up England to the Jewish refugees and to his wealthy Sephardic friends; he desired to see the Jews scattered even to the "end of the earth" (Angle-Terre = England cf. Deut. 28:64) and thus hasten the coming of the Messiah who would bring relief to the distressed and the broken of heart. For indeed migrations and Messianism are never far removed from each other, even though their geographical destinations appear to be far apart.

It is a queer paradox of fate that the stricken Eastern Jews of the middle seventeenth century in their yearning turned still further East but were physically compelled to seek some semblance of safety in the West. Out of this quirk of history came that spiritual flight eastward which was focused in the person of Shabbathai Zebi as the Messiah who would lead the lost sheep of Israel back to the ancestral home, Palestine. The Jewish masses of Eastern Europe have never ceased since those days to search for some form of spiritual escape. The exposure of Shabbathai Zebi as an impotent visionary made no difference: escape had to come. There had to be a way out. In the eighteenth century this way out was Hasidism, a religion of self-emancipation, a renunciation of the *galut* philosophy of salvation solely through patience and atonement. Hasidism created its own dream world of happiness by dragging God down from His transcendant throne and making Him dance on the house-tops with a desperate people who are determined to be gay in spite of everything. When this failed to meet the needs of the masses, myriads of Jews fled in spirit or flesh into the folds of the Zionist movement during the next century. This was their declaration that the Messiah would be compelled to come before his appointed time. Others, unable to regard migration as a satisfactory solution for the ills of their people, sought the salvation of mankind in the revolutionary movements of their time. Of these a number sat in the high places of the Russian regime during the fateful years of the last two generations. The bulk of the Russian Jews, however, sought an avenue of escape in the nineteenth century through settlement in the Promised Land of the Americas.

It may have been that the flight of the Jew in 1648, spiritually to the east and politically to the west, marked the first faint, symbolic intimation of the future decline of Europe. If this be true, then it bespeaks some uncanny quality of premonition on his part, for Western Europe at this time was just beginning to embark on its career of artistic, literary, commercial, scientific, and technical achievement. Is it possible that the Jew has a keen sensitivity to impending disaster because he is frequently the first victim of change in the social order? Is it possible that because of some mysterious sense beyond reason itself he sensed death and decay in Eastern, even in Central Europe, and that he began to move almost unwittingly to the West? Or did he know through some strange insight that the future lay with the new colonial powers? One thing is certain: the pendulum of Jewish migration slowly reversed itself.

Since the days of the expulsion of the Jews from England in 1290, it had slowly but inexorably moved eastward. Now it began to move westward: to Central and Western Europe and the tiny colonies of the New World.

Today the pendulum is still moving, irresistibly, almost implacably, in the same direction, but this time it is describing an ever larger arc. Today a New East and a New West have come into the sphere of its motion. It is no longer Eastern Europe and Western Europe across whose face the shadow of the pendulum of historical movement falls; it is the New America and the New Asia that are now the goals of aspirations of a distraught and helpless people in Europe.

Their need for security is urgent and compelling today as it has never been before. Jewry is in the throes of the greatest agony it has known in all its history. The present crisis, which represents the climax of all the catastrophes that have racked the body of European Jewry for centuries, fills us with pain and trepidation. The hopes of the past are no longer at our command to cushion the impending disaster. During the latter part of the nineteenth century, emigration did offer some surcease from poverty, war, and persecution. The very knowledge that the gates of the United States were open was itself a ray of hope to buoy up the spirit of doomed men and women. But the clouds soon gathered again on the horizon of Jewish life. The first World War came with its trail of destruction, mass deportations, and the breakdown of the normal channels of trade. It was followed by the Ukrainian pogroms with their slaughter of almost a hundred thousand Jews. In the next two decades, Poland and Rumania, brutally chauvinistic, clearly indicated what a burden their Jewish population represented and deliberately tolerated anti-Semitic movements as a means of driving them out. Flight was the sole hope for survival and the last great wave of migration swept upon our shores in 1921 when 119,036 Jews came to the United States.

Three years later, however, the Immigration Act of 1924 became the law of this land. It was a piece of legislation inspired only in part by the desire to protect American labor against the fleeing hordes of Europe. In reality it was actuated by racial prejudice against the peoples of Southern and Eastern Europe, particularly the Italians, the Slavs, and the Jews. Consequently, the European stream of migration was deflected toward Canada, Cuba, Mexico, and South America. Yet in a few years even these outlets for the surplus populations of the Old World were closed tightly as the Act of 1924 struck a pattern which was followed by other American states. The result has been that today practically all the immigration laws of the Western continent are racially restrictive or economically selective. In both cases they discriminate against the Jews because of their origin and economic background.

Following this turn of events, the masses of oppressed Jewry flocked to Palestine, especially after the National Socialists seized control of Germany. Yet during this period stretching between the two World Wars, emigration never became a solution to the European Jewish problem, for the annual number of emigrants finally was not even sufficient to exceed the natural increase of the Jewish population. How much more then is the status of this people tragic now, during this Second World War, when all avenues of escape are closing up.

As we survey the plight of European Jewry today, we see a picture of unrelieved tragedy and despair. German Jewry, economically and politically crushed, is holding on tenaciously to the little that is left. Half of its number leads a precarious sort of existence wherever it has been able to find a resting place in the world, from New York to Shanghai. Thousands languish in the concentration camps of Germany, the work camps of Poland, and the restricted areas of the Allied lands where they are regarded as enemy aliens. Bohemian and Moravian Jewry has been deported in large numbers to the Polish reservation of Lublin. Its 120 or more Jewish communities have been reduced to a mere dozen or so. Slovakia, Hungary, Rumania, and Italy, are gradually depriving their Jewish citizens of their political and economic rights, while the future of the Jews in Norway and Denmark, in Belgium, Holland, and France, subjected to German control or threat is likewise dark and foreboding.

Throughout southern Europe, moveover, thousands of Jews have sought refuge in conversion to Catholicism. This is exactly what happened in Spain in 1391, a century before the final expulsion period. It would not be at all surprising if some day a new Marrano problem were to arise to plague these states with spiritual rebellion, mass maladjustment, and widespread heresies. But the greatest tragedy has occurred in Poland, where a war of horror and devastation has swept across the land bringing death, sadism, famine, and epidemics.

The only section of Polish Jewry whose lot is tolerable and whose outlook is not altogether one of grim terror and destruction is the million or more who have found refuge in the Eastern part of the land now contained within the domain of the Soviets. At this hour, Russia shelters almost four million Jews, the second largest Jewry in the world. We are indeed thankful that they have been spared the blight of war, but there is little prospect that Russia with her vast territories, will open her borders to the refugees of war-torn Europe. Neither is there ground for the belief that the Jewish population of Russia will some day assume leadership in Jewish life. There is not the remotest possibility that either of these contingencies will occur. The Union of Soviet Socialist Republics has no desire to complicate her social and economic problems by the addition of new bourgeois elements. She will never tolerate the construction of a Jewish cultural center founded upon a religious basis. Nor will world Jewry, for its part, accept any leadership that is not rooted in the traditions of the past.

We may also confidently expect further economic dislocation as well as an intensification of the Jewish political and economic crisis after the Second World War has come to an end. The only hope for a post-war amelioration—and this only in the event of an Allied victory—is that the whole question of the Jew in Europe will be seriously considered at the council of peace. It may well be asked if it is worthwhile to subject the Central and East European Jewish masses to a new post-war wave of chauvinism and to place our faith in the questionable guarantees of the pseudo-liberal democracies; yet it is the hope of all men that a more permanent basis for the peace and security of the world will be laid when this holocaust is over. The possibility of transporting great masses of Jews from hostile, culturally inferior lands, for colonization in other territories under friendly auspices, will no doubt likewise need to be carefully discussed. If such a transplanting of the Jewish masses is to be other than a cruel deportation, it is essential that world Jewry create a powerful representative organization that will be in a position to convert this dramatic event into the beginning of a new chapter of hope in the history of the Jewish people.

But until such a state of affairs comes to pass, the Jews will need to remain confined and oppressed in their huge Pale of Settlement that we call Central and Eastern Europe. Most assuredly, however, this suffering among the masses of Europe, rooted in the Messianic tradition, will bring forth a new cry for deliverance, a new yearning for Palestine as a physical refuge and as a spiritual home. Yet we must realize in the light of the War and the realistic politic that is being played today in the Mediterranean, that Palestine may not, in our generation, develop into a center for mass flight. One need not be reconciled to this eventuality, but one must face it. Palestine must prepare for a unique rôle, a rôle that calls for a sharp break with Jewish tradition. There is no longer to be a choice of Palestine *or* the *diaspora,* for in a realistic sense we must be prepared to accept *both* Palestine *and* the *diaspora.* The two are not mutually exclusive.

For the *diaspora* has spread and will continue to spread while at the same time a movement for national return grows apace. The *diaspora* must not occupy an inferior place in the scheme of Jewish things. The *galut,* in theory and practice, must become the equal of Palestine. To achieve this condition, the word *galut* will have to be invested with new meaning. It must now connote not absence from a physical Palestine, but the yearning for an attainable ideal. If the Jew is to attain any sort of inner peace and security, he must renounce the old idea of *galut.* He must part company with the notion that he is totally different and has been cast out by the nations. To accept such a pessimistic view is to surrender to the anti-Semite, to make the totally false assumption that the anti-Semite speaks for the peoples of the earth. Our present life in the democracies can by no stretch of the imagination be termed a *galut* existence. We have no desire to escape such a world. Indeed it is unfortunate that we who reside in the free lands of the world have allowed ourselves to brood over Europe's present state of decay and have become susceptible to the corrosive effects of morbidity. We see old centers crumbling and their population hemmed in by the sword of destruction. As a result our own sense of security is deserting us. We are fashioning a *galut* psychology of our own and are submitting to a neurosis of alien-mindedness that is poisoning our lives everywhere. There is a paramount danger here against which we must build the strongest fortifications of the spirit. We must under no circumstance permit the forces of evil to send us into spiritual exile.

Similarly is it essential to re-evaluate the position which Palestine is to fill in the Jewish life of the future. It may not become a great and powerful state; it may never contain more than the three percent of world Jewry which it holds today. Certainly, on account of the difficulties of immigration, war, and the upsurge of nationalism in the Near East, it cannot aspire to become a Jewish center exercising hegemony through economic and political power. It would be a mistake to conceive of the Holy Land in terms of vast numbers of inhabitants. It neither should nor can it ever hope to compete politically and economically with American Jewry. Surely that is not the type of influence which we envision for Palestine in the world of tomorrow.

Palestine will fall short of the mark, if its mission be merely to provide physical asylum, if it seeks only to become a catch-basin for desperate refugees. It will then be the *galut* itself, in the worst sense of the word. Palestine can attain fulfillment only if it becomes Zion. Devotion to the ancestral ideals and traditions, the search for prophetic conviction and practice, the spread of the Hebrew language as a medium of Jewish expression, the furtherance of Jewish solidarity by serving as a unifying bond for hundreds of scattered communities—this must be its function and rôle in the future.

The Palestine of the past where pious men went to die was pitied for its senility. But the day is past when Palestine served merely as a universal Jewish burial ground. The immigration since the first World War has brought thousands of cultured men and women from the great centers of Europe and even from America. Refugees with learning and skills have come in, bringing new life to the old home land, even as did the ancient exiles in the days of Nehemiah who brought back to Jerusalem the culture that once was Babylon's. Palestine Jewry has been further enriched by the talents and abilities of the German emigrés, who brought with them the science, precision, and high intelligence that had always distinguished German research. Through these things Palestine has become, even more than the United States, the spiritual heir of German-Jewish scholarship.

As a result of this influx, Palestine, if it can escape the devastation of war, will be prepared to exercise a strong influence on world Jewry despite its small Jewish population. It should be noted that the Palestine of Judah

Jacob Rader Marcus (extreme right) at a meeting of the Cincinnati chapter of the Inter-collegiate Menorah Society in 1914. In the front center of the picture, holding his gloves, is Henry Hurwitz, president of the society, and to the right in the fur cap is the well-known sociologist Professor Horace Kallen.

Marcus, as a second lieutenant, served as a member of the American Expeditionary Forces during 1918 through 1919.

Marcus's Ordination diploma from Hebrew Union College in 1920.

Dr, Marcus with confirmation class (from left: Grace Adams, Maurice Weil, Jr., Esther Green, Esther Levy) of Temple Adath Israel (Lexington, Kentucky), 1927.

Courtesy of Temple Adath Israel.

Marcus was in Europe from 1921 to 1925 studying for his doctorate. This picture was taken near Beaulieu, France.

Marcus's student identification card from Friedrich Wilhelms Univerität in 1923.

Just prior to Marcus's wedding to Antoinette (Nettie) Brody in 1925. Seated left to right are friends Paula and Maurice Eisenberg, Rose Brody (Nettie's mother), Nelson Glueck (the future president of Hebrew Union College), Joseph Brody (Nettie's father), Nettie Brody, and Marcus.

Minister's License

THE STATE OF OHIO, } ss. **PROBATE COURT.**
HAMILTON COUNTY

Be it remembered, that at a session of the Probate Court of said County, held at Cincinnati on the 26th *day of* January *19*29 *it having been made to appear to the satisfaction of said Court that* Jacob R. Marcus *is a regularly ordained* ~~Minister of the Gospel~~ Rabbi *of the religious society or congregation known* ~~as~~ the Jewish Congregation *and that he is officiating to a society or congregation of said denomination in said County, and that agreeably to the Rules and Regulations of said society, he is authorized to solemnize marriages.*

Now, on application, License is hereby granted unto the said Rabbi Jacob R. Marcus *as provided by law, authorizing him to solemnize marriages within the State of Ohio so long as he shall continue a regular minister in such society congregation.*

In Witness Whereof, *I have hereunto set my hand and the seal of said Court, at Cincinnati, this* 26th *day of* January *19*29

William H. Lueders
Probate Judge

D W Williams
Deputy Clerk

Rabbi Marcus: Clergy license from the State of Ohio (1929). Note that "Minister of the Gospel" is crossed out and replaced with the handwritten word "Rabbi."

Marcus (first row, second from the left) attending his first meeting of the Central Conference of American Rabbis in Rochester, New York, 1920. Professor Gotthard Deutsch, Marcus's mentor at HUC, is in the second row, eighth from the left, and David Philipson, who sponsored Marcus to the HUC faculty, is the second from the right.

Marcus the public historian: Throughout his career Marcus believed that Jewish history had to be accessible to the public and he gave numerous talks on a variety of subjects.

The American Jewish Tercentenary Committee (1954) promoted the study of American Jewish history. Marcus, a member of the Tercentenary Committee on Research and Publications, made numerous presentations, some with his friend and colleague Rabbi Abba Hillel Silver.

Founding Director of the American Jewish Archives. Marcus dictating to his personal secretary Sarah Grossman in the early 1950s.

Marcus speaking at the CCAR convention in Jerusalem (1981), where he received special recognition for his contributions to the education of rabbis.

Marcus lecturing to a class during his early career, 1930s.

Marcus lecturing to a class later in his career, 1979.

Marcus on his ninetieth birthday, still active in teaching and publishing.

Marcus walking near his home in Cincinnati. The city of Cincinnati renamed the corner of Middleton and McAlpin Avenues, Marcus Square, in 1987.

the Prince, in the second century C.E., probably did not shelter more than 15 or 20 percent of the world's Jews. Yet it held undisputed sway over the scattered communities of Israel, and this at a time when rapid transportation and instantaneous communication did not knit the would closely together as they do now.

It is to this new and growing Palestine that the world looks with interest and expectation. It challenges this youthful and virile settlement, rich in Hebraic lore and tradition, to impress itself spiritually upon our times and to rise to a position of leadership in the affairs of world Jewry.

The only other land which may dare to stand spiritually with Palestine is the United States. Indeed this land is already fulfilling the hope that the world had placed in Palestine. For a generation or so American Jewry has been forging ahead to world leadership. It has the advantages of economic superiority, prestige, and numbers. It contains great educational institutions, a growing press, a deepening appreciation for the Jewish people as a whole. Jewry in this country, building new hopes on the foundations of our democracy, has already enriched our cultural heritage immeasurably. What we have envisioned in the Palestine of the future has actually begun to take on tangible form here in America. Without setting forth consciously to do so, the American-Jewish community has actually begun to measure itself by the standards which were intended originally for the ideal community-to-be in the Holy Land. Without philosophizing or theorizing about it, America is taking up the charge which world Jewry has directed at Palestine. America has eagerly accepted the challenge to spiritualize itself and to become the great nursery of Jewish learning, aided as it has been in recent years by the many German-Jewish scholars who have found a home on these shores.

It is good that it should be so, for we have no real assurance at the present moment that out of the conflict which now engulfs the European world Palestine will emerge as the savior-nation of world Jewry. America is our insurance against possible failure in Palestine. And if in the history of tomorrow the seeds planted in Palestine should come to full fruition, the existence of still another great spiritual and cultural center here in America cannot but be a great boon.

The challenge of the hour is no longer how the American-Jewish community may become a great center of Jewish life. We have already reached that state. The task now confronting us is to became that type of center which will initiate for world Jewry a new Golden Age of learning, inspired by the finest in the civilization of this generation.

We realize that to accept this challenge is to fly in the face of current history, to build while others destroy, to seek for light while others writhe in the darkness of despair, to strengthen the bulwarks of civilization while others seek to shatter them. But we who have been trained in the crucible of the centuries to struggle with courage and dignity have no alternative. In accepting this challenge we voice our hope not only in ourselves but in the larger humanity about us. Let the spiritual leaders of *American* Jewry consider this in their innermost hearts, for they hold the key to the destiny of Israel. The answer to the charge must well forth in one single overwhelming chorus: "I shall not die but live and declare the works of the Lord" (Ps. 118:17).

New Literary Responsibilities

(1941)

Editor's note:

Written in 1941 during the darkest days of World War II, the following essay may be understood as a prescription for the post-war years. It is important to note that, long before the war's end was at hand, Jacob Marcus recognized the magnitude of the loss that the Nazi Holocaust was inflicting on the Jewish people. Moreover, he understood that North American Jewry would need to become a new center of Jewish gravity in the wake of European Jewry's devastation. In preparing themselves for a new postwar Jewish world order, American Jewry would need to assume new literary responsibilities.1

This essay was originally an address delivered to the members of the Jewish Publication Society of America (JPS) at its annual meeting. Marcus re-emphasizes his often repeated conviction that cultural efflorescence is the cardinal feature of a great Jewish spiritual center. In evaluating the cultural achievements of any Jewish community, literary progress and intellectual attainment are the basic standards of measure. Books are essential tools for achieving cultural vibrancy. Without the publication and propagation of learned books, it is practically impossible for a society to acquire knowledge and disseminate it widely.2

The history of the JPS sheds much light on the long struggle to provide American Jewry with "significant, worthwhile, and informative books of Jewish interest in the English language, so that the Jewish religion, history, literature, and culture will be understood, and read, and known."3 The JPS's past accomplishments have been considerable, Marcus observes, but communal greatness can never be viewed as "an accomplished fact," but rather it must be "a noble promise." Just as the JPS reflects American Jewry's "first traces of a high destiny," so too, wrote Marcus, does this institution embody the promise of "tomorrow's glory."

1. For more on those who began to anticipate the importance of American Jewry's new role in a post-war Jewish world order, see Jonathan D. Sarna, "The Twentieth Century through American Jewish Eyes: A History of the *American Jewish Yearbook*, 1899–1999," in David Singer and Lawrence Grossman, eds., *American Jewish Yearbook 2000*, 100: 45–49.

2. At the time, Marcus was a member of the JPS's Publications Committee. For more on the history of the Jewish Publication Society, see Jonathan D. Sarna, *JPS: The Americanization of Jewish Culture, 1888–1988* (Philadelphia: Jewish Publication Society, 1989).

3. See ibid., 292.

Until the ascension of Hitler, European Jewry had been the acknowledged intellectual center of world Jewry. Jews throughout the Diaspora made use of European Jewry's literary produce. In the midst of the Holocaust's whirlwind, Marcus notes bluntly "that [European] Jewry with all its beauty lies rotting in the ground." Now American Jewry was destined to fill the intellectual void that the destruction of European Jewry created. Marcus's message was simple and direct: "[World Jewry] will need books . . . and we [American Jewry] must supply them."

That Marcus makes no mention of the prospective role that a Jewish homeland in Palestine might one day play is indicative of the historian's predilections. With a dramatic flair that he would regularly employ in his mature years, Marcus insisted that the destiny of the Jewish people around the world was in the hands of American Jewry: "The literary future of the Jewish people has been placed squarely upon our shoulders."

Marcus's expectations for American Jewry would indeed be fulfilled in the post–World War II years. By the last quarter of the twentieth century, the vast majority of Jewish scholarship in the English language—the international language of academe—was published in the United States of America. Although the JPS has played a unique and significant part in this propagation of Jewish scholarship, it is also true that this literary expansion was due in large measure to the activities of many serious publishing houses, some general and some Jewish. These publishers discovered that Jews and, yes, non-Jews around the world were willing to purchase books in English on Jewish topics. Marcus was among the very first voices to urge United States Jewry to embrace its post-war duty by becoming a major literary center so that Jewish culture would live and survive in America and, indeed, throughout the world.

∼

It would be no violation of the surface truth to say that the Jewish Publication Society of America is unquestionably the greatest institution of its kind that modern Jewry has created. But utterances of this sort involve a subtle danger, for they assume a state of final and definitive accomplishment which might be taken as an appropriate signal for relaxation into an attitude of smug and unproductive complacency. These are times when every present moment is a battleground on which opposing forces are struggling to gain possession of the future. In such times, to evaluate ourselves and our institutions in terms of past accomplishment alone is to fall into a fatal error from which there can be no recovery. The merits of the past no longer constitute by themselves a reliable index of true greatness. That alone is great which bears within itself the seeds of mighty achievement in the days to come. Greatness, then, is not an accomplished fact; it is a noble promise.

It is this variety of greatness which the times demand of our Publication Society as of all Jewish institutions. And it is only in this sense that it is meaningful today to speak of the Jewish Publication Society of America as a great organization. With this in mind, we turn to an examination of the record of this Society and its antecedents, not out of a desire to gratify our conceit, but because we believe that we shall find in that record the first traces of a high destiny and an imperative which will drive us forward to tomorrow's glory.

The Jewish Publication Society has, during its lifetime, issued more than two hundred different books of Jewish interest to its subscribers totaling over two million copies. Its educational influence and spiritual import have been almost incalculable. It has provided the source from which two generations of Jews have received cultural stimulus and nourishment during the formative and crucial decades of American Jewish life. Thousands of men, women, and children have streamed to these shores in the last fifty years, after they had been torn up with their roots from their tradition-bound orthodox homes in Eastern Europe. To many of these immigrants and their children the volumes which have issued from our press have provided the materials out of which these wanderers have erected new and secure dwellings of the spirit.

We are proud of that record. We have every reason to be proud, especially since the struggle to keep alive has not always been easy. The present Society came into being only after two other valiant attempts had been made in this land and had failed, though bravely.

Let it never be said that American Jewry, even a century ago when it was a community of less than 20,000 persons, was not conscious of its obligation to further its literature and to expand its teachings. Jewry in the '40's in this country was just getting on its feet. It was vitally interested in everything Jewish, even if that interest took it to the other side of the world. Thus, for example, when the news came that Jews were being tortured in far-off Damascus on the absurd charge of ritual murder, mass protest meetings were held in New York, Richmond, and Philadelphia in the summer of 1840.

At the Philadelphia meeting, held on Thursday, August 27th, in the vestry rooms of historic Mikveh Israel Synagogue, the leading spirit was

Isaac Lesser. It was this same man who, five years later, bent his efforts to create an American Jewish Publication Society. The motivations which characterized his age were different from those which operate in our own. It is true that they also wanted to educate their fellow Jews, but their primary impulse to action grew out of a genuine fear of the Christian missionary and his free literature. The Jewish religion was in danger because there were no Jewish books. During that very generation in the gold fields of distant California, a pious Jewish mother who wished to give her children a religious education, took a typical Christian catechism, carefully struck out the word Jesus wherever it occurred, and penciled in above it the word "God" and then proceeded to educate a family which later became notable in American Jewry.

It was necessary in that era to confound the missionaries, to save the younger Jewish generation, to develop a group of American Jewish writers, and to create unity in a religiously discordant Jewish world: all of this through the creation and development of common literary interests. That age had a passion for union and a dread of the effects of religious discord. That was why Henry Jones—who was born plain Heinrich Jonas—created the Independent Order of B'nai B'rith in 1843. He not only wanted to further morality among Jews, but he was also determined to bring a unity into American Jewish life by creating for all Jews a common meeting ground where religious polemics and credal disharmony would be conspicuous by their absence.

And so the American Jewish Publication Society was created in 1845, patterned in all probability after one of the missionary and tract societies of the time. In London in 1840 or 1842, a publishing house called the "Cheap Jewish Library" issued a story entitled *Caleb Asher* which had been written for the moral improvement of the laboring classes. A reprint of this book was the first venture of the new American press.

Under the brilliant leadership of Isaac Leeser, this first society managed to maintain itself and to publish fourteen volumes and pamphlets in about five years. It was an uphill struggle: at one meeting in 1849—in which the uncle of a present leader in our Society was active—there were bitter complaints of a lack of support. The Jews, it seems, were too busy making money to buy books. The subscribers paid but a dollar a year and some of them expected a new publication every month. The book-of-the-month idea must have been born with them. They were a thrifty lot and they expected every dollar to do yeoman service. Then on December 27, 1851, a fire broke out in the building of Mr. Hart on Chestnut and

Sixth and with the building there went up in flames the plates and the stocks of books. The only insurance was an apparently childlike faith in the ability of books to survive flames. The Society was dead.

Four years later the Jews of this country must have been stirred when they read of the success of the Institute for the Furtherance of Israelitish Literature in Germany. Under the able leadership of Ludwig Philippson, the organizer of German liberal Jewry, this society issued eighty volumes, including the larger part of the monumental *History of the Jews* by Heinrich Graetz. And Jewry here knew that this European press had had to overcome difficulties which could never arise in free America. In 1855 the Imperial Government at Vienna prohibited Jews in the Austrian Empire from joining the society, and three years later, when Ludwig Philippson was in Milan—then Austrian territory—seeking support for his enterprise, he was arrested and given twenty-four hours to leave the country. When the astonished rabbi asked the Italian policeman what he had done, that official eyed him grimly and said: "You have established a publication society and that the Austrian government does not want. We do not tolerate such people."

Eleven years after this, in 1869, Isaac Mayer Wise engaged in a strong campaign to reestablish a publication society here. He entertained a grandiose scheme which envisioned the translation into English of every rabbinic and medieval Jewish classic, and when in London the Society of Hebrew Literature began to operate under F. D. Mocatta and David Salomons, he took credit for it. He felt that if he could only create a conference of American congregations, a theological seminary, and a publication society, he could bring the Messiah! Rabbi Wise, you see, was a man of great enthusiasms . . . and, we may add, of keen perception. Listen to what he wrote that year in his *American Israelite:*

> All the public speaking of all our co-religionists in this country will not do us as much good in removing prejudice, diffusing correct knowledge, and attaching liberal minds to our cause, as five good English books will do. All the talk in the stores and elsewhere, and all the crying over spilt milk will do us no good. If you do not inform yourselves, if you do not inform the world of what you are, think, want, expect, and hope, you can never expect to be understood or to understand yourselves.

Two years later, in 1870, a group of New York Jews brought about the resurrection of the American Jewish Publication Society. Its second advent was a brief one, for it died in the panic of 1873, but its death was only the prelude to its rebirth in 1888 as a triumphant, vigorous, and vital organism. This was the genesis of our present organization.

I do not think that it ever entered the mind of any one of those men who met in 1888 to create this present Society, that in the year 1941 Jewish scholarship, learning, and book-making would be dying on the European continent. But this is precisely what has come to pass. The Soncino Society of London, which translated the *Talmud* and the *Midrash* has reached the end of its tether. The plates of its fine translation of the *Zohar* were blasted into fragments by a Nazi bomb, and the library of the Anglo-Jewish Historical Society has been destroyed. The Society for Jewish Studies in France is mute after sixty years of dignified labor, and Jewish cultural life in Poland is at a desperately low level. In 1934, over 560 books of Jewish content were published in Poland; 175 Jewish newspapers and periodicals flourished in that land; in Warsaw the Judaistic Institute furthered rabbinic scholarship; in Vilna the Yiddish Scientific Academy explored the social history of the Jewish masses. All that has been swept away as if by a raging torrent.

As late as 1934, in the second year of the Hitler Reich, there were still sixty Jewish newspapers in Germany. There may be two or three today. There were important publication societies in Frankfurt-am-Main and in Berlin. Two important German Jewish scientific periodicals were widely read. One German Jewish encyclopaedia had been finished and another had already reached the tenth volume. Hundreds of books of Jewish interest rolled off the presses annually. The Academy for the Science of Judaism undertook to restudy the history and literature of world Jewry, and the Society for the Furtherance of the Science of Judaism, established in 1902, had already published dozens of works which laid the foundation for a sounder understanding of the age-long culture and contribution of the Jewish people. The Jewish world lived by the inspiration of German Jewry. Now, that Jewry with all its beauty lies rotting in the ground.

To be sure, those who seek comfort in this present tragedy will say: "Zion still stands upon the everlasting hills and her banners flutter defiantly in the breeze." And it is true. We do have our great university on Mt. Scopus, and a magnificent national library; we have our Palestinian scientific periodicals, and a Hebrew publication society that recalls to wakefulness the old masters who have been too long asleep. Yes, it is true: Israel is not altogether orphaned. Thank God for that. Yet what person would be so bold as to declare that the City of David is not to have its hour of agony—an agony which may for the fleeting moment paralyze that new life which has been built out of the blood and sweat, the tears and hopes of so many of our people. Even so, if the agony should come—and pray God it may not—I repeat: Israel is not yet lost. American Jewry still stands, and with it, modestly, but I hope determined, there stands this Publication Society.

There was never a time in our American life that the work of this press was more vital and necessary than it is today. Almost everywhere Jewish books are being destroyed. Almost nowhere outside the United States are they being printed. The Jewish Publication Society is the only surviving literary medium of mass instruction west of Jerusalem. Five million Jews on this continent must find much of their inspiration through us. And lest the magnitude of this task escape us, it should be pointed out that we are not merely five million. At this moment we are Jewry—the only Jewry free to act. We are the whole army: the vanguard, the main body, and the rear guard. We are the heart of a Jewish life which must be maintained and whose spirit must be strengthened ever anew. This is the hour of our crisis. And the crisis is a double one.

The burden is solely ours to carry: Jewish culture and civilization and leadership are shifting rapidly to these shores. Men will need books, books in the vernacular: we must supply them. Here on these shores, the scholars we have bred and the scholars we have sheltered will write new books, steeped in the wisdom and lore that have flourished in Europe since that day a thousand years ago when the Babylonian luminaries first brought the torch of learning to the Mediterranean lands. These books we will publish. This is our privilege, our sacred obligation, and our magnificent opportunity.

Nor shall we fail in this duty. I know that because I know you and the American Jewry that walks with you. We shall continue to assist in the work of educating our fellow Jews, and we shall do our part here in this land to give world Jewry the guidance it must have. The crisis will be met, but this is only one crisis—and the lesser one.

At this moment there is flourishing in Germany a National Socialist Empire that is determined to rule Europe and the world. This powerful state seeks to gain friends in every land by preaching a gospel of hate. It moves calmly and deliberately but beneath the quiet surface of its activity there is couched an implacable malice that is burning at white heat. We know that. Anti-Semitism is to be the wedge that will clear the way for the philosophy of despotism. It is to be the tie that will bind all free nations of the world together in a bond of common sympathy with this new Hitlerian Reich. In Germany's international crusade for anti-Semitism the Jew is denounced as the curse of modern civilization, damned as the source of liberalism and democracy, and anathematized as the cause of all social misery and human misfortune. It is affirmed therefore that the destruction of the Jew and of democracy are the only hopes for this war-ridden world. The Reich is bending all of its energies to convince the world that it is the beneficent mission of Germany to assume European hegemony, to prove to the nations that the destruction of the Jew in present-day Europe is a necessary step in the furtherance of civilization.

One of the most important instrumentalities to this end was the erection in 1935 of an Imperial Institute for the History of the New Germany (Reichsinstitut für die Geschichte des neuen Deutschland). Within this institute there is no section more vigorous than the Department for the Study of the Jewish Problem. It has already published several volumes and pamphlets on the Jewish question; it proposes to rewrite the entire history of the Jewish people and to interpret it as it sees fit. If the volume, *Die Juden in Deutschland,* which was published in 1935, is to be typical, then the world is to be taught that Jewish history is the history of prurient criminals, conspiring against mankind and battening like horrible vultures on the bodies of a suffering humanity. That is the grosser type of presentation. But the Imperial Institute is also the master of techniques that are not so flagrantly crude. Some of the writings of this new school assume a dispassionate objectivity that is all the more sinister because it pretends to be fair, impartial, and scientific. The final impression of the reader is intended to be that the Jews are an unworthy people. The further inference is inescapable: those who destroy them are historically justified.

It is easy to underestimate this type of attack on the Jew. Subtle works of this type definitely can and do undermine the status of the Jew. If the tremendous resources of the new Germany are placed behind this Imperial Institute, its influence can be widespread; if this new empire succeeds in perpetuating itself in Europe its teachings can become a serious menace to American Jewry. This is the second crisis: a more serious one, but it too can be met and overcome.

There is but one effective answer to lies and to half-truths—and that is the whole truth. It is our task to publish books, both popular and technical, the scientific integrity of which is beyond the shadow of suspicion. Objective scholars possess the criteria to determine with whom lies the truth. Every volume that comes forth from Munich must be countered by a volume from the City of Brotherly Love. This is a new and added responsibility, a grave responsibility that requires vision and courage and unyielding tenacity.

The record of our past accomplishment and the desperate exegencies of the present alike summon us to heroic achievement. The literary future of the Jewish people has been placed squarely upon our shoulders. There can be no question but that we must and shall carry that burden gallantly and to the greater glory of our people and of an intellectually free humanity. I have said that ours is a grave responsibility; it is also a great opportunity. I believe we shall be worthy of it.

The Program of the American Jewish Archives

(1948)

Editor's note:

As we have seen, Jacob Marcus's long-held belief that American Jewry possessed the wherewithal to make itself into a major "spiritual center" for world Jewry intensified dramatically in the aftermath of the Holocaust. After the tragic annihilation of European Jewry and its cultural apparatus, American Jewry had become "the largest surviving body of Jews in any one country" and, as such, it was duty-bound to assume new cultural responsibilities. The source of Marcus's determination to establish an "American Jewish Archives" on the campus of the Hebrew Union College may be traced back to this very same conviction.

In addition to the new literary responsibilities that Marcus urged United States Jewry to assume, he simultaneously recognized that the records of the American Jewish past must be collected and preserved. As American Jewry entered a new and significant stage in its cultural development, it was imperative that the community be furnished with the resources it required to sustain the field of American Jewish historical research.

With the help of his friend and schoolmate, Rabbi Walter E. Rothman (1898–1966), Hebrew Union College's librarian, Marcus began collecting records relating to the American Jewish experience in the early 1940s. HUC began requiring its rabbinic students to complete a required course on "The American Jew" in 1942. In 1946, Marcus urged his colleagues in the Central Conference of American Rabbis to initiate a systematic effort to collect and preserve the records of their synagogues. The ascension of his close friend, Nelson Glueck (1900–1971), to the presidency of the Hebrew Union College in 1947 paved the way for Marcus to realize his desire to establish a major archives in Cincinnati. The College's Board of Governors formally called that archives into existence as the American Jewish Archives on 1 December 1947, and Marcus was named as its director.[1]

1. Chyet, "Jacob Rader Marcus," 17. Marcus's required course appears in the 1941–1942 *HUC Catalogue*, 44. The minutes of the HUC Board of Governors note the establishment of the American Jewish Archives in January 1948. See Minutes of the Hebrew Union College Board of Governors, Box B-1, Folder 1, HUC-JIR Records, Mss. Coll. #20, AJA, Cincinnati, Ohio.

In 1948, the new archives began issuing a scholarly journal named American Jewish Archives.[2] In the publication's inaugural issue, Marcus published the following brief essay, which outlines the basic elements of his vision for the newly created American Jewish Archives. He begins by acknowledging the "pioneering" contributions of the American Jewish Historical Society (AJHS), which, since its establishment in 1892, laid "a foundation for scientific scholarship in the field." He makes note of the fact that because the AJHS was geographically situated in the New York City, its "excellent collection . . . served primarily, though by no means exclusively, those who dwell in the New York metropolitan area." The massive Jewish community that lived along the northeastern seacoast was, at the time, the primary focus of the AJHS's holdings while Jewish life distant from New York City in the middle and western portions of the United States had been comparatively neglected. In addition to these geographic concerns, Marcus was acutely aware that the AJHS suffered from limited financial resources and inadequate facilities. As AJHS president Bertram W. Korn observed in 1960, "To every objective student, it must have appeared that [the AJHS was] falling deeper and deeper into a pit from which there could be no rescue."[3]

For these reasons, Marcus was driven to act. He emphasized the pressing need for the establishment of a new repository that would preserve the history of the nearly 1,100,000 Jews who lived "between the Rockies and the Cumberland plateau." It was therefore quite fitting that an "American Jewish Archives" be established in Cincinnati, Ohio—"the oldest Jewish settlement west of the Alleghenies." From its inception, Marcus directed the AJA

---

2. The journal's name became *The American Jewish Archives Journal* in 1998.

3. When Lee M. Friedman, a past-president of AJHS, died in 1957 he made the Society the principal beneficiary of his estate. This bequest transformed the organization in significant ways and ultimately resulted in the establishment of the Society's first permanent home. Prior to this point, however, the AJHS endured numerous financial crises. Its archives were housed in cramped quarters at the Jewish Theological Seminary, and later in a rented warehouse in New York City. Bertram W. Korn graphically recollected how researchers "were denied every kind of personal comfort" when they needed to use the AJHS's holdings. See Bertram W. Korn, "Prelude to Progress: Address of the President," *Publication of the American Jewish Historical Society* 49 (March 1960): 148. On the history of the AJHS, see also Nathan M. Kaganoff, "AJHS at 90: Reflections on the History of the Oldest Ethnic Historical Society in America," *American Jewish History* 71 (1982): 466–85; and Jonathan D. Sarna, "The Archives of the American Jewish Historical Society: A Report to the Committee on Goals and Objectives Necessary for Success of the American Jewish Historical Society," ca. 1985, SC-282, AJA, Cincinnati, Ohio.

and practically every aspect of its operation for the first forty-eight years of its existence.

In explicating his vision for the AJA's program, Marcus offered a synopsis of the dynamics that affect the study of the American Jewish experience and which, by extension, must inform the mission and vision of the new archival institution. This incisive summary provides readers with a synopsis of Marcus's approach to the study of the American Jewish experience as well as an understanding of how the AJA's program would service that methodology.

Marcus delineates five vital elements that any student of American Jewish history must bear in mind: (a) American Jewish history is fundamentally an examination of the interrelationship of the individual Jew and the Jewish community as well as the interaction of the Jewish heritage and the American environment; (b) this symbiosis of Judaism and Americanism is a vital subset of a larger universe, American history; (c) the study of the American Jewish experience is vitally important to American history because, though numerically small, Jews have been uniquely visible in the American nation; (d) to properly understand American Jewish history, scholars must study its life as a "community"—and the synagogue is the most tangible expression of this "living-togetherness"; and (e) the study of the typical American Jew necessarily provokes a kind of historical strabismus—wherein one eye must focus on the American Jew's amorphously American characteristics (Marcus estimates that this constitutes about 90 percent of the totality) while the other eye must simultaneously concentrate intently on the individual's specifically Jewish characteristics (about 10 percent of the whole).

The American Jewish Archives (renamed "The Jacob Rader Marcus Center of the American Jewish Archives" in 1995 to honor the institution's founder) has pursued the programmatic course outlined here by Marcus. Instead of concentrating on the "contribution of Jews to American life," the AJA sought to collect every sort of material that shed light on how the American Jew interacted with the American environment.

Finally, it is important to note that Marcus provided the AJA with the financial resources it needed to fulfill its mission. A skillful and clever fundraiser, he successfully amassed a number of endowment funds that provided the AJA with the monies it needed to publish its journal, to host visiting scholars, and to fund a variety of programmatic activities.[4] Upon his death

---

4. Marcus's annual fundraising letters to the alumni of the Hebrew Union College were published posthumously. See Abraham J. Peck, ed., *All Hail to a Prince of a Schnorrer: The Collected Schnor Letters of Dr. Jacob Rader Marcus* (Cincinnati, American Jewish Archives: 1996).

in 1995, Marcus left a major trust fund for the benefit of the AJA. By 2003, fifty-six years after its establishment, the AJA had grown from a very modest collection of documents that fit neatly on a half-dozen shelving units to a major research center housed in a 50,000-square-foot building complex with nearly 10,000 linear feet of catalogued archives.

~

During the late winter of 1947—in December—Dr. Nelson Glueck, President of the Hebrew Union College, authorized the establishment of the American Jewish Archives. He appointed Dr. Jacob R. Marcus, the Adolph S. Ochs Professor of Jewish History, to serve as director; Rabbi Bertram W. Korn, the Ella H. Philipson Fellow in American Jewish History, to serve as associate director; and Dr. Selma Stern-Taeubler, the well-known historian of German Jewry, to serve as archivist.

Prior to this time the only institution devoted exclusively to the field of American Jewish historical research was the American Jewish Historical Society, founded in 1892. The activities of this organization have been pioneering ones; it has already published thirty-eight volumes of essays, source materials, and indices, thereby laying a foundation for scientific scholarship in the field. No historian or sociologist who attempts to understand the American Jew can afford to neglect these productions; they are basic and invaluable, although admittedly of uneven quality. The library of the American Jewish Historical Society, situated in the city of New York, has an excellent collection of both manuscripts and printed records, but because of the accident of its geographic situation, it serves primarily, though by no means exclusively, those who dwell in the New York metropolitan area. The time has now come to make provision for those students and researchers living between the Rockies and the Cumberland plateau, and to offer study opportunities to the 1,1000,000 Jews living in the Mississippi basin.

The creation of this new Jewish depository in Cincinnati, the oldest Jewish settlement west of the Alleghenies, is but one phase of the inevitable geographic expansion of American Jewish culture. We may assume that it is but a matter of time before a similar archive will be established on the Pacific coast. This Jewish academic expansion is a repetition of the story of the development of the general—non-Jewish—American historical societies and archives throughout the nation. Today there are literally hundreds of such organizations and libraries throughout the land; several states have dozens; New York state alone has 142 of them.

The establishment of Jewish historical and archival centers is a particularly fortunate development. American Jewry is at this moment the largest surviving body of Jews in any one country. These United States today shelter 5,000,000 Jews, almost one-half of the 11,000,000 who have survived the Hitler era. American Jewry has become the "center" of world Jewish spiritual life. When the Jewish historian of the next generation reaches the year 1939, he will begin a new chapter in the history of his people, a chapter which must be called, "The American Jewish Center." This Jewish community has now become the pivotal and controlling factor in that historic development which began in the thirteenth pre-Christian century in Palestine and has continued throughout the interventing centuries in Babylon, Spain and Germany-Poland. The present position of American Jewry was thrust upon it in 1939 when the Jews of Poland began to perish in the wake of the German invasion; its roots, however, as an American Jewish expression, go back to the middle of the seventeenth century and even earlier if we include those individuals who sailed with Columbus, who marched with Cortez, or who lived and died as crypto-Jews in the great settlements of South America, the Caribbean, Mexico and the old Spanish southwest.

It is rare for a historian to be granted the privilege of watching and "filming" history as it actually occurs. Yet that is our privilege today. This is a young country; incredibly young. The Gratz brothers—distinguished enterprisers who helped open the trans-Allegheny country in the eighteenth century—first came to these shores in 1754, at a time when there were less than two million souls in the American colonies; today, in this land of one hundred and forty millions, there are hundreds of people still living who enjoyed the friendship of, and listened to the romantic reminiscences narrated by, Mrs. Tom Henry Clay, a granddaughter of one of those merchant venturers.

It is still possible today to collect considerable amounts of colonial Jewish material and thus to document much of the life of American Jewry from its very first moments. Only too often in the past the study of Jewish history has been a post-mortem autopsy. We propose to collect the records of this great Jewish center, not after it has perished, but while it is still young, virile, and growing, It is a remarkable opportunity and challenge.

~

The study of American Jewish history is primarily the study of the inter-relationship and interaction, within the life of the individual Jew and the

Jewish community, of the Jewish heritage and the American environment. Judaism, the expression of Jewish life, took root 3,500 years ago in a Near Asiatic environment. This religion and its followers have lived through a variety of cultures and tremendous inner changes down to the present day. The American Jew with his composite background, stemming from Slavonic East Europe, or Germanic Central Europe, or Iberian Southwestern Europe, is now in the process of evolving a type of Judaism in this new Anglo-Saxon, Christian environment which will permit him to be all-Jewish and all-American. He is attempting to create a successful adjustment. The opportunity to observe this process in its "becoming" offers a fascinating and instructive field of study.

The perception, analysis and recording of the symbiosis of Judaism and Americanism is obviously a part of American history. To be sure, it does not comport with the orthodox historiographic tradition. It will not have much to do with Congress, with statute law, with sieges and blockades, although individual Jews have participated in almost every event in American life since the earliest days. But American history is also the record of the various social, religious, cultural, ethnic and racial groups who have moved in crisscross fashion through the confusion of American life. The story of this nation is not a straight Anglo-Saxon line beginning in England and stretching primly and unwaveringly across the centuries. It is also the history of a host of influences, peoples and institutions moving and darting in from all angles and converging in one central agglomerative mass to create an American people and epos.

In this polilineal series, American Jewry is but one hair-thin line, numerically small, but distinctly visible because of its early urban character, its commercial proclivities, its high degree of literacy, and its struggle for civil and economic liberties. Whether this small group has made any special "contribution" to American life is yet to be determined. We shall first have to agree on a definition of the term "contribution." But whatever the definition, many of us are not particularly interested in studying American Jewish history from this viewpoint. Whether the immigrant Jew came in 1654 to New Amsterdam or in 1924 to New York, we seek to understand how he lived, how he worked, how he established his own cultural-religious community, and how he interacted in this novel environment, creating a new Jewish life and at the same time helping to give birth to a new American world.

In order better to understand and study the history of American Jewry, we shall have to study its life as a "community." American Jewry is "fellowship" (Gemeinschaft), a closely knit ethnic-religious commonality. (We do not mean a legally-recognized religious corporation like the European Gemeinde or Kehillah, or the Catholic church in Quebec.) This living-together of Jews finds its most tangible expression in the religious core, the independent religious congregation. The American Jewish Archives, therefore, will concentrate on the acquisition and study of synagogal minute books, trustees' minutes, financial and cemetery records, charters, constitutions and their amendments, temple dedication and anniversary booklets, and similar literary materials. Since the leadership of these religious institutions was frequently their most obvious form of expression, the Archives will also assemble collections of rabbis' manuscript files, sermon notes, and other rabbinical papers.

Of course the synagogue does not exhaust the field of Jewish corporate expression or communal manifestation. While it is true that originally all Jewish institutions were religious in the sense that they operated within the periphery of religious control and were ostensibly religously motivated, it should constantly be borne in mind that with the dawn of the French Revolution and the breakdown of the oligarchical, corporate Jewish community, the secular Jew and secular Jewish societies made their appearance. Today, therefore, there are numerous American Jewish fraternities, lodges, Landsmannschaften, and clubs of a cultural, social, philanthropic, economic, and civic defense nature that have drawn large numbers of Jews into their ambit. It is essential that the records of these organizations—at least typical examples—be collected and preserved.

Every Jewish community is in many ways the aggregate of a series of individuals. Consequently the intensive study of the individual is indispensable. We are interested, therefore, in collecting the papers and studying the lives and careers of individual Jews and their families, particularly if we are able to trace them from their earliest appearance on the American scene. It is true that we shall often enough find nothing specifically "Jewish." (We are still not certain that we can define this adjective!) Any student of American history knows that only too frequently the typical Jew, like the typical Catholic or Protestant, Swede or Italian, Mason or Knight of Columbus, is about 90 percent amorphously American and about 10 percent an example of his specific religious group, lodge, or club. Very often—in the majority of cases, to be exact—the records of an individual Jew do not throw any light on his relation to his religious past, or to the ethnic-nationalistic culture from which he or his forebears stemmed. The very fact that many records of this type studiously avoid all Jewish references is highly significant, for if personal reminiscences like manuscript and privately printed autobiographies do not express the Jewish reactions of their authors, we may draw interesting conclusions about their conscious or unconscious assimilation and submergence into the main stream of American life. The larger American history, particularly, will profit from the preservation and examination of this type of material.

These Archives have been established primarily for the collection of manuscript and unpublished materials. It is not intended to compete with the Hebrew Union College Library—in whose building it is housed—in the assembling of printed works touching on the American scene. But, because it has been designed to serve as a research center for established scholars, for students of the Hebrew Union College, and for others who wish to explore the American Jewish field, every effort will be made to assemble—in open shelves—a working library of the standard reference books on general and American Jewish history where the scholar may find the essential tools at arm's reach. To further this purpose it is also planned to build up a file of American Jewish periodicals, magazines and journals. Gifts of significant general and Jewish reference books, and of runs of American Jewish periodicals will therefore be gratefully accepted.

In order to inform the interested public and co-workers in the field of American history of our progress and activities, we will publish this semi-annual bulletin: including lists of our more important accessions and, in each issue, at least one article of scientific calibre.

We will welcome the cooperation of all persons interested in this venture, whether laymen or scholars, and will gratefully welcome contributions of funds and materials, loans or copies of significant records, and above all we solicit references to Jews—however that word may be defined—in the history of the United States.

We seek to ascertain the facts as they actually are; and we desire to promote the study of those materials which will further a knowledge of the American Jew, not only for the purpose of understanding this present period in the millenial history of the Jewish people, but also so that we may grasp the ethos of Americanism and thus make another contribution to the history of humanity.

Three Hundred Years in America

(1955)

Editor's note:

By 1954, the very year that American Jewry celebrated the tercentenary of its communal life in North America, Jacob Marcus was at the height of his professional career. Not only had he gained broad recognition as one of the most prominent historians of the American Jewish experience, he had also assumed a number of important communal offices that gave him considerable national influence. In addition to his faculty post at the Hebrew Union College and his role as director of the American Jewish Archives, Marcus served as the president of the American Jewish Historical Society (1955–1958), chairman of the Jewish Publication Society's influential Publication Committee (1949–1954), and president of the Central Conference of American Rabbis (1949–1951). Collectively, these positions provided Marcus with a visible national platform for promoting the significance of the American Jewish community as it marked the three hundredth anniversary of its communal existence.[1]

When Temple Beth El of Detroit, Michigan, celebrated the centennial of its founding in 1955, Marcus was invited to serve as the keynote speaker. The address he delivered, "Three Hundred Years in America," would later be published.[2] This essay constitutes a summary of Marcus's vision of American Jewish history, a historical conception that stressed: (a) the Jew's enduring fight for the principle of "equal rights and equal responsibilities"; (b) the Jew's thorough embrace of America as home; and (c) the Jew's ongoing commitment to preserving the basic elements of the Jewish heritage—"generosity, honor, and loyalty"—in the American nation. In doing so, Marcus argues, American Jews have never ceased to achieve "exemplary" status as citizens of the country. As a summary of American Jewish history, this article remains, fifty years after it was composed, a tour de force.

1. In 1952, Marcus began serving as a member of the "Committee on Research and Publications" for the American Jewish Tercentenary Committee. See Minutes of the American Jewish Tercentenary Committee, 15 November 1952, American Jewish Tercentenary Nearprint Collection, AJA, Cincinnati, Ohio.

2. For a description of Marcus's appearance at Temple Beth El of Detroit, see *300: A Monthly Newsletter of the American Jewish Tercentenary* (March 1955): 6.

Understandably, Marcus concludes his tercentenary summary of Ameri-
can Jewish history with a glance toward the future. Will American Jewry
continue to flourish and thrive? Marcus's answer to this question would be-
come one of the historian's recurring leitmotifs: four thousand years of Jew-
ish history, of Jewish spiritual teachings, of the Jewish religious enterprise
has inspired the American Jew with an unflagging determination "to fight
for right and for liberty and for decency and happiness, not only for Jews, but
for every living being; for every man, woman and child that breathes, black
and white, Jew and Gentile."

This singular conviction embodies the point at which Marcus the rabbi
and Marcus the scientific historian intersect. The critical study of Jewish his-
tory leads inevitably to the conclusion that despite the endless array of Ha-
mans, Torquemadas, and Hitlers, "Jews glory in their survival. They refuse
to disappear."[3]

∾

Temple Beth El is really a pioneer congregation. This is the oldest extant
Jewish institution in this great state of Michigan. We Jews are proud of
such pioneer institutions—proud of the fact that we are pioneers, in the
literal and truest sense of the word, in this great republic which we cherish. We came to this country—our spiritual ancestors—long before there
were Baptists and Lutherans. We held religious services in New York City
long before even the Roman Catholics gathered together to worship God.
We were an organized community three hundred years ago in 1654. Our
ancestors came from Brazil. They were refugees from the Portuguese In-
quisition, because, in 1654, Brazil had been taken—retaken—by the Portuguese; and the Jews, who had settled there under the Dutch, had been
compelled to leave. Most of them returned to the old homeland—to Holland. One particular ship was captured by Spanish pirates. The Spanish
pirate ship, in turn, was taken by a French man-o-war. Captain de la Mot-
the, the captain of this French ship, the *St. Charles,* asked these Jews what
their citizenship was, and when he found out they were Dutchmen, Hol-
landers, he took them to the nearest Dutch port, and he literally dumped
them, in September, 1654, on the Battery at New Amsterdam, a town
which ten years later became New York. That was the beginning of our
communal life in this country.

3. Jacob Rader Marcus, *The American Jew, 1585–1990: A History* (Brooklyn: Carlson Publishing, Inc., 1995), 383.

I know that some of you will ask me if those Jews who came in September 1654 were the first Jews in the colonies. My friends, you know what the basic principle in all Jewish history is—no Jew is ever the first Jew anywhere. There has always been one who has been there before him—and that was true at this particular time, because one Jew came down to take a look at these "greenhorns." His name was Jacob Barsimson. He was an oldtimer, prepared to teach them the ropes, because, after all, he had been in the country for almost three weeks!

Among those who landed in September 1654 was a butcher by the name of Asser Levy. A very competent man, he was a *shochet*—a very bold man, a very courageous man. I've often suspected, too, that there was in him something of the old Hebrew Prophets. He could foresee the future. He must have known what was going to happen to the poor Jews of New York in November 1929, and a few gentiles, too, at the time of the great stock market crash, because when this butcher built his slaughterhouse, he built it on what is today Wall Street. It was "Wall" Street, because it was the last street in town. It was the street that had the wall to keep off the English and the Swedes on the Delaware and the Indians.[4] Asser Levy found out that, when he was prepared to do his duty within the trainband—with the militia men—and to fight against Indians, he was told by Peter Stuyvesant that because he was a Jew he couldn't fight. They wouldn't let him fight, but they expected him to pay a special tax that was exacted only of Jews. He said that he would not pay the tax but that he was determined to fight with his fellow burghers on the wall. He went to court, fought through his case, and won his case. He laid down a principle that we Jews have attempted to maintain to the present day— *equal rights and equal responsibilities.*

The first congregation, which was established in 1654, was a Sephardic congregation, a Spanish and Portuguese congregation. Among the Jews who followed this Spanish and Portuguese ritual in the next century, was a very well known family of merchants in Philadelphia. This was the firm of B. &. M. Gratz Bros. The Gratzes first were merchant shippers. But when the English began to enforce the blockade against smugglers and when they applied British laws with respect to international commerce, most of the Americans found themselves in difficulties. The Gratzes

---

4. The meaning of this sentence, printed here as in the original, is obscure. It seems likely that Marcus had intended to say: "It was the street that had the wall to keep off the English, the Swedes, and the Delaware Indians."

turned their attention to trading with the Indians across the Allegheny Mountains. After trading with the Indians, they acquired large grants of land and attempted to establish great colonies here in this country. Ben Franklin, Washington, the Gratzes and others were engaged in this colonial activity. At one time the land speculators thought of establishing a fourteenth colony, called Vandalia. There were to be 20,000,000 acres in this colony. The Gratzes and their Jewish associates engaged for a time in the attempt to start another colony on the Illinois and Chicago rivers. They, at one time, owned all of the site of the present city of Chicago, in Cook County. Unfortunately, they were not able to hold on to the lands which they owned in those days.

In spite of the fact that they were officers of the Spanish and Portuguese congregation in Philadelphia, which was known as "The Hope of Israel," the Gratzes were, in reality, not Spanish or Portuguese Jews; they were, in truth, Polish Jews, who had come from the German border. What was it that brought German Jews to this country in the 1750s? They came here for the same reason the German Jews came here in 1939—they were experiencing persecution. Just about the time that we were getting ready to write our Declaration of Independence, the German independent principalities were publishing and promulgating laws such as the following, and I quote one literally: "All jugglers, beartrainers, tramps, German Jew peddlers and Polish Jews are forbidden access to this country, under penalty of being sent to the penitentiary. All gypsies caught will be hanged or shot." This was the type of legislation that was by no means unusual in Germany in the eighteenth century, and it was the type of legislation that induced Jews, German Jews, to migrate to this country at that time. The Jews, however, as a rule, never leave the land of their nativity, until they are forced to leave.

Many of the German Jews hoped that after the American Revolution conditions would improve in Germany and that Germany would ultimately establish republics along the American line. The Revolution of 1848 convinced many German Jews, however, that there was no possibility of an improvement in the conditions in central Europe. So, by that time, the more cultured and wealthy German Jews, who had held on with the hope of a change in the political life, also thought it advisable to migrate and to come to these shores.

We know the stories of some of those German Jews who migrated during the year 1848 and shortly after. There was one very interesting family in the city of Prague, and they were determined to come here; but before they came they thought they would send a young member of the family to see what the country was like. This young man was sent over in the fall of 1848. His first name was Adolf. He came to the great metropolis of New York. Actually, at that time, in the winter of 1848, it had 400,000 people. He wandered up and down the streets, and he saw something that interested him very much. In front of every brown stone house he saw a jug—a milk jug. In each milk jug were two or three cents for a quart of milk. He was very much interested as he watched for a while—nobody went up and down the streets taking the two or three cents out of the jug; so he wrote back to the family, "Come on over to America. This is an honest country—it is the only place to raise a family." And so the clan came over, in the spring of 1849. But they were "funny" Jews (you know, there are some Jews who are very strange), and these Jews didn't like New York City. They didn't care to remain there, so they went up the Hudson River to Albany, where they probably ran into a *landsman* from Bohemia by the name of Isaac Mayer Wise, stayed there very briefly, took the canal boats west, and finally landed in the "Queen City of the West" (and, as all of you know, the "Queen City of the West" is none other than Cincinnati, Ohio), stayed there briefly, then moved to Madison, Indiana, on the Ohio, and finally crossed the Ohio to the city at the falls of the Ohio, which we know today as Louisville. There, in 1856, Adolf, already married, had a son, and he called him Louis Dembitz Brandeis.

Now the Brandeis and the Goldmarks, who came over in '48, were really not characteristic of the typical Jew who emigrated in the '30s and '40s and after that time. The average German Jew who came over in the middle of the nineteenth century was a poor man—some Jewish background (not too much)—a person who had never had the advantages of any real education. We know a great deal about them, because that Bohemian rabbi, Isaac Mayer Wise, in the city of Albany, liked to write, and he has written his memoirs. He told us about his congregation. Most of them were peddlers. He wrote of his experience with these peddlers. If the peddler had any capacity, after a while he graduated from being a peddler. He became what was called, in those days, a "merchant baron." A merchant baron was a man who didn't carry his pack upon his back but actually had a horse and buggy. Then, he would find some likely crossroad spot and settle down. After he settled down, he would open a little retail store. After he was successful, if he was—and frequently they were not; but if he was successful, he would expand. He had two choices: he could decide to open a larger store and become a jobber for other peddlers, finally a wholesaler and even a manufacturer; or he could decide to stay strictly in the retail business, open a larger store and, finally, became a department store owner. Now of course it is important for men to make a living. That was the first thing that they had to do. But once they had made a living, they thought of other things. They began to open their synagogues and their little meeting places, just as this little community did in Detroit, in 1850, when they established Beth El (which, of course, you know, means "the House of God"). Once they had built their *shuls*, their little synagogues, and their charities, they began to think in larger terms of national religious organizations, and the first national organization of the Jews came in the 1850s, because of an incident that occurred over in Italy.

In Italy, in the little university town—famous for its law school—of Bologna, which belonged to the Papacy, there was a family called the Mortaras. In 1856 the Mortaras had a four-year-old boy by the name of Edgar, who became very sick and, when it was feared that Edgar might die, the nurse, a very pious Roman Catholic, secretly baptized the child, without the knowledge of the parents. Two years later, the girl left her employer, the Mortara family, and informed the Papal authorities of what she had done. The Pope, at that time, therefore, issued a warrant, sent the Swiss guards with the warrant for the arrest of young Edgar Mortara, and this child of six, in 1858, on a June night, about 10 o'clock, was literally taken out of the arms of his mother and never returned again to the home of the Mortaras.

When this became known all through the world, the American Jews felt that, even in this free land, "eternal vigilance is the price of liberty," and so they organized *the first civic defense organization for Jews*, which was known as the Board of Delegates of American Israelites, and that was in the following year, in 1859. Within two years, they had plenty of work to do, because the great Civil War broke out, and in this war thousands upon thousands of Jews volunteered. There were nine men of Jewish origin in the Northern army, the Union army, who were generals. In spite of the fact there were so many Jewish generals and so many Jews who fought and died to preserve the Union, no rabbi could serve as a chaplain in the United States Army, because of the fact that the law passed by Congress limited that right and privilege only to the Christian clergy. The Board of Delegates went to work and changed that law.

Even as the people in the North fought for what they thought was right, the Jews in the South fought for the Confederacy, and the Jews in the South had a very notable record. The Quartermaster General of the Confederate Army was Colonel Myers of Charleston, the Surgeon General was Dr. Camden De Leon. There was one Jew in the South who was Attorney-General, Secretary of War, and finally, Secretary of State. Many people maintain that he was the brains of the Confederacy, and he was the Jew, Judah P. Benjamin.

After the war was over, all the struggle and effort that had gone into destruction went into building this great country. By 1869 the last spike was driven into a railroad in Utah. That created a transcontinental railroad system. The people of this country were united, and, as the people were united, they believed, that is, the Jews believed, that we should also be united. In 1873, Isaac Mayer Wise, that young Bohemian, who had gone to Cincinnati, the second largest Jewish community in America, there succeeded in uniting all of the Hebrew Congregations of America into a union. Two years later, he built the Hebrew Union College, the largest and oldest Jewish theological seminary in the Western World.

This man Wise was a rather remarkable person. He was also a great journalist. He had a newspaper called *The American Israelite,* which went into almost every Jewish home in this country. In 1877, he had an interesting bit of news to report to his readers. He reported the fact that the richest Jew in America, and a man who had been one of the outstanding bankers helping the Union during the Civil War, Joseph Seligman, of the firm of Seligman Brothers, had been refused a night's lodging in the Grand Union Hotel in Saratoga, the Spa in New York State. Wise and the Jews of this country were very much disturbed—not because Mr. Seligman would not have a place to sleep, because he could well afford to buy all the hotels in Saratoga and not miss the money (he was reputedly worth $30,000,000)—but they were indignant at the thought that a man should be discriminated against because of his religion. They considered that bigoted and un-American. What did the Jews of this country do when they noted this action? They didn't do what our generation has been accustomed to do. In our generation, we do things differently. When we notice any discrimination of that type, we call a meeting of the most prominent Jews, we very carefully lock the door, we look under the chairs and tables, to be sure nobody is listening to us, and then we do—absolutely nothing! These Jews were conscious of the fact that the firm that owned the Grand Union Hotel was a firm that also owned the largest dry-goods wholesale concern in America, known as A. T. Stewart and Company. A great many of the Jews in the 1870's were in the drygoods and in the furnishings businesses. They were determined to boycott that un-American institution. They didn't do it secretly; they came out with notices in the press, and they signed their names. It wasn't long after that, because of this boycott in all probability, that A. T. Stewart went into bankruptcy and was brought by a more enterprising and more liberal business man by the name of John Wanamaker.

The Jews of that generation were able to do what they did because they were a small community of about 250,000. Most of them were central Europeans, most of them were small business people, most of them were members of the Reform synagogues. That whole picture, the picture of 1877, changed radically four years later, when someone threw a bomb in Russia and destroyed one of the rulers of Russia—one of the Czars. That started a wave and a flow of immigration. Today, as a result of that immigration of East European Jews, we are no longer a group of 250,000, but we are a group of 5,000,000. This is the largest group of Jews, in all probability, that has ever existed at any one time in any one country. All of these Jews, no matter what their background or affiliation, are attempting, to the best of their ability, to make their contribution to the American scene. They have their ideals, and they are attempting to lead exemplary lives.

I believe that their ideal can be typified, to a large extent, in the life of one particular American family that I have in mind. This family came here also after 1848 and they settled in the South, in Alabama. One of the most important members of this family was a young Jew whose first name was Mayer. Mayer became a very ardent Southerner. During the period of the Civil War, he heard that a great many of the Alabama soldiers were suffering in the Northern prison stockades for lack of proper care, medicine and nutrition. He knew, as we know, there was no proper agency for them, because this was long before the days of the American Red Cross. He determined to do something about it. He went to see Governor Watts, at Montgomery. He said, "Governor, I've got an idea—let's take half a million dollars worth of good Southern cotton, and ask the North to accept the cotton, turn it into gold, and use the money solely for humanitarian purposes. The North needs the cotton awfully bad." The Governor agreed with him, and decided to see Jefferson Davis, at Richmond. Davis approved of it, and he opened negotiations with Grant, who had just been transferred from the West to the East, and was before Richmond. Grant refused to do anything, and nothing could be done. Young Mayer returned, back to Montgomery, without having accomplished his purpose. After the war was over, Mayer knew that it would be years before the South would rise again. He moved to the city of New York, married, and had a family. His youngest son, who is still alive today, has been governor of New York State for four terms, and is now in the United States Senate. The father, Mayer Lehman, did everything he could, in his own humble way, to feed some hungry, starving and sick Alabama soldiers in Northern prison stockades. The father was unsuccessful. The son, Herbert Lehman, as director general of the United Nations Relief and Rehabilitation Administration, successfully fed hundreds of millions of suffering human beings all over the world.

This is the story of one American family. We are proud of the Lehmans—we are proud of all Jews who have, with honesty and integrity, attempted to be and to maintain themselves as good citizens. Sometimes, however, in the quiet and the solitude of our thoughts, we lift up our eyes and we recall what has happened abroad since 1939, particularly in central Europe. We are disturbed by the fact that a Jewry that we thought was secure has been destroyed; that five million Jews have been destroyed. We sometimes ask ourselves, How can we attain security? How can we survive as Jews and as an integral part of this great American Republic? What is the formula for survival for our children? Of course, there are many Jews who have the answer. Some tell us that we ought to go into politics, like Bernard Baruch, and secure the gratitude of our fellow citizens. There are others who maintain that we should engage in scientific activity. There are some who have learned so little from the pages of history that they believe that the only salvation of the Jew lies in the acquisition of the almighty dollar. I am the last person in the world to decry the influence of wealth, of political power, of scientific achievement, but I maintain that if the Jew is to survive he can survive only through *the integrity of the individual.* If American Judaism is to rise and not to fall, it will depend upon the individual Jew in his relation to his Jewish community and the larger community into which he is integrated.

This personal integrity of which I speak I believe to be a compound of three elements—*generosity, honor,* and *loyalty.* There is no need today, anywhere in the United States, to speak to American Jews about generosity. Do you realize that, since 1914, these facts, these figures, are literally true—one thousand million—one billion dollars—has been sent abroad by American Jews for the support and sustenance of other Jews, whom they have never known and will never know, purely out of a fine sense of kinship and fellowship? There is nothing like it in all the pages of recorded history!

Certainly I have not come all the way from the "Queen City of the West" to talk to you people about integrity; although I know that you will be the first to say to me that no individual, no Jew, is so righteous and so perfect that he cannot possibly be a little bit better. I know that some of you will say to me that it is hard for us to pull ourselves up by our very own boot straps—that there is a certain amount of social prejudice against us. That is true—and I happen to have a large, unabridged dictionary on my desk that was published in the early part of this century, and it still carries the term "Jew" as a synonym for "scoundrel and usurer," but the fact that such prejudice does exist—that the term "Jew" is for many people a term of reproach—all of that should serve as a challenge to us to take that term of reproach and transmute it into a patent of nobility. If you tell me that it cannot be done, I would like to tell you that there was once a Protestant sect in this country that was hated and despised as the Jew has never been hated and despised. Individuals of this group were actually lynched in the American colonies, but these people persevered in their integrity and today throughout the world, there is no group that is more respected than the Society of Friends, the Quakers. What they have done we can also do. Every Jew should so live and conduct himself as if the future welfare of his people were dependent upon his own personal moral activity. Of course that takes courage, my friends. We have our great spiritual leaders, such as you have in this congregation; we have our great religious institutions; we have our Bible, our Talmud, our Rabbinic traditions, all of which have taught us for the last 4,000 years, to fight for right and for liberty and for decency and happiness, not only for the Jews, but for every living being; for every man, woman and child that breathes, black and white, Jew and Gentile.

And you may say to me, "If I am generous and honorable, and a decent human being, is this an absolute guarantee that I am going to have a future for myself and my children?" My friends, I wish I could give you that guarantee, but there are no guarantees for individuals, no guarantees for great empires and great states; but, if there is a road which the Jew should tread, I believe it is the path which I have described.

I believe that when every Jew is distinguished among his fellow citizens for his personal integrity—then I believe, I hope, that nothing in God's green earth will ever shake or disturb his position. *Character is the most important thing in life.* If you are good men and women, then all the winds and storms of prejudice may whistle and howl about your ears, but, when the din and the noise and turmoil have passed away, and the dawn of a new day comes shining over the horizon, you will still be standing here erect, unflinching, undaunted—An eternal people.

Pedagogue's Progress

(1957)

Editor's note:

Jacob Marcus was convinced that by using a scientific/critical methodology the historian could hope to arrive at the truth. "The fact scrubbed clean," he wrote, "is infinitely more beautiful than perfumed words." Yet Marcus was simultaneously a rabbi. As such, he was a spiritual teacher and leader. In his historical publications, he consciously avoided rabbinical interloping. From the podium or in the classroom, however, he allowed this aspect of his personality to emerge.

On 9 June 1957, it was Marcus the spiritual teacher who rose to deliver the Baccalaureate Address at State Teachers College of the State University of New York in Fredonia. The sixty-one-year-old historian used this occasion to discuss the large mission of education and, particularly, of the educator. The lesson he imparted to these new teachers was a reflection of the political climate of that day in which the United States was locked in a fierce and all-encompassing ideological confrontation with the Soviet Union. Concerned about the apocalyptic Cold War rhetoric that typified this clash of the titans, Marcus warned his young listeners to be wary of jingoism that depicted the conflict as "a battle of the Good against the Evil, of God against Antichrist." Decrying the exploitation of religion for political purposes, Marcus viewed this tendency as a dangerous ploy to gather Americans under a false banner of ideological unity.

The philosophical justification for this rhetorical trend was called the "Reason of State." For Marcus, this rationale constituted a worrisome assault against the separation of church and state—an onslaught that was frequently occurring in the public school system. If state-sponsored religious rhetoric were to gain a real foothold in the public schools of the United States, minority religions (including some Christian sects) would ultimately withdraw their children and enroll them in parochial schools. Should this occur, American Jews and other minority religions would be evermore inclined to seclude themselves and avoid participation in general society. The end result of this self-imposed exile of minorities from the realm of public education would be increased social prejudice—the very affliction that a good system of education should strive to remedy. Despite the impressive growth of Jewish day school education during the last quarter of the twentieth century, Marcus's ideas remain remarkably salient. At the dawn of the twenty-first century, the vast majority of American Jews still educate their children in public or non-sectarian private schools, and the role that religion should play in the life of these institutions continues to engender strong debate.

Yet Marcus is no advocate of a culture devoid of religious life. Religion and the world of the spirit is more vital than ever as Americans confront their existence in an age of nuclear warfare wherein "all men will be cremated equal." A good teacher will indeed influence students in the realm of the spirit, but Marcus the historian/rabbi admonishes his audience to adopt the prophet Habakkuk's perspective as their own: "The righteous shall live by their faith." The greatest religious teachings, he insists, are never imposed on others. The teacher who lives an exemplary life is a teacher who can change the world and, ultimately, the pedagogue's progress will be measured by this standard.

~

We all know that there is a new world dawning. We all know that it is a world of incredible speed in transportation and of progress in the conquest of disease. It is also a world of a rapid growth of schools and colleges. By 1970, six million students will be hurrying through the halls of the universities of this country. This will be a sophisticated lot. Eager and impressionable worshipers at the altar of television, they will begin their graduate studies when they enter kindergarten. This new generation of alert youngsters, as familiar with the outer realms of space as they are with their own back alleys, will offer a tremendous challenge to the teachers of tomorrow. The responsibility of educating children will not be new. But the conscientious teacher, grimly aware of the challenge of a generation prolific with prodigies, will gird his loins and intensify his preparation.

I am not talking about a larger store of knowledge. No! As important as knowledge itself is the approach to it: such things as the capacity to think, to doubt, to reject, to decide intelligently. I have always believed that a student has not begun to mature until he glows with a healthy skepticism, until he bristles when he hears the moron's proverb: "I know it's true; I seen it in a book."

The student of history can learn from the past not only what to do, but also what not to do. History has pragmatic value. It has something to teach us. It can guide us as we seek to bring out the potentialities of one of our basic national institutions, the public school.

It is a fact of our times that we are confronted by a gigantic empire much larger than ours and possessed of tremendous potential power. Its materialistic philosophy is at variance with our way of thinking, and, what is far more significant, there are many indications that this rival state is implacably hostile to us. Religious uniformity, many believe, is imperatively necessary to unite us spiritually for the inevitable Armageddon. The impending struggle, so we are told, will be a battle of the Good against the Evil, of God against Antichrist.

Whether the forces of Western democracy can survive in the same world remains to be seen. There is in our country today a politically motivated attempt to draw the people of this land closer together through common national religious practices. I question whether this is a healthy development. In essence it is the beginning of a move to evolve uniformity in religious folkways, to further a *rapprochement* of Church and State, and thereby do violence to one of the most sacred of American traditions.

Let the pedagogue never forget the slough of religious bigotry out of which we have climbed. Almost three hundred years ago, three men and a woman, Quakers, were executed in Massachusetts because of religious fanaticism. In eighteenth-century Maryland, on the death of a Protestant father, his infant child might well be torn from the arms of its Catholic mother to be reared by Protestant strangers. As late as 1774, on the eve of the American Revolution, Baptists were beaten and imprisoned in Anglican Virginia because they persisted in worshiping God as their consciences dictated. In his famous Memorial and Remonstrance of 1784, James Madison reminded his fellow-Americans: "Torrents of blood have been spilt in the Old World in consequence of vain attempts of the secular arm to extinguish religious discord by proscribing all differences in religious opinion." When men like Madison sat down to write the American Constitution, they were very conscious of the ever-present dangers of compulsory religious uniformity. They took to heart the bitter lessons of the past. It is for this reason that the Federal organic statute of this country imposes no test oaths and tolerates "no law respecting an establishment of religion, or prohibiting the free exercise therof." In 1788, after a majority of the states had already accepted the new Constitution, the people of this land realized that they were initiating political changes of epochal significance. "The citizens of the United States of America," said George Washington, "have a right to applaud themselves for having given to mankind examples of enlarged and liberal policy, a policy worthy of imitation. All possess alike liberty of conscience and immunities of citizenship." To commemorate the adoption of the Constitution, the citizens of Philadelphia held a federal parade on July 4, 1788. On that day in the capital city, they saw a sight that no country and no culture had hitherto witnessed. The clergy of the metropolis, Protestants, Catholics, and Jews, walked in that colorful procession arm in arm. That act was symbolic of the dawn of a new civilization where men would be free to live and practice their religion without let or hindrance. And because that is the American spirit, it is my opinion that it is a violation of our way of life to impose religious practices on children in the public schools.

Religion is one of the most sensitive areas of the human psyche. Someone has said, almost cynically, that acerbities are keenest where differences are least. The absolutes of religion and theology cannot be taught except in an historical and sectarian context. The mysteries of Trinitarianism, of sin, of salvation, of the Atonement, are "of singular magnitude and delicacy." It is inevitable that if they are taught in a public school, violence will be done to the consciences and convictions of many students.

There will always be a substantial minority of Americans of all faiths who will resent and oppose the introduction of the most innocuous of religious teachings into the American public schools. If for religious and nationalistic reasons the schools become a battleground for conflicting religious groups, the chief sufferer will be the school itself. Various dissidents among all faiths, Protestants, Catholics, and Jews, will withdraw, as all three are doing today in some measure, and will expand their own school systems. To diminish the influence of our public schools would indeed be tragic. They are admirably fitted to further unity and a sense of community. I know of no institution where a child may better learn to know his fellow-American and thus divorce himself from his social prejudices.

The more highly one regards the public-school system of our country, the more concerned one must be to protect its integrity. If the primary goal of the public school is to create an enlightened, united American people—that goal, I believe, will not be reached if we continue to foster and introduce religious teachings and practices into our public-school system. Religion should be taught in the home, in the church, in the synagogue, not by the State. And if the institutions of religion turn to the State for aid in attaining their purposes, it is indeed a sad commentary on their effectiveness. The eternal verities of religion cannot successfully be taught to school students of diverse religious backgrounds; the patriotic values inherent in religious conformity are illusory; the attempt, in a democratic state, to impose religion on captive listeners can lead only to spiritual confusion and to political oppression.

The effort to bring formal religion into the public schools of the country is being made on two levels. The first of these, the desire to integrate more closely religion and the State, is motivated by laudable but mistaken intentions. On the second level, the effort reflects a hushed but very real rivalry between the forces of Protestantism and Catholicism. Men of zeal in the great Protestant churches may not themselves be fully aware of what they seek, but I am convinced that they are striving, in a nonsectarian sense, to impress their Protestant religious personality on the American public school, so that it may serve as a countervailing force to the dynamic Catholic school system. Because of this effort to religionize the schools, the liberal Protestants, the unchurched elements, and the Jews are caught between the upper and nether millstones of two competing religious groups. It is an uncomfortable, unenviable position.

You who are conscious of your high purpose in life may turn to me and say reproachfully: "Can a teacher exert no influence in the realm of the spirit"? You know full well the answer to that. Whether you will or not, you influence them profoundly. Your personality impinges upon your students every moment that you are with them. Because they look to you, you must live exemplary lives. The most effective form of religious instruction is to be our better selves. We must live by our faith, not impose it on others. And, if you must have a religious credo for your classroom, permit me to recommend that of the Baptist, Roger Williams. I know of nothing finer:

> I desire not that liberty for myself which I would not freely and impartially weigh out to all the consciences of the world besides. Therefore, I humbly conceive that it is the express and absolute duty of the civil powers to proclaim absolute freedom of conscience in all the world.

As teachers it is not sufficient to know the pitfalls of divisiveness that threaten us. If we are going to influence people, we must evince a more positive attitude. Our program must envisage the future. In the light of our needs in the world in which we are going to live, it may be necessary to re-evaluate traditional beliefs and ideals.

One of the dominant convictions of the American today is the sacrosanct nature of the State. There is a tacit acceptance of a concept known as "Reason of State." That is an awkward, weird phrase, but its connotation is simple: the State is the highest good, not God. The State is the highest good, not the human being, not morality, not religion. Accordingly, to magnify the State and to help it achieve its manifest destiny is the end of all political action. Moreover, the morals of the State are determined by the needs of its preservation. Acceptance of such ideas underlies much that we teach and possibly believe in the social sciences.

How shall we characterize such convictions, and what do they really mean? Do they not amount to a relativistic, opportunistic, subjective morality? Can they result in anything but amorality? Does it not all add up to impiety?

The dogma of Reason of State, taking on flesh, has made statesmanship, diplomacy, politics, nationalism, terms of derogation in our modern vocabulary. It leads to cant and hypocrisy, to an inner struggle between virtue and guilt, to a brutalization of the human conscience. It begets a conflict within us that will corrode us spiritually. We cannot be moral as individuals and immoral as a group. We must hammer into the minds and souls of those we teach the supreme law that every State is bound by the same ethical principles that determine the mutual relationships of enlightened moral individuals.

It may be necessary for us today to re-evaluate that love of homeland which we call patriotism and nationalism. Is it not time once more to ask ourselves: What is love of country? Who is my countryman? To whom do we owe our highest loyalties—to the State, to God, to conscience, to our common humanity? These are questions which every thinking person must answer for himself. And there is this fact that he might well bear in mind. In 1620, when the "Mayflower" sailed for America, it traveled at the rate of two and one-half miles per hour and arrived off the coast of Massachusetts after sixty-seven days. Today the average transatlantic plane crosses the ocean in ten or twelve hours. The thought that boundaries are defensible is antiquated. Every man, wherever in the world he may be, is now my neighbor. He may be a bad neighbor, but he is my neighbor. Years ago we were taught by the Roman Horace that it is sweet and honorable to die for one's country. I would like to believe that in this new world of ours the greatest love of country is to learn to live with my neighbor.

If by the magic of rapid communication and transportation every man is my neighbor, killing people as a method of solving international problems is of questionable morality and hazardous statesmanship. However, I must admit, war is a tribute to our superior intellect. As far as

I can recall, man is the only animal in nature that bands together periodically and systematically to destroy one another. And we now have the added comforting and consoling assurance that the atomic wars of the future will be carried on in the spirit of pure democracy: all men will be cremated equal. The war of tomorrow will be ill-advised because we can no longer isolate ourselves or keep our enemies out. The rest of the world is too big for us to kill; and there is always the possibility of defeat. At the turn of the century, Kipling, in his "Recessional," solemnly warned his countrymen on whose dominions the sun never set:

> Lo! all our pomp of yesterday
> Is one with Nineveh and Tyre!

A generation later the British Empire was a second-class state. Not even the mightiest of nations has won every battle and every war; the pathway of history is littered with the shattered fragments of great states that have risen and fallen. It is a sad and sobering thought.

Perhaps wars are inevitable. As a hard-bitten historian, I have few illusions about the imminent dawn of a Messianic world. Self-preservation is still the first law of nature. Yet I believe that if people are to be taught to hate anything, they must be taught to hate evil, and war is evil. They must be taught to hate, to despise, to loathe violence. They must learn that you cannot effectively convince a man by clubbing him into insensibility.

There are those who tell us that we must learn to love our neighbors. I must admit that I despair of raising my sights to the great command enjoined in the Mosaic code: "Thou shalt love thy neighbor as thyself." It is almost too much to require that we love our fellowman. The most we can hope for is to try to understand him. In evaluating the command, "Thou shalt love thy neighbor as thyself," I like the interpretation offered by an eighteenth-century Jewish scholar. He pointed out that the Hebrew original in the Bible permits the following translation: "Thou shalt love thy neighbor. He is just like." Let us begin modestly in our approach to our neighbors who have just begun to crowd into our backyard. It is not too much to ask for tolerance for every human being who breathes, black and white, Jew and Gentile. I know that tolerance is not an ideal virtue, but it is a virtue, and it is infinitely better than rejection, suspicion, and hate.

In thinking of that which is within the realm of possibility, I have often asked myself what is the most that we can hope for. The answer is: respect for the individual, the realization of the sanctity of personality. It is true that men are not created equal by nature, but all alike they carry in themselves the same spark of divinity. To reject man as a man is to reject Him who made man. We must stand in awe at the very thought of the uniqueness of every individual and of his inherent capacity to love and to be loved, to be kind and generous and helpful.

We who believe that man is teachable and perfectible know that the whole world lies spread out before us. Let us set out to conquer it: with love, with gentleness, with understanding. There is nothing more beautiful than the thought of helping others grow within, that they, too, may make conquests of the spirit. No more exalting mission can fall to the lot of any dedicated human being. No profession is more noble than that of the teacher.

About seventeen hundred years ago a rabbi once said: "The world is sustained by the breath of the mouths of school children" (*Talmud Babli Sabbath 119b*). To you are entrusted the children, to you is entrusted the world. I pray you, give life to the children that all of us may live.

Genesis

College Beginnings (1978)

Editor's note:

In 1975, the Hebrew Union College celebrated the centennial anniversary of its founding. Professor Marcus, the most senior member of the faculty, was asked to reminisce about the school's beginnings. He titled his talk "Genesis," drawing an allusion to the Biblical story of Genesis wherein we learn how the world come into existence from nothingness. So goes, in a poetic sense, the beginnings of Hebrew Union College (HUC) as narrated in a most personal fashion by Jacob Rader Marcus.

Marcus's biography and the College's history had overlapped for sixty-five of the school's one hundred years. With the loss of his wife, Antoinette (Nettie) in 1953 and his only daughter, Merle, in 1965, the HUC community had literally evolved into Marcus's family, his home, and his habitat. Like the distinguished philosopher, Harry Wolfson (1887–1974), who was frequently referred to as "Wolfson of Harvard," Marcus's name had become inexorably linked to HUC. In this entertaining, light-hearted overview of the school's beginnings, Marcus certainly does not suggest that the College was created by the hand of the Almighty. Nevertheless, his loving narrative leaves no doubt that Marcus's personal universe and HUC were, in fact, one and the same.

As a lecturer, Marcus was nonpareil. His sense of humor was legendary, and he loved to mine historical documents for side-splitting anecdotes that enabled him to illustrate his historical lesson while regaling his listeners with delightful yarns. He incorporated a remarkable array of clever sayings, bon mots, which he dubbed "Marcusian wisecracks," and he wielded them skillfully when he lectured in public or in the HUC classroom. In recounting, for example, how mischievous HUC students loved to crawl under the bathroom doors and lock them from the inside just for the pleasure of seeing their teachers push at those doors while writhing in agony—Marcus observes that some people believe this was how the Charleston dance began. "That's all wrong," the Doctor intoned solemnly, "it was the Virginia reel!"

The contents of this essay give credence to Marcus's contention, repeated time and again in the last two decades of his life, that he not only wrote American Jewish history, he was American Jewish history. Indeed, Marcus's memoirs about the College remind us that American Reform Judaism's historical personalities—Kaufmann Kohler, Gotthard Deutsch, Jacob Lauterbach, Julian Morgenstern—were among the leading characters in his life's drama.

In addition to the anecdotes he preserved, Marcus delineates his own analysis of the school's unique "point of view," the institution's commitment to the principles of American Reform Judaism. The school is, above all, an academic institution wherein the modern facts of science must always trump "yesterday's rabbinic and religious traditions." HUC is a scholarly academy that depends on the atmosphere of liberal Judaism for its very existence. According to Marcus, HUC is a school wherein the belief in the oneness of God affirms a love for "our common human family." It is a seminary that cherishes no "sacred cows"; there is no fixed religious authority. HUC strives to imbue its students with a personal faith and challenges them to live by it. One hundred years after the school's humble beginnings, Marcus proclaimed American Reform Judaism the "largest liberal religious movement in the world." Indeed, he never tired of reminding listeners that "the sun never sets on a graduate of the Hebrew Union College," and then he added, "and pray God that sun never will set."

The octogenarian Marcus concluded this essay by inviting listeners, with tongue in cheek, to attend the bicentennial celebration of the school's founding (in 2075!) at which time he eagerly anticipated reviewing the history of HUC's second century of existence. Marcus's wisecracks aside, one point seems unassailable: Whenever the history of the College is discussed, the impact of Jacob Rader Marcus's seventy-five-year-long career on the school's faculty will be a subject of considerable historical interest.

∼

We're here for a birthday party. Our College was a hundred years old this week. We were born on October 4, 1875. That's apparently a long time ago, but if you think in biblical terms, it doesn't mean a thing, because Methuselah lived to be almost a thousand years of age; so, you see, we've just really started our career.

Some of you might ask this question: Why did we have a college in the first place? Why did they start a school? And to understand that, we have to go back a bit. We know why Harvard started. It started in 1636 because the Puritans wanted a learned ministry. That, too, was part of our problem in the decades before the Civil War. We not only wanted a learned ministry; we wanted a respectable ministry.

Some of you may say to me, "Just what do you mean by that word 'respectable'? Just what happened in the past?" Well, I'm thinking of a friend of mine who lived in the 1840s, a man named "Roley" Marks. Roley was a nickname. Actually, his name was Albert J. Marks. He made a living as an actor and he was also a part-time rabbi. He was more or less a full-time fireman, also, with a volunteer fire company, and when he heard that bell ring, he left the pulpit, ran and grabbed his coat and hat, and joined his company. When reproached, he always had a good argument. His argument was that God could take care of himself, but the burning building could not.

I have often suspected, also, that he not only worshipped at the altar of Judaism but also at the altar of John Barleycorn. At all events, on one Rosh Hashanah Eve in the 1840s, he preached and he didn't do so well. Maybe he wasn't altogether there, and he was reproached by some people who were present. This angered him very very much. The following morning he rose and instead of preaching indulged in a tirade against his critics; his climactic phrase was, "Jesus Christ, who says I'm not a rabbi?"

Conditions like that continued for quite a long time. Early in the twentieth century, Beaumont, Texas, advertised for a rabbi. They wanted a man who could get along socially with everybody; a man who was a good mixer; and after their advertisement appeared Jewish editors began to comment: "What Beaumont wants is not a rabbi but a bartender."

The man who realized what this country needed was Isaac Mayer Wise. He was a Bohemian who came to these shores in 1846; an exceedingly attractive young man, a charming fellow, a beautiful person.

Wise was a rebel. In his day there was a law in Bohemia called the *Matrikel Gesetz*. Rabbis could only marry one person in the family because the government didn't want the Jews to propagate. They wanted to "kill them off." Wise paid no attention to laws; he got in trouble with the authorities and finally decided to come to America where he could develop and do what he wanted to do.

He was more or less a stormy petrel. He was always in trouble; got himself an Orthodox congregation, 1846, Albany, and soon became a religious radical. He did things no respectable Orthodox Jew would do. He would write on the Sabbath. He would swing in a swing on a holiday. That's all work. You're not supposed to do those things. And he had ideas, a newfangled ideas about art music. In those days not only the Orthodox Jews looked askance at art music, but so did some of the Christians, people whom we today would call Fundamentalists. Wise himself tells of an incident in a church, no doubt in Albany, where instrumental music was forbidden, and where a choir leader had smuggled a little two-pronged tuning fork into the choir loft and had used it to get the pitch. When a deacon noticed this he stood up in the congregation and yelled at the choir leader in a stentorian tone: "Take that instrument of Hell out of this house of God," and that tuning fork had to be removed.

Wise made one terrible mistake. He fought with the president of his congregation. That's always a mistake, for the president got his cronies together and they fired Isaac Mayer Wise shortly before Rosh Hashanah 1850, but the rabbi refused to stay fired. He knew he had the congregation with him, so when Rosh Hashanah morning came, and he went up to the pulpit to perform the services, the president took a poke at him. If I know Isaac Mayer Wise, he poked him back. I have always maintained that those were the blows that were heard around the world. In a way that was the beginning of organized Reform Judaism. Wise seceded the following day with his friends and established a Reform congregation. Eight years after he had come to his country he was such a notable leader that Cincinnati's Bene Yeshurun Congregation invited him to come down here to be their rabbi. What's important about this is that—with the possible exception of New Orleans—Cincinnati was the largest community between the Allegheny and the Pacific Coast, the Pacific Ocean. So here was a man who was catapulted almost immediately into a tremendously big and important job.

That was in 1854. In 1866 he built that magnificent cathedral downtown which we call the Isaac Mayer Wise Temple. It was in that decade of the 1860s that something happened which was to have a tremendous impact upon American life and upon American Jewish life. A group of capitalists got together in an obscure little village in the Rocky Mountains in the Territory of Utah at a place called Promontory Point. There, one man reached into his pocket and pulled out a golden spike. Another had a silver sledgehammer; and they drove that golden spike into an oak tie and by that symbolic act they completed the first transcontinental American railroad. The Atlantic and Pacific were now united, and a land that had been through four years of Civil War and had been cemented in blood was now reinforced by bands of steel. More important, space and time were annihilated. People could move anywhere in a hurry; and it was then that Isaac Mayer Wise decided there was a need to unite all of the Jewish congregations here in the United States.

He had the complete support of a group of enlightened lay people here in Cincinnati. Without them he could not have done anything. They helped him; they advised him; they supplied the money; and so they organized a union of American Jewish congregations, but did not call it a union of Jewish congregations because the word "Jew" in those days was a dirty word even for Jews. Much more respectable was the term "Hebrew"; so they named it the Union of American Hebrew Congregations.

That was in 1873. The prime purpose of the Union was to create a college to train American rabbis in the American spirit, respectable rabbis and learned rabbis. That was its job; and so they created a seminary. It was not a Reform college; that was made perfectly clear. The word "Reform" or "Liberal" does not occur anywhere in the early literature. It was a school to unite all the Jews of America. They needed unity; so it was to be a Union College, but they couldn't call it a Union College because there were several Christian Union Colleges in the country, so it was to be called a Jewish Union College, but inasmuch as Jews refused to call it a Jewish Union College, it had to be a Hebrew Union College, and thus on October 4, 1875 they held their first session in the cellar, the vestry rooms of the Mound Street Temple. They had about ten young folk, teenagers, when they opened the doors. Shortly after they opened they got a recruit, a girl. She wasn't a teenager. She was in the seventh grade of the public school, and she was eleven years of age. She should have been home sitting on the kitchen floor juggling jacks instead of juggling Hebrew irregular verbs.

They also had a library. What's a college without a library? And they locked the library up every night in a two-and-a-half-foot wooden box, and they locked it up not because they were afraid the youngsters would go off and steal the books, but they were afraid down there on Mound Street that the mice would come out of the panels and eat the books.

A few years later they were so successful—they really were successful—that they bought an elegant mansion down on West Sixth Street, not too far from Baymiller, and they opened it in 1881, and I went to that school the last year that they kept it open. By this time the library had really grown tremendously and they had bookcases in almost every room in the building. Of course the boys busted the panes in the bookcases, but I found that very convenient because when I came to my classes, which started at 3 o'clock, I would simply saunter into what Dr. Kaufmann Kohler used to call the "lunching room"—he meant the lounging room, of course—and I would prop up my chair against one of the broken bookcases, and I knew which one I liked; I wouldn't even look; I'd reach back and take out a volume, one of the six volumes of Graetz's *History of the Jews,* and I would read as I would a dime novel, and that was the beginning of an American Jewish historian.

Those of you who know these old houses, and some of you do know them, know that the third floors were usually very large and spacious, and they were used as dancing rooms. You could have a reception there, but the College didn't use the third floor as a dancing hall; it used it as a chapel, and they put in pews there, and occasionally Bernard Bettmann would come and would talk to the boys. He was the chairman of the Board from 1875 on till well into the twentieth century. He was a fine gentleman, a very cultured gentleman. He had a slight German accent and spoke with a heavy guttural intonation, and it wasn't in my time—possibly a year or so before me, so it was told me—that he had come to school and addressed the boys, telling them all to go out and dissimulate Judaism, and they took his advice and have been doing it ever since.

Now, you may be surprised by the fact that the first students were very young. They were very few and they were very young. Don't be surprised at the paucity of the numbers. The typical American academy or college of the seventeenth, eighteenth, and nineteenth centuries had but a handful of students. As a matter of fact, when Oliver Wendell Holmes wrote a poem celebrating the bicentennial of Harvard in 1836, two hundred years after it opened, this is what he said:

> And who was on the Catalogue
> When College was begun?
> Two nephews of the President,
> And *the* Professor's son. . . .
> Lord' how the seniors knocked about
> The freshman class of one!

So it wasn't unusual to have such a small number of students and such young ones.

We were in no hurry to graduate. We were young and willing to wait. The College, after a few years, became a nine-year school. You went four years to high school; you went four years to the university; and then, because we were getting along in a scholastic sense, you enjoyed one year of graduate work.

We boys all lived in Avondale or Walnut Hills, and we used to walk down from those suburbs all the way to the school, about two miles or more. My classmate who is, thank God, still living, Abe Shinedling, when he had his shoes soled, used to put on two soles because he not only walked down from the hills to near Baymiller but walked all the way back after school was over. We were so poor we couldn't afford the nickel for the car ride, so we walked to high school. We went to Woodward High School downtown near Liberty. Then at 2:15, when we were let out, we ran to make our 3:00 class, and we stayed at the school from 3:00 to 6:00, and then like princes, we would spend a nickel, and we would take the streetcar back home.

Now, you must understand that most of us were about fifteen or sixteen. We worked very hard, twenty-five hours a week at least at high school, fifteen hours at the College; and of course we got tired and we got bored. Occasionally we were unhappy; and because we had high spirits and were full of beans, we sometimes cut up a bit.

Before my time they had a German-born professor who was rather naive, and the boys would play the same trick on him often. During the winter season they would take some snow and mold it into a hard ice ball and put it under the gas jet; and when, after awhile, that snow began to melt, the Herr Professor would turn solemnly to his class and say, "Boys, the gas is leaking."

We had other forms of divertissement. What we would do is this: The smallest among us, and some were only in kneepants, would crawl under the batwing doors of the toilets and lock them from the inside. At 5:00 the faculty would rush down—they were a bunch of elderly men—and would frantically start to push at those doors writhing in agony. There are some people who maintain that this was the beginning of the Charleston dance. That's all wrong. It was the Virginia reel.

My favorite professor—and we all liked him—was Dr. Jacob Z. Lauterbach. The Doctor frequently had the 5:00 to 6:00 hour, and we liked him because he was a voracious eater, and we knew that when he got hungry he would always let us out a little bit early. When we moved up here on the hill and we finally had a dormitory, he was the man who was always called upon to recite the blessing over the bread and the wine on a Friday night, the *kiddush*. One Friday night he wasn't there, and he was always the first man at the table. The boys knew something was wrong. They looked around, and they finally found him outside the door of the dormitory. He was talking to a black cat on this Friday night and he was saying, "Shoo, cat; go way cat; go way cat," but the cat wouldn't go away, so the boys helped him in his misery. They drove the cat away, and he rushed in, hurried through the prayers, and after he had dug into the food and finished, the boys turned to him and they said, "Dr. Lauterbach, you are a distinguished Talmudist, you're a folklorist, a cultural anthropologist of note. How could you possibly believe such a superstition?" He looked at them quizzically, and in his heavy Austrian accent he said, "I'm modern and I'm scientific, but vy takes chences."

In 1912 we moved up here on the hill. The grounds had not been finished. They were still full of knolls and hummocks. We boys were recruited, got pick and shovel, and we had to level off the place. We made a nice ballfield. Most of the buildings we have today weren't standing then, and because there were so many hills here—and the hills were as high as those across at Burnet Woods—the catalogue of the College always said quite correctly, "The College is built on a bluff."

That wasn't true. The College was not built on a bluff. We boys had to work hard. You had to make a ninety-four average to get a scholarship or you were out of luck; and bear in mind you never carried less than thirty hours, fifteen at the university and fifteen at the College. The presidents of the school maintained the highest standards. There were Kohler, Morgenstern, Glueck, succeeded by our friend, the president of today, Dr. Alfred Gottschalk, who is driving us as we have been driven in the past, demanding that we do the best we can to maintain the high scholastic standards that have always distinguished the College.

When I went to the University of Berlin in 1922 to do graduate work and to get my doctorate, they refused to give me any credit for my University of Cincinnati studies. Of course, that was arrogant. The University wasn't that bad. It was a good school, and I was very happy there, but the Rector in Berlin would not give me a single credit for my work at the local university. They did give me all the credits I needed for the classes I had taken at the Hebrew Union College. Our school had a good name in Germany.

Although the students were young, many were exceptionally able. In the first class I taught, in 1920, I had a student who was so small he was still in kneepants; his feet would not reach the floor. His name was Joshua Loth Liebman. He graduated from the school and wrote a book called *Peace of Mind* that sold over a million copies.

Well what did the school actually do during the last hundred years? What did it accomplish. What did it teach? It has always had a point of view all its own. We are a liberal school. Theologically, we're unitarian. We believe that God created the world and that there is but one God. We believe, since God is the father of everyone, that every human being—man, woman, or child—is our brother, is a member of our common human family; we have no prejudice against anybody or against any religion, and that is why we are sympathetic to all religions and certainly sympathetic to Christianity.

Well, you may say to me, "That's a very liberal point of view, but you must have some body of knowledge, some body of theology. You must have something specific in which you believe. You must believe in revelation." Yes, we believe in revelation. We believe in the Ten Commandments, which were given to our fathers three thousand years ago. We think it's a magnificent code and a fine body of ethics. We do not believe, however, that the first and the last word was said at Mount Sinai. We believe that every new generation has its Mount Sinai, and every age produces its own Ten Commandments, that every generation has something new and beautiful to offer to us, and we reach out everywhere, to Christianity, to Islam, to any faith or to any good book or any beautiful picture, and take what we find beautiful and exalting and use it to enrich ourselves. We have our rituals; we have our ceremonies and we love them, but we have always maintained that the moral law is far more important than the ritual law.

Some of you may ask me, "Does Reform have a hierarchy? Does it have authority; isn't there somebody who can say go and somebody who can say stay?" No, we have no fixed authority. The only voice we recognize is the consensus, the ethical consensus of every generation. The only voice to which we listen is that which lies within us. Well, you may say to me, "If that's true, and there are 5,800,000 Jews in the United States, then there are 5,800,000 Judaisms in the United States," and my answer is, yes, thank God. Every man has his own faith and he lives by that faith.

We believe in science; and if there is anything in our past beliefs that is not congruent with the facts of science, then we revalue yesterday's rabbinic and religious traditions. Because we are modern and because we accept the findings of science, we are willing to divorce ourselves from some of the prejudices of the past, particularly where women are concerned. We have granted women a larger part in our synagogues and in our religious practices. We look upon them as equals. There have been women presidents of congregations for at least a generation. We have just graduated some women in our seminary, and we are determined to continue the policy of according them complete and absolute equality.

We do not believe in the physical resurrection. We do believe in some form of immorality. We do not believe in the concept of a personal Messiah, that some individual, a monarch, a member of the House of David, will yet appear, rule over us, and tell us what to do. That we completely reject. Though we do not accept the concept of a personal Messiah, we do believe in a Messianic age. We hope and pray and work for social justice. We strive to improve this world to the end that the masses, hundreds of thousands and millions in this country and abroad, may not remain ill-fed and ill-clothed, and ill-housed.

What has Reform to do with the ushering in of the Messianic age? We believe we have a mission to perform. It is our job to help bring it about. Does that mean that we Jews believe that we are *the* Chosen People? Certainly not. We reject that concept, yet we believe that every people in a way is a chosen people. Every people believes it has something to say, a job to do, and we believe it has been our obligation, since the days of the prophets, to preach social justice, righteousness, decency, opportunity for every human being, black and white, Jew and Gentile. This is our job. That is the mission that we have to perform; and because we have that task, that goal, we believe that we can perform it wherever we are. A generation ago, Reform maintained that the only place you could have fulfilled that mission was in the land where you lived and where you wanted to be. There was no need to go back to Palestine, and for that reason many of our leaders of yesterday were anti-Zionists, strongly anti-Zionistic.

Today we have a better understanding. We believe that a man can be a good friend of Israel, do everything he possibly can to help our fellow Jews in the Holy Land live their lives to the fullest, and at the same time we, wherever we are, work as human beings to make this world a better place for everyone. And because we live in this world and affirm it and its positive values with vigor, we have embraced education. We are passionate partisans of the arts and sciences. It is no accident, therefore, that the Jews of the United States, with less than 3 percent of the population, have won at least 15 percent of all the Nobel Prizes in the physical sciences.

We are—you'll excuse me for saying it—a successful religious group. This may shock you or surprise you, but it is true. We are the largest liberal religious movement in the world. We have grown internationally. There is no continent where you will not find graduates of the Hebrew Union College. You'll find them in Australia, South Africa, South America, Canada, and I like to parody the statement that was made about the

British Empire: the sun never sets on a graduate of the Hebrew Union College, and pray God that sun never will set.

Thus endeth the first book, the Book of Genesis, after a hundred years. I do hope that all of you come back here at the end of the next hundred years and permit me to review that new century.

Testament

(1989)

Editor's note:

Jacob Marcus was ninety-three years old when he delivered "Testament," his last major address to an audience of more than a thousand people who had filled the pews of Cincinnati's historic Plum Street Temple. Ostensibly, Marcus wrote this address to mark the centennial anniversary of the Central Conference of American Rabbis (CCAR).[1] For months, he had been ruminating over the content of this message; he told many students and colleagues that he realized he had actually been preparing himself to deliver this particular address for many years. As the name suggests, Marcus fully expected this essay to be a valedictory address reflecting a lifetime devoted to the study of the American Jewish experience. And so it was.

In his "Testament," Marcus's now familiar optimism about prospects for Jewish life in America has given way to a more fatalistic air. On the one hand, the aged historian still insists that America is "the greatest country in the world"—a nation in which Jews and Judaism have flourished in numerous ways. By way of example, he points to the expansive Jewish organizational structure that serves American Jewish life. There are so many Jewish institutions functioning in the American nation that every rabbi in the CCAR could "hope some day to become a president"!

Yet Marcus also confesses that his lifelong love affair with America has not been without its hurts and disappointments. As a young man, Marcus explained, he was convinced that America—good old Uncle Sam—was the Messiah, the veritable source of Jewish redemption. Over the years, however, he realized that "poor Uncle Sam" was most assuredly not the Messiah. Throughout the twentieth century, as the world repeatedly brutalized Jews, the United States government let Marcus down by failing to actualize the lofty ideals on which the republic was founded. Alluding to the country's failure to rescue the Jews who were fleeing from Nazi barbarism, Marcus laments: The United States government "held life and death in [its] hands; [it] chose death."

In a noteworthy paragraph, Marcus underscores the historical significance of the third Jewish commonwealth, Israel. By reminding his audience

---

1. 21–26 June, 1989.

that the rebirth of the Jewish state in the last half of the twentieth century was "the most glorious moment in all Jewish history," Marcus acknowledges the centrality of Israel to the American Jew. Nonetheless, he reminded his audience that no one community—not even the modern State of Israel—was a panacea for the Jewish people. He asserted a principle that he had repeatedly emphasized throughout his career: Omniterritoriality. Jews must continue to live in every part of the world. Just as this principle preserved the Jewish people in the past so too, he believed, it would safeguard its survival in the future.

Jacob Marcus concludes his testament by confessing he has complete faith in only two ideals; the indestructibility of the Jewish people and its unflagging ethical legacy for humankind. For when all is said and done, what is the meaning of the Jew's place in the history of human affairs? In responding to this query, the nonagenarian refuses to equivocate: no matter how pitifully human civilization may degenerate, the study of Jewish history testifies to the Jew's indestructibility. The Jewish people will endure forever, he concludes, and hold fast to their ethical raison d'être:"humanizing" the planet Earth.

∼

I am grateful in spirit and thankful in heart to the Central Conference of American Rabbis for inviting me to address them in this their centennial year. You are all my immortality; you have kept me alive. Now you know why I believe in *Tehiyas Ha-mesim*, resurrection. It is a privilege to talk to this conference, the oldest and certainly the most liberal rabbinical assembly in the world. We are absolutely free, under no authority except the dictates of our own conscience. That is why we are great. We glory in the knowledge that we are today the largest liberal religious movement in the world. We preach a gospel of ethics and rationality. When I realize what the Jews have done for this great republic I am happy. The whole course of American history would have changed if the Egyptians had survived in the Red Sea and we had been drowned.

We live in great times, in the greatest country in the world. Politically we are powerful; the State of Israel lives through the breath of the American Jew. We are affluent and generous. Every year we send $500,000,000 across the seas to help fellow Jews; relatively speaking, this is the greatest philanthropic feat in all history. Our cultural achievements in this land are almost incredible. Fifty thousand Jewish men and women teach in the colleges of America; Nobel Prize winners abound. Three hundred universities list Hebrew and Judaic studies in their catalogues. There are more Jewish books in the United States than in all Israel; one Reform congregation alone in the Far West has a library of 25,000 volumes. There are over 10,000 Jewish organizations in this country. Thank God, every member of this conference can hope some day to become a president.

The Third Jewish Commonwealth has been established; Israel is the only country in the world where a Jew can go as a right. This is truly a golden age. How fortunate you are to be alive in this the most glorious moment in all Jewish history. *Ronu le-yaakov simhoh*, sing with gladness for Jacob (JER.31:6).

In the lifetime of many of the adults in this conference, in the early 1930's, there was only one other country as liberal as the United States. This was Weimar Germany; a Jew was the primary architect of its constitution. There it was, in 1932, that 11,737,185 German citizens cast their ballots for a candidate who had dedicated himself to the destruction of World Jewry. Just about a decade later, these Germans began the murder of at least 5,000,000 Jews. It is the most horrible crime in all history. In effect, in what purported to be a Christian state, the rulers said: suffer the little ones to come unto us and we will lead them into the incinerators. This nation, the most cultured in all Europe, murdered its Jewish God, its symbol of love and compassion. Many years ago Isaac Mayer Wise, who occupied this pulpit from which I now speak, wrote the following sentence: "The world has sinned more against the Jew than 100 Christs could atone for on the cross."

I grew up believing in the Messiah. When I cupped my ear I could almost hear the clop-clop of the hooves of his white steed as it galloped into the sunlight. I knew exactly what he would look like. He would be six feet four inches tall; he would have a long thin white beard, he would wear a stovepipe hat, his cutaway and trousers would be red, white, and blue. Poor Uncle Sam! In 1903 when he passed through Kishineff, the Russians clubbed him to his knees; in 1943 when he finally reached Central Europe, the good citizens of Germany cremated him. The Messiah did not die alone; Benjamin Franklin, Thomas Jefferson, Abraham Lincoln perished with him. President Franklin Delano Roosevelt, the Congress, the State Department held life and death in their hands; they chose death. The United States Government closed its gates to potentially the most gifted émigrés who had ever knocked at its doors. In the grand design of defeating the Germans, the Jews were expendable.

In 1920 when I was appointed an instructor in rabbinics at the Hebrew Union College I taught *Pirke Ovos, The Sayings of the Fathers*: "Who is wise? He who foresees the future." We are not paranoid, but what happened in Europe, in Germany, makes us wary. A philosopher once said: "Those who do not learn from history are doomed to repeat it." The message of the Holocaust is implicit; let us draw our conclusions. If it could happen in liberal Weimar Germany it can happen anywhere in the world. Recall what I taught many of you in my classes: ultimately no land in all Jewish history has ever spared Jews. There are no guarantees for survival; there never were; there never will be. As rabbis, leaders, the *azile bene yisroel*, the Princes of the House of Israel, envisaging the millennial future of our people, what shall we tell our children?

We have two options: the geopolitical and the religiospiritual. For the geopolitical, I offer you a new word which I have introduced into the English language. It has eighteen letters: omniterritoriality. I discovered this word in the Talmud, in Pesahim 87b, thirty-five lines down from the top of the page: God showed his goodness to the Jews by scattering them among the nations. The comment of the medieval scholar Rashi is enlightening: "If they are scattered they cannot all be annihilated at one fell stroke." Over the centuries, omniterritoriality has saved Jewry. There must be no land without some Jews.

Then there is the religiospiritual option. Let us disregard the persecutions of the past 1900 years. Maybe God will perform a miracle and we here will never experience any disaster. I am fully aware that most of the polls indicate that a substantial minority of Americans do not like Jews. Nevertheless, it is obvious in this centennial year that our lines have fallen in pleasant places. Thank God for fortress America.

However, we face a serious problem—not oppression to be sure—but constant attrition, assimilation. Yes we are assimilating, declining numerically. Don't draw any false conclusions. Do not misread Jewish history. In the last three to four thousand years there was never a day when the majority of Jews were practicing religionists, not even in ancient Israel in the ninth century before the Christian era. The majority of all Jews in Palestine were then virtual pagans. In the days of Elijah there were only 7,000 practicing Jews in all Israel, men and women who had not bowed the knee to Baal. Today we are few not because we were murdered throughout the ages but because we seceded, acculturated, voluntarily. I surmise that most Jews in history assimilated, succumbed to the attractive appeal of the host culture. Otherwise we would not be a mere 13,000,000 but 1,000,000,000, as numerous as the Chinese. In all the centuries the handful who survived was the norm. Jochanan ben Zakkai was no fool; when he defected to the Romans all he asked for was a little schoolhouse and a few disciples. Forget about numbers. Numbers are a myth. We have always lived through a few, a saving remnant.

Jewish history points a statistical moral. If we are determined to survive—and we are—we must cultivate those few who are devoted to our religion, our culture. When you survey your congregation on a Friday night, don't count bodies, count souls. These chosen few, this elect, has a job to do: these Jews are our future; they have to save us; even more they have something to tell the whole world, to distill for all humanity what the Jew has learned after 3,000 years of bitter experience. We are presumptuous enough to bring our gift to the Gentiles, to those who, we believe, are desperately in need of what we have to offer. We do not wish to missionize the nations; we want to humanize them.

And what is this that we have learned; what are the implacable, the inexorable verities? It is our hope to further traditional values, not traditions as such. We must become proud exponents of the best in our Jewish heritage. That legacy reached its height in the ethical demands of the Hebrew prophets. They taught us to abhor hatred, violence, brutality, to avoid every aspect of any concept that manifests itself in contempt for fellow human beings. Let us be men and women of dignity, kindliness, learning, gentility, moral courage. It is imperative that we respect the sanctity of every human soul. Let us never forget that the weapons of the Jew are truth and the irrefutable logic of decency. We emphasize the cosmopolitan, the universal; we insist on social justice, on political and religious freedom. It may well be that we cannot love our neighbor as we love ourselves—that is a counsel of perfection—but the least we can do is to tolerate him and his differences. Never lower your ethical sights. If we are not a moral people, then we are like so many others, billions of pounds of organic matter, nothing else. Our ultimate goal is to strive for a universal society which will require political states to maintain the same ethical standards that distinguish moral individuals. We Jews pride ourselves that we are a civilized humanitarian folk. Let us manifest it in all of our actions. Our history demands that we continue our quest for Zion. Zion is our highest Jewish self in projection; it is the ideal we seek but we can only glimpse.

Rabbi Marcus, *divre nehomoh*? Comfort? The true *nehomoh* is to face reality. We address ourselves to eternity. We have an enduring faith. We have no choice; for this were we created. The bodies consumed in Auschwitz may yet light up a world that lives in darkness. "Our ancestors received the law on Sinai's mount amidst thunder and lightning and cloud and flame, and amidst thunder and lightning and cloud and flame we will keep it." Our prophetic exhortations are the last and best hope of humanity. If we raise but a handful of disciples who treasure our ideals we will survive. We are an *am olom*, an eternal people; the world can never, never destroy all of us. And in that fateful moment when the earth begins to shatter, when the very heavens tremble, when the sun, the moon and the stars turn dark, when the last bomb falls and the last mushroom cloud evaporates, we, we will emerge erect, undaunted, dedicated to the hope that a day will yet come when "they shall not hurt or destroy in all my Holy Mountain, for the earth shall be full of the knowledge of the Lord as the waters cover the seas" (ISA.11:9).

PART III

Marcus's Bibliography

Writings of Jacob Rader Marcus

A Bibliography

— EDITED BY FREDERIC KROME,

COMPILED BY GERI NEWBURGE AND JEFF WILDSTEIN

A bibliography of the writings of Jacob Rader Marcus (1896–1995) runs to over thirty typewritten pages and encompasses a chronological span of some eighty years. His first article appeared in 1916, when he was still a student at the Hebrew Union College (HUC), while his last book was published posthumously in 1996.[1] During those eighty years, the American Jewish community, indeed world Jewry, underwent fundamental transformations, and Jacob Rader Marcus's historical writings bear witness to the dramatic developments that marked the twentieth century.

In 1978, a bibliography of Marcus's oeuvre was compiled by Dr. Herbert C. Zafren, then director of Libraries of the Hebrew Union College-Jewish Institute of Religion, and Dr. Abraham Peck, who served as Administrative Director of the American Jewish Archives.[2] When the bibliography appeared, the then-eighty-two-year-old Marcus was already being referred to as the "Dean of American Jewish Historians," and few realized that he had more than fifteen years of productive scholarship still ahead of him. The Zafren/Peck bibliography had been periodically updated in typescript by Marcus's long-time personal secretary, Ethel-Jane Callner (1912–1999), who continued tallying his publications year after year.

Although the Zafren/Peck bibliography served as the basic starting point for this work, certain changes were made. For example, the previous bibliography listed the journal *American Jewish Archives* (now *The American Jewish Archives Journal*) as one of Marcus's publications every year from 1948 on. Even though Marcus edited the journal from its

This bibliography could not have been completed without the assistance of Judith Daniels and Kathy Greenberg.

1. Marcus's last original piece of scholarship appeared in 1996. Some of his publications, however, continue to be reprinted.

2. *The Writings of Jacob Rader Marcus: A Bibliographic Record,* compiled by Herbert C. Zafren and Abraham J. Peck (Cincinnati: American Jewish Archives, 1978).

founding until his death in 1995, it was decided not to list it as a separate publication. Instead, this bibliography lists the editorial statements, articles, book reviews, and documents that Marcus personally contributed to the journal. The 1978 Marcus bibliography also listed *Studies in Bibliography and Booklore* every year between 1953 and 1957 as one of his publications. Since Marcus was a member of the board, and did not contribute any written material to the journal, this reference has also been dropped.

The Zafren/Peck bibliography listed some of Marcus's syllabi and public relations announcements as part of his publications record. Although such material is valuable for understanding Marcus's approach to history, and are still worth reading as historical documents, they too have been cut from the new bibliography.[3] The Zafren/Peck bibliography sometimes listed offprints of Marcus's articles, supplied by journal publishers, as separate publications. These references have been removed.

Certain features of the original bibliography have been retained. It was decided, after numerous discussions, that the chronological organization of Marcus's publications would still be used. This has the advantage of providing the reader with a sense of the progression of Marcus's scholarly interests, and by extension, that of American Jewish historical research.

A major problem facing any Marcus bibliographer is that many of his works have been republished, some on more than one occasion. This often leads to confusion when reading the Zafren/Peck bibliography. In order to avoid repetition, reprints are listed with the initial publication, unless the reprint was substantially revised, or its appearance at a specific point illuminates some important aspect of Marcus's career. In some cases an explanatory note is used to explain the significance behind the editorial decision.

Initial work on checking the Zafren/Peck bibliography and then compiling material that was missed in the 1978 publication was begun in the summer of 1998 by Jeffrey Wildstein, a rabbinic student at Hebrew Union College-Jewish Institute of Religion, then serving as a summer intern at The Jacob Rader Marcus Center of the American Jewish Archives. In the summer of 2000, rabbinic intern Geri Newburg continued the project, not only searching for lacuna in the initial bibliography, but also incorporating material Marcus wrote post-1978. Once the raw data was collated, it was then entered into a database and the services of Judith Daniels were

---

3. Marcus's syllabi and other class related material are available in the Jacob Rader Marcus Collection, Ms. # 210, in the AJA.

solicited. Judith Daniels worked with Dr. Marcus for over a decade, overseeing numerous publication projects (Marcus referred to her as his "Chief of Staff"). Daniels checked to ensure that everything Marcus published during the last ten years of his life was included. She also checked the rest of the bibliography for accuracy.

An examination of Marcus's writings reveals that his work fell into several broad categories:

1. Popular Writings

From an early stage of his career, Marcus believed that a historian's primary task was to bring the knowledge of history to people outside the Ivory Tower. In addition, Marcus needed to earn a living at a time when the salaries of HUC faculty were extremely low.[4] Thus he combined his talents for writing with his need to earn a living, and published a number of short popular essays on Jewish history in the Anglo-Jewish press for pay. A number of these articles were reprinted, primarily in the Cincinnati based *American Israelite*. It has proven impossible to determine with exactitude where each reprint appeared, as some undoubtedly were used for Temple Bulletins that show up on no periodical index. A direct relationship with *The Scribe* of Portland, Oregon, and the *American Israelite* in Cincinnati, Ohio, is evident from reading the bibliography.

2. Contemporary Opinion/Observations

Some of Marcus's earliest writings reflect his developing opinions on topics that would occupy him throughout his career, for example his 1918 article "Lost: Judaism in the A.E.F.," which was published in the *American Hebrew*. Such columns are not historical work per se, yet they do reflect Marcus's understanding of the role that history played in the Jewish experience.

Beginning in 1929, Marcus also wrote a column for the *CCAR Yearbook* entitled "A Survey of Contemporaneous Jewish History." Marcus served as chairman of the Contemporaneous Affairs committee of the Central Conference of American Rabbis through 1948, and wrote the historical part of the reports. Since they were an annual contribution each has been given its own citation in the bibliography.

4. I owe this point to Kevin Proffitt, Chief Archivist of the Marcus Center, for directing me to information from Marcus's personal diary, which is part of the Papers of Jacob Rader Marcus, Ms. Col. #210, The Jacob Rader Marcus Center of the American Jewish Archives (hereafter, AJA).

3. Scholarly Articles

Early in his career, Marcus wrote a number of scholarly articles for academic-based journals, such as the *Publications of the American Jewish Historical Society*. These essays represent some of Marcus's most original and analytical work, and cover a variety of topics, from American Zionism to the periodization of American Jewish history. Several of these articles were subsequently reprinted in pamphlet form by the American Jewish Archives. We chose to list most of these American Jewish Archives pamphlets separately from their original publication in the belief that the timing of their appearance reveals something of the growth of American Jewish scholarship, or at the very least Marcus's efforts to sponsor the study of American Jewish history.

4. Documents/Document Collections

In July 1959, Marcus wrote that his experience as editor of *American Jewish Archives* "has demonstrated that it is very difficult to secure original, worthwhile scientific articles. In lieu of such articles, we have resorted to the publication of documentary material."[5] Marcus's decision to publish documents was based on his belief that primary sources formed the bedrock upon which any historian, professionally trained or not, built a historical narrative. Furthermore, he believed that American Jewish history had to be told from the bottom up, rather than recount the story of great men at the top. Thus Marcus's publication of these documents, in *American Jewish Archives* and elsewhere, must be understood in part as reflecting the immaturity of American Jewish history as a scholarly discipline. Since Marcus was attempting to move the study of the American Jewish experience away from the filiopietism that was so commonly found in existing publications, it is not surprising that he would sometimes publish three or more documents in an issue of his journal. In such cases every attempt has been made to group these documents together in a given year so it is clear to the researcher what type of source material was published. It is also significant to notice that, after 1965, Marcus's publication of documents in the journal began to fall off, an indication perhaps that the field had begun to mature.

5. Jacob Rader Marcus to Solomon Grayzel, 23 July 1959, American Jewish Archives Records, AJA.

5. Scholarly Books

When Marcus was in his seventies, he was asked if he intended to publish many more articles. Marcus replied that he was not going to worry about writing articles, rather he would focus his energy on writing books.[6] Although he would never entirely give up being an essayist, often writing the forward to books produced by other, younger scholars (many of them his disciples), Marcus turned the majority of his attention to developing a narrative history of American Jewry. The fruit of this labor was his three-volume *Colonial American Jew, 1492–1776,* and Marcus's four-volume opus *United States Jewry, 1776–1985,* which was published between 1989 and 1993.[7] In the latter case, the decision was made to list all four volumes under 1989, rather than spread out the references over the four year period.[8]

Marcus's publishing accomplishments loom large in comparison to the efforts of almost any other single individual. This bibliography reveals not only the broad sweep of his interests, but also the specific topics that interested him at different times during his career. Even a quick perusal of these pages reveals Marcus's legendary productivity. It is hoped that this bibliography will provide a guide to researchers interested in studying both American Jewish history, and the impact of one of the field's most prolific and influential scholars.

1916

"America: The Spiritual Center of Jewery" [sic]. *Jewish Community Bulletin* (Wheeling, W. Va.) 1, no. 3: 4–5, 8.

Review of *The Evolution of Modern Hebrew Literature,* by Abraham S. Waldstein. *Hebrew Union College Monthly* 2: 304–305.

Review of *The International Standard Bible Encyclopedia,* edited by James Orr. 5 vols. *Hebrew Union College Monthly* 3: 20–23.

Review of *The Jews of Russia and Poland,* by Israel Friedlaender. *Hebrew Union College Monthly* 2: 171–72.

Review of *Yearbook (Central Conference of American Rabbis),* vol. 25. *Hebrew Union College Monthly* 2: 175–76.

---

6. Information provided by Kevin Proffitt to Frederic Krome.

7. Detroit: Wayne State University Press, 1970; reprint 1994.

8. The four-volume set was also published by Wayne State University Press; volume 1 in 1989, volume 2 in 1991, and volumes 3 and 4 in 1993.

"Mendele Mocher Seforim." *American Hebrew* 98: 410–11.

Personal letter from Jacob Rader Marcus to *The Jewish Community Bulletin* (Wheeling, W.Va.) 1, no. 6: 23.

1917

"The Jewish Soldier." *Jewish Comment* (Baltimore) 50, no. 18: 433–36. Reprint. *Hebrew Union College Monthly* 4: 115–22.

"Judaism and Struggling Christianity." *Hebrew Union College Monthly* 3: 181–94.

"Martin Luther and the Jews." *Hebrew Union College Monthly* 3: 69–80, 122–33.

Review of *The Jews among the Greeks and the Romans,* by Max Radin. *Hebrew Union College Monthly* 3: 159–60.

1919

"Lost: Judaism in the A.E.F. [American Expeditionary Forces]: The Urgent Need for Welfare Workers." *American Hebrew* (New York) 104: 448, 456–57.

"Religion and the Jewish Soldier." *The Community Voice of the Allentown [PA] Jewish Community Center* 1, no. 1: 6, 8, 14.

Review of *Chosen Peoples: The Hebraic Ideal Versus the Teutonic,* by Israel Zangwill. *Hebrew Union College Monthly* 6: 22–23.

1920

"An Investigation into Polish Jewish Life of the Sixteenth Century with Special Reference to Isaac ben Abraham, Author of Hizuk Emunah." Rabbinic thesis, Hebrew Union College.

Review of *The Inward Light,* by Allan Davis and Anna R. Stratton. *Hebrew Union College Monthly* 6: 119–20.

"Valedictory." *Hebrew Union College Monthly* 6: 182–84.

1921

"Current Events (Month Ending 3 December 1921)." *B'nai B'rith News* (Chicago) 14, no. 4: 5–6.

"The Jew Enters Spain." *The Scribe* (Portland, Ore.) 5, no. 8: 4. Reprint. "Sketches of Jewish History, IX. The Jew Enters Spain." *American Israelite* 74, no. 38 (1928): 4.

"Jewish Diplomats in Moslem Spain." *The Scribe* (Portland, Ore.) 5, no. 11: 4, 11. Reprint. "Sketches of Jewish Diplomats in Moslem Spain." *American Israelite* 74, no. 42 (1928): 1.

"The Karaites." *The Scribe* (Portland, Ore.) 5, no. 5: 5, 13–14.

"Making a Living in Ancient [i.e., Medieval] Spain." *The Scribe* (Portland, Ore.) 5, no. 15: 5, 12–13. Reprint "Sketches of Jewish History, XII. Making a Living in Ancient [i.e., Medieval] Spain." *American Israelite* 74, no. 44 (1928): 4.

"Mohammed and the Jews." *The Scribe* (Portland, Ore.) 4, no. 26: 5. Reprint. "Sketches of Jewish History, VIII. Mohammed and the Jews." *American Israelite* 74 (1928) no. 37: 4.

"The Poets of Spain." *The Scribe* (Portland, Ore.) 5, no. 9: 5, 11. Reprint. "Sketches of Jewish History, X. The Poets of Spain." *American Israelite* 74, no. 40 (1928): 4.

"Polish Situation Not Hopeless." *Jewish Tribune* (New York) (August 26): 2, 17.

1922

"Current Events." *B'nai B'rith News* (Chicago) 14, no. 5: 5–6, 16; no. 6: 5, 16; no. 8: 5–6; no. 9: 5–6; no. 10: 5, 16.

"An Exponent of Hebraic Culture: Gotthard Deutsch." *The Cincinnati Menorah*, 18–19.

"Jewish Histories Series: Before the Roman Conquest." *The Scribe* (Portland, Ore.) 5, no. 22: 5, 14. Reprint. "Outline Sketches of Jewish History: Jewish History before the Roman Conquest." *American Israelite* 74, no. 30 (1928): 4.

"Jewish History Series: The Rise of the House of Hillel." *The Scribe* (Portland, Ore.) 5, no. 24: 5, 13. Reprint. "Sketches of Jewish History: The Rise of the House of Hillel." *American Israelite* 74, no. 31 (1928): 4.

"Jewish History Series, III: The Inner Life of Palestinian Jewry." *The Scribe* (Portland, Ore.) 5, no. 26: 5, 14. Reprint. "Sketches of Jewish History: The Inner Life of Palestinian Jewry." *American Israelite* 74, no. 32 (1928): 4.

"Jewish History Series, V: The Jews in the Diaspora." *The Scribe* (Portland, Ore.) 6, no. 2: 5, 13–15. Reprint. "Sketches of Jewish History, IV: The Jews in the Diaspora." *American Israelite* 74, no. 33 (1928): 4.

"Jewish History Series, VI: The Jewish Constitution." *The Scribe* (Portland, Ore.) 6, no. 9: 5, 12–13. Reprint. "Sketches of Jewish History, V: The Jewish Constitution." *American Israelite* 74, no. 35 (1928): 4.

"Jewish History Series, VII: The Passing of Palestine." *The Scribe* (Portland, Ore.) 6, no. 9: 5, 13. Reprint. "Sketches of Jewish History, VI: The Passing of Palestine." *American Israelite* 74, no. 35 (1928): 4.

"Jewish History Series, VIII: The Rise of Babylon." *The Scribe* (Portland, Ore.) 6, no. 12: 5, 13. Reprint. "Sketches of Jewish History, VII: The Rise of Babylon." *American Israelite* 74, no. 36 (1928): 4.

1925

"Die handelspolitischen Beziehungen zwischen England und Deutschland in den Jahren 1576–1585," by E. Eberling. Berlin: Ph.D. diss.

"Notes on Sephardic Jewish History of the Sixteenth Century." *Hebrew Union College Jubilee Volume*. Cincinnati: Hebrew Union College.

1928

"Israel Jacobson." *Central Conference of American Rabbis Yearbook* 38: 386–498.

1929

"A Survey of Contemporaneous Jewish History (June 1928 to June 15, 1929)." *Central Conference of American Rabbis Yearbook* 39: 230–53.

1930

"The Love Letters of Bendet Schottlaender," edited by J. R. Marcus. *Hebrew Union College Annual* 7: 537–77.

Review of *The Origins of the Synagogue and the Church,* by Kaufmann Kohler. *Jewish Quarterly Review* (1929) n.s. 21: 197–98.

1931

"The Americanization of Isaac Mayer Wise." An address delivered on Founder's Day, March 28, at the Hebrew Union College (Cincinnati).

"Jewish Palestine: A Study in Becoming." In *History of Palestine and Syria to the Macedonian Conquest,* by A. T. E. Olmstead, 497–520. New York, London: C. Scribner's Sons, 1931. Reprint. *Jewish Palestine: A Study in Becoming. The New Orient,* vol. I, 289–312. Chicago: Open Court Publishers, 1933.

"A Layman's Jewish Library," by Israel Bettan, L. I. Egelson, and J. R. Marcus. *Jewish Tracts: The Tract Commission of the Union of American Hebrew Congregations and the Central Conference of American Rabbis,* no. 18.

1932

"Report of Committee on Contemporaneous History and Literature." *Central Conference of American Rabbis Yearbook* 42: 86–88.

1933

"Impacts of Contemporary Life upon Judaism." In "Religion Tomorrow: A Symposium." *Papers delivered at the XXXIII Council U.A.H.C.* (Chicago), 20–28.

"Report of Committee on Contemporaneous History and Literature." *Central Conference of American Rabbis Yearbook* 43: 99–103.

"Zionism and the American Jew." *American Scholar* 2: 279–92.

1934

The Rise and Destiny of the German Jew. Cincinnati: Union of American Hebrew Congregations, Department of Synagogue and School Extension. A second edition was published without E. Gamoran's Introduction and Topics for Study, discussion, and papers. Another edition appeared in 1973 titled *The Rise and Destiny of the German Jew. With a postmortem*. New York: KTAV Pub. House, 1973. An extract appeared in "Les Juifs et le nouvel Etat allemand." *L'Univers Israélite* 90 (1935): 327.

"Report of Committee on Contemporaneous History." *Central Conference of American Rabbis Yearbook* 44: 282–89.

1935

"A Brief Introduction to the Bibliography of Modern Jewish History. A selected annotated list of the standard books in several languages on the period from 1960 to modern times." Hebrew Union College, Department of Jewish Religious Education, no. 16.

"Report of Committee on Contemporaneous History." *Central Conference of American Rabbis Yearbook* 45: 452–58.

1936

"Report of the Committee on Contemporaneous History and Literature." *Central Conference of American Rabbis Yearbook* 46: 318–26.

1937

"An index to *Jewish Festschriften*," by Jacob R. Marcus and A. [T.] Bilgray. Hebrew Union College.

"Report of the Committee on Contemporaneous History and Literature." *Central Conference of American Rabbis Yearbook* 47: 394–404.

1938

The Jew in the Medieval World: A Source Book: 315–1791. Cincinnati: Union of American Hebrew Congregations Jewish History Source Books.[1]

"Report of the Committee on Contemporaneous History and Literature." *Central Conference of American Rabbis Yearbook* 48: 302–11.

"Jacob R. Marcus. Interview by Henry Rabinowitz." *The Hebrew Union College Monthly* (February 13): 4, 12.

---

1. *The Jew in the Medieval World: A Source Book: 315–1791* was originally written for the UAHC's Synagogue and School Extension program, which was concerned with what we today call Adult or Continuing Education. Ironically, the book is perhaps Marcus's most enduring work as it is utilized in college classes. It has been republished at least a dozen times, currently by the Hebrew Union College Press (2000), where it is the best-selling title in their catalogue.

1939

Is Anti-Semitism Justified in Germany? n.p.

Review of *The Jewish Contribution to Civilization,* by Cecil Roth. *Jewish Social Studies* 1: 263–64.

Review of *A Social and Religious History of the Jews,* by S. W. Baron. *Jewish Quarterly Review* n.s. 29: 45–50.

"Report of Committee on Contemporaneous History and Literature." *Central Conference of American Rabbis Yearbook* 49: 65–71, 365–83.

1940

"Mass Migrations of Jews and their Effects on Jewish Life." *Central Conference of American Rabbis Yearbook* 50: 277–99.

"Report of Committee on Contemporaneous History and Literature." *Central Conference of American Rabbis Yearbook* 50: 67–73, 383–85.

1941

"Jacob Mann." *Central Conference of American Rabbis Yearbook* 51: 247–49.

"Judaism and Western Civilization." *Contemporary Jewish Record* 4: 501–10. Condensed from an address delivered 30 July 1941, at the Harvard Summer School Conference on Religion and the World Today.

"New Literary Responsibilities." *American Jewish Year Book 5702,* 784–91.

"Report of Committee on Contemporaneous History." *Central Conference of American Rabbis Yearbook* 51: 68–73, 331–33.

"A Century Ago and Today." *The Jewish Herald-Voice* Rosh Hashanah ed. (5702): 22, 50. Reprint. "A Century Ago and Today." *The Jewish Exponent* (September 19): 36, 45.

1942

"Defenses Against Antisemitism," in *Essays on Antisemitism,* edited by Koppel S. Pinson, 175–86. New York: Conference on Jewish Relations. Reprint. *Essays on Antisemitism,* edited by Koppel S. Pinson, 49–58. With a foreword by Salo W. Baron (1946).

"Report of Committee on Contemporaneous History." *Central Conference of American Rabbis Yearbook* 52: 60–63, 354–56.

Review of *Rome,* by H. Vogelstein. *Review of Religion* 6: 311–15.

"Saving Europe in Spite of Itself." *Hebrew Union College Bulletin* 2, no. 1: 1–2, 14–15.

1943

"A Brief Bibliography of American Jewish History." Reprint. *Jewish Book Annual, 1943-1944,* 23–30. Reprint. *Jewish Book Annual, 1950.*

A Brief Bibliography of American Jewish History. Rev. ed. New York: Community
Education Service of the American Jewish Historical Society, sponsored by
the National Jewish Welfare Board, 1949. Reprint. New York: National Jewish
Welfare Board, published jointly by the American Jewish Tercentenary Committee and the Jewish Book Council of America, 1954.

"Jews," in *Encyclopaedia Britannica* 13: 58–64. Includes "Culture and Community
in the Medieval Jewish World," "Modern Period," "The Age of Reaction Beginning 1920," and "The Jews in the United States." Issued as preprint and reprinted in many subsequent issues of the *Encyclopaedia.*

"Report of the Committee on Contemporaneous History." *Central Conference of
American Rabbis Yearbook* 53: 52–55, 258–61.

"United Planning for a United World." *Hebrew Union College Bulletin* 2, no. 3: 5–6.

צמישצ רר7אנמ שפינלצו *Yivo Bleter* 21: 201–14.

1944

"Report of Committee on Contemporaneous History." *Central Conference of
American Rabbis Yearbook* 54: 62–64, 257–60.

Review of *History of the Jews in England,* by Cecil Roth. *Jewish Quarterly Review*
n.s. 34: 483–86.

1945

"The Contribution of the Jew to American Civilization." Broadcast on *Message of
Israel,* New York, April 8.

"Democracy in Judaism." *Liberal Judaism* 13, no. 8: 11–19.

Jews in American Life. New York: American Jewish Committee. Rev. ed. 1955.

"An Old People in a New World: The Story of How the Jew Came to America."
Broadcast on *Message of Israel,* New York, April 1. Reprint. "An Old People in a
New World." *Current Religious Thought* (Oberlin, Ohio) 5, no. 6 (1945): 16–18.

צמישצ וו7אנמ שפינלצו *Yivo Bleter* 25: 367–71.

1946

"Report of Committee on Contemporaneous History." *Central Conference of
American Rabbis Yearbook* 55: 59–61, 212–14.

"The Triesch Hebra Kaddisha, 1687–1828." *Hebrew Union College Annual* 19: 169–
204.

1947

Communal Sick-Care in the German Ghetto. Cincinnati: Hebrew Union College
Press.

"The Modern Religion of Moses Hart." *Hebrew Union College Annual* 20: 585–615.

"Report of the Committee on Contemporaneous History." *Central Conference of American Rabbis Yearbook* 56: 72–76, 343–46.

Review of *In Time and Eternity: a Jewish Reader,* edited by N. N. Glatzer. *Jewish Social Studies* 9, no. 3: 257–58.

1948

"The Forty-Eighters." In *Charting Freedom's Course* (1947). *The Forty-first Annual Report of the American Jewish Committee* (New York), 79–90.

"From Peddler to Regimental Commander in Two Years: The Civil War Career of Major Louis A. Gratz." *Publications of the American Jewish Historical Society* 38: 22–44.

"The Program of the American Jewish Archives." *American Jewish Archives* 1, no. 1: 2–5.

"Report of the Committee on Contemporaneous History." *Central Conference of American Rabbis Yearbook* 57: 57–60, 450–53.

1949

A Brief Bibliography of American Jewish History (1943). Rev. ed. New York: Community Education Service of the American Jewish Historical Society, sponsored by the National Jewish Welfare Board.

"Fifty Years of the Year Book." *Committee Reporter* 6, no. 3: 4.

"Light on Early Connecticut Jewry." *American Jewish Archives* 1, no. 2: 3–52.

"Looking Back 60 Years." *Jewish Exponent* (Philadelphia) 119, no. 14: 17.

The President's News Letter (Central Conference of American Rabbis) 1, no. 1.

1950

"A Brief Bibliography of American Jewish History." Reprint. *Jewish Book Annual.*

A Brief Supplement to the Standard Hebrew Dictionaries of Abbreviations, Alexander Marx Jubilee Volume. New York: Jewish Theological Seminary of America, 447–80.

"Dedication Address," in *Chicago Sinai Congregations Bulletin* 7, no. 31: [4].

"The President's Message to the 61st Annual Convention of the Central Conference of American Rabbis." *Central Conference of American Rabbis Yearbook* 60: 237–46.

The President's News Letter (Central Conference of American Rabbis) 1, no. 2.

1951

"Dr. David Philipson's Place in American Jewish Historiography." *American Jewish Archives* 3, no. 2: 28–31.

Early American Jewry. 2 vols. Philadelphia: Jewish Publication Society of America, 1951–1953. Vol. 1: *The Jews of New York, New England, and Canada, 1649–1794.*

"The Man Who Created Reform Judaism." *Liberal Judaism* 19, no. 1: 1–5.

Review of *The Great Synagogue, London, 1690–1940,* by Cecil Roth. *American Jewish Archives* 3: 112–16.

"Solomon Landman." *Central Conference of American Rabbis Yearbook* 61: 254–55.

"The Rabbi's Basic Library," selected by Jacob R. Marcus and Sheldon H. Blank. מפד יורצ, *Bulletin of the Central Conference of American Rabbis Committee on Jewish Literature and Art* no. 1 (Purim, 5711): 1–7.

1952

"Bright Star Shining in the West." Union of American Hebrew Congregations, United Jewish Layman's Committee, Inc. Broadcast on *Message of Israel,* 9 March 1952.

"European Bibliographical Items on Chicago," in *The Chicago Pinkas,* edited by S. Rawidowicz, 177–97.

1953

"After Five Years." *American Jewish Archives* 5: 3–4.

"Henry Cohen (1863–1952)." *Publication of the American Jewish Historical Society* 42: 451–55.

How to Write the History of an American Jewish Community. Cincinnati: American Jewish Archives.

Early American Jewry. 2 vols. Philadelphia: Jewish Publication Society of America, 1951–1953. Vol. 2: *The Jews of Pennsylvania and the South, 1655–1790.*

Review of *Portraits Etched in Stone: Early Jewish Settlers, 1682–1831,* by David de Sola Pool. *William and Mary Quarterly Series* 3, vol. 10: 259–61.

Review of *The Sephardim of England,* by Albert M. Hyamson. *American Jewish Archives* 5: 126–29.

"The West India and South America Expedition of the American Jewish Archives." *American Jewish Archives* 5: 5–21.

Documents selected and edited by Jacob Rader Marcus:

"American Jewry in 1753 and in 1853." *American Jewish Archives* 5, no. 2: 115–20.

"The Land of Israel in 1985." *American Jewish Archives* 5, no. 2: 139.

"Rebecca Gratz on Religious Bigotry." *American Jewish Archives* 5, no. 2: 114.

1954

"After One Hundred Years: Isaac Mayer Wise in the West." *American Jewish Archives* 6, no. 1: 14.

"A Few Notes from the Record." *National Jewish Monthly* (Washington) 69, no. 1: 10–11, 16, 20.

Foreword to *A Jewish Tourist's Guide to the U.S.,* by Bernard Postal and Lionel Koppman. Philadelphia: Jewish Publication Society.

Preface to *Jewish Americana. A supplement to An American Jewish Bibliography,* by A. S. W. Rosenbach. Cincinnati: American Jewish Archives.

"Jews in American Life." *The Bulletin of Temple Beth El* (Detroit) 17 (December 31). Extended version. "Jews in American Life." *The American Jewish Committee* (New York).

"A Brief Bibliography of American Jewish History." A reprint published jointly by the American Jewish Tercentenary Committee and the *Jewish Book Council of America.*

"Tercentenary, 1654–1954." *American Jewish Archives* 6: 75–76.

"Judah Touro: Retrospect after a Century." *American Jewish Archives* 6, no. 1: 3–4.

Documents selected and edited by Jacob Rader Marcus:

"The New York Jew." *American Jewish Archives* 6, no. 2: 105–106.

"Unwritten History: Reminiscences of N. Taylor Phillips." *American Jewish Archives* 6, no. 2: 77–104.

"Letters to Moses Montefiore." *American Jewish Archives* 6, no. 2: 166.

"That Ebrew Jew." *American Jewish Archives* 6, no. 2: 148–50.

"A Poem," by Joseph Lyons. *American Jewish Archives* 6, no. 2: 106.

"Rules for Levi Cohen's Perusal when He Has Leisure." *American Jewish Archives* 6, no. 1: 13.

1955

"Important Historic Records." *JPS Bookmark* 2, no. 4: 4–6.

Introduction to *Year Without Fear,* by Martin M. Weitz. New York: Bloch Publishing Co.

Jews in American Life. Rev. ed. New York: American Jewish Committee. Original edition published in 1945.

Memoirs of American Jews, 1775–1865. The Jacob R. Schiff Library of Jewish Contributions to American Democracy. 3 vols. Philadelphia: Jewish Publication Society of America.

"Three Hundred Years in America." In *The Beth El Story, with a History of the Jews in Michigan before 1850,* by Irving I. Katz, 151–64. Detroit: Wayne University Press.

"Who Are We American Jews?" *Hebrew Union College-Jewish Institute of Religion Bulletin* 7, no. 4: 15–17.

"Historical News." *American Jewish Archives* 7, no. 1: 130–33.

"History Speaks." *Temple Israel Voice Bulletin* (Memphis) 10, no. 6: 1.

Review of *Jewish Life in America: A Panoramic View as Seen by the American Jewish Year Book,* vol. 56 (1955). *The Committee Reporter* (New York) 12, no. 3 (May 1955): 1.

Documents selected and edited by Jacob Rader Marcus:

"Samuel Oscar Alexander: California Merchant." *American Jewish Archives* 7, no. 2: 85–89.

"An Appeal to Loyalty." *American Jewish Archives* 7, no. 2: 232–33.

"The Federal Parade of 1788." *American Jewish Archives* 7, no. 1: 65–67.

"Isaac Harby on Religious Equality." *American Jewish Archives* 7, no. 1: 68–72.

"The Jews in the United States 1848." *American Jewish Archives* 7, no. 1: 82–84.

"Albert Moses Luria: Gallant Young Confederate." *American Jewish Archives* 7, no. 1: 90–103.

"The Stark-Minis Duel." *American Jewish Archives* 7, no. 1: 73–81.

"That'll Be the Day!" *American Jewish Archives* 7, no. 2: 231.

"Judah Touro Saves a Church." *American Jewish Archives* 7, no. 1: 64.

"Victory in Maryland." *American Jewish Archives* 7, no. 1: 67.

1956

"The Christian Shylock." *The Jewish Digest* (September): 61–64.

"M. Myer Singer, 1895–1956: In Memoriam." *American Jewish Archives* 8, no. 2: 133.

"Selma Stern-Taeubler: Archivist Retires." *American Jewish Archives* 8, no. 2: 132.

"The Future of American Jewry." *American Israelite.* One Hundredth Anniversary Edition (February 23) 101, section 1: 1; section 2: 8, 10–13.

Documents selected and edited by Jacob Rader Marcus:

"Elegiac Sonnet." *American Jewish Archives* 8, no. 1: 22.

"Hebrew Marriage Contract." *American Jewish Archives* 8, no. 1: 23.

"Trail Blazers of the Trans-Mississippi West." *American Jewish Archives* 8, no. 2: 59–130.

"The Unsolved Murder of Benjamin Nathan (1924)." *American Jewish Archives* 8, no. 1: 14–21.

1957

"Address of the President." *Publication of the American Jewish Historical Society* 46: 465–66.

Foreword to *Precious Stones of the Jews of Curaçao. Curaçaon Jewry, 1656–1957,* by Isaac S. Emmanuel, 7–8. New York: Bloch.

"The Future of American Jewry." *The Jewish Statement* (Jersey City, N.J.) 26, no. 18 (March 29): 3–4.

"The Goals of Survival: What Will U.S. Jewry Be Like in 2000?" *National Jewish Monthly* (Washington, D.C.) 71, no. 9: 4, 6.

"Letters as a Source of Biography." In *The Writing of American Jewish History*, edited by Moshe Davis and Isidore S. Meyer, 420–25. New York: American Jewish Historical Society.

"The Newmann Memorial Publication Fund of the American Jewish Archives." *American Jewish Archives* 9, no. 2: 139–40.

Pedagogue's Progress. Cincinnati: American Jewish Archives.

Preface to *Life Without Strife,* by Martin M. Weitz, New York: Bloch Publishers.

Review of *The History of the Jews of Philadelphia from Colonial Times to the Age of Jackson,* by Edwin Wolf, II and Maxwell Whiteman. *Jewish Exponent* (Philadelphia) 127, no. 38: 15.

"Ten Years After." *American Jewish Archives* 9: 126–27.

Documents selected and edited by Jacob Rader Marcus:

"Congregation Beth Shalom, Richmond, Va.: Extracts from the Minute Book September 1863–January 1864." *American Jewish Archives* 9, no. 2: 141–43.

"Abe Goldbaum and the General: An Incident of the Old West." *American Jewish Archives* 9, no. 1: 43–45. Reprint. *The Jewish Digest* (Scarsdale, N.Y.) 5 (November 1959): 68–70.

"Jewish Immigrant Life in Philadelphia: From *The Sunday Mercury,* August 10, 1890." *American Jewish Archives* 9, no. 1: 32–42.

"The War between the States: Reminiscences of Edward Rosewater, Army Telegrapher." *American Jewish Archives* 9 no. 2: 128–38.

1958

"Address of the President." *Publications of the American Jewish Historical Society* 47, no. 3 (March). Reprint. *The Periodization of American Jewish History.* Cincinnati: American Jewish Archives Pamphlet.

"Lee M. Friedman, 1871–1957, in Memoriam." *American Jewish Archives* 10: 12–13.

American Jewry Documents, Eighteenth Century. Cincinnati: Hebrew Union College Press.

Foreword, *The Journal of the Southern Jewish Historical Society* 1, no. 1 (November): 1.

"Historian's Credo." *Temple Israel Voice* (Memphis, Tenn.) (October 20).

Documents selected and edited by Jacob Rader Marcus:

"A Prayer for Peace." *American Jewish Archives* 10, no. 2: 133–34.

"War on the Willamette, 1880." *American Jewish Archives* 10, no. 1: 121–24.

"An Arizona Pioneer: Memoirs of Sam Aaron." *American Jewish Archives* 10, no. 2: 95–120.

1959

Isaac Mayer Wise and the College He Built. Cincinnati: American Jewish Archives Pamphlet.

"The Theme in American Jewish History." *Publication of the American Jewish Historical Society* 48, no. 3 (March 1959): 141–46.

"Joshua Bloch." *Central Conference of American Rabbis Yearbook* 68: 231–32.

"A Spiked Water Cooler." *Hebrew Union College-Jewish Institute of Religion Bulletin* 11, no. 4 (May).

Review of *The Standard Jewish Encyclopedia,* edited by Cecil Roth. *American Jewish Archives* 11, no. 2: 189–90.

Documents selected and edited by Jacob Rader Marcus:

"Berthold Auerbach and the Hilton-Seligman Affair." *American Jewish Archives* 11, no. 2: 184–87.

"Autobiography: Abraham Cronbach." *American Jewish Archives* 11, no. 1: 3–4.

"Brotherly Love: 1854." *American Jewish Archives* 11, no. 2: 202–203.

"On the Religious Proscription of Catholics." *American Jewish Archives* 11, no. 2: 176–83.

"On Novel Reading," by Isaac Frank. *American Jewish Archives* 11, no. 2: 123–24.

1960

"My Favorite Hero." *The Jewish Digest* (Scarsdale, N.Y.) 5: 38–40.

"The Valenzin Affair." In *The Joshua Bloch Memorial Volume,* edited by Abraham Berger, Lawrence Marwick, and Isidore S. Meyer, 140–50. New York: Bloch.

Foreword to *Americans of Jewish Descent,* by Malcolm H. Stern. Cincinnati: American Jewish Archives in conjunction with the Hebrew Union College Press.

"A Selected Bibliography of American Jewish History." Reprint. *American Jewish Historical Quarterly* 51, no. 1: 97–134

"The American Jewish Archives." *The American Archivist* 23, no. 1 (January 1960): 57–61.

"Shalom Aleichem, Peace Be Unto You." *The Ohio Sentinel.* Part I, Thursday, 22 September; Part II, Thursday, 29 September.

Documents selected and edited by Jacob Rader Marcus:

"Anti-Jewish Sentiment in California." *American Jewish Archives* 12, no. 1: 15–33.

"The Call for a Hebrew College." *American Jewish Archives* 12, no. 2: 143–49.

"Decorum in the Synagogue." *American Jewish Archives* 12, no. 1: 120.

"Early Legal Records of Jews of Lancaster County, Pennsylvania," by Irwin S. Rhodes. *American Jewish Archives* 12, no. 1: 96–108.

"Texas Merchants after the Civil War." *American Jewish Archives* 12, no. 1: 71–74.

"Yiddish-Speaking Socialists in America: 1892–1905," by Bernard H. Bloom. *American Jewish Archives* 12, no. 1: 34–68.

1962

Introduction to *Seventeenth-Century Brazilian Jewry: A Critical Review,* by Isaac S. Emmanuel. *American Jewish Archives* 14, no. 1: 32–68.

Preface to *Five Families and Eight Young Men (Nashville and her Jewry 1850–1861),* by Fedora Small Frank. Nashville, Tennessee Book Co.

Documents selected and edited by Jacob Rader Marcus:

"Pages from My Stormy Life: An Autobiographical Sketch," by Melech Epstein. *American Jewish Archives* no. 2: 129–74.

1963

"Major Trends in American Jewish Historical Research." Reprint. *Jewish Exponent* (Philadelphia) 133–34 (June 21): 21–22.

"The Oldest Known Synagogue Record Book of Continental North America 1720–1721." In *The Time of Harvest: Essays in Honor of Abba Hillel Silver.* New York: Macmillan, 227–34.

Preface to *Reform Movements in Judaism,* by Abraham Cronbach. New York: Bookman Associates.

Documents selected and edited by Jacob Rader Marcus:

"A Letter from Bavaria: 1846." *American Jewish Archives* 15, no. 1: 17–20.

"Old Billy." *American Jewish Archives* 15, no. 1: 3–5.

"Are You a Jewess?" *American Jewish Archives* 15, no. 1: 59.

"Patriotism in Triplicate." *American Jewish Archives* 15, no. 1: 58–59.

"The Jews of Alaska," by Jessie S. Bloom. *American Jewish Archives* 15, no. 2: 97–116.

1964

"Background for the History of American Jewry." In *The American Jew: A Reappraisal,* edited by Oscar I. Janowsky. Philadelphia: Jewish Publication Society of America. Reprinted as a pamphlet by the American Jewish Archives.

On Love, Marriage, Children . . . and Death, Too . . . Intimate Glimpses into the Lives of American Jews in a Bygone Age as Told in Their Own Words. Cincinnati: Society of Jewish Bibliophiles.

"Principales Tendencias en la Investigación Histórica Judía en América del Norte. DAVAR Revista Literaria." *Publicacion Trimestral Editada Por La Sociedad Hebraica* (Argentina) (Julio-Septiembre). First published in *Jewish Exponent* (Philadelphia) (1963).

"Major Trends in American Jewish Historical Research." *American Jewish Archives* 16, no. 1: 9–21. First published in *Jewish Exponent* (Philadelphia) (21 June 1963) 133–34: 21–22.

Documents selected and edited by Jacob Rader Marcus:

"Five Gates: Casual Notes for an Autobiography," by Jacob Sonderling. *American Jewish Archives* 16, no. 2: 107–23.

"Even in Puritan Boston." *American Jewish Archives* 16, no. 1: 50.

"Growing Up in Syracuse," by William Lee Provol. *American Jewish Archives* 16, no. 1: 22–40.

"Down with the Jews!" by Harry H. Marks. *American Jewish Archives* 16, no. 1: 3–8.

1965

Documents selected and edited by Jacob Rader Marcus:

"The One Oasis." *American Jewish Archives* 17, no. 2: 180–81.

"A Word from Waco." *American Jewish Archives* 17, no. 2: 169.

"Words and Phrases." *American Jewish Archives* 17, no. 1: 76, no. 2: 140.

"Tomorrow's Prospect." New York: *Central Conference of American Rabbis Yearbook.*

"A Colony in Kansas 1882." *American Jewish Archives* 17, no. 2: 114–39.

"Ludwig Lewisohn: In Memoriam." *American Jewish Archives* 17, no. 2: 109–13.

"The Face of the American Jew." *American Jewish Archives* 17, no. 1: 17–26.

1966

"David Neumark." *Hebrew Union College Annual* 37.

Foreword to *DeSola Odyssey: A Thousand and One Years,* by Anita de Sola Lazaron. Richmond, Va., n.p.

"The American Colonial Jew: A Study in Acculturation." The B. G. Rudolph Lectures in Judaic Studies (Syracuse University), 24 pp.

The Quintessential American Jew. Cincinnati: American Jewish Archives Pamphlet. First published in *American Jewish Historical Quarterly* 58, no. 1.

Documents selected and edited by Jacob Rader Marcus:

"The Task of the Jews in the United States 1851." *American Jewish Archives* 18, no. 2: 155–59.

"Strangers to a Strange Land." *American Jewish Archives* 18, no. 2: 133–38.

"A Gentleman of the Law 1773." *American Jewish Archives* 18, no. 2: 132.

"War on Lodge Street." *American Jewish Archives* 18, no. 2: 128.

"The American Jew in 1872." *American Jewish Archives* 18, no. 1: 29–40.

"Immigrants in Buffalo." *American Jewish Archives* 18, no. 1: 20–28.

1967

Documents selected and edited by Jacob Rader Marcus:

"My Memories of Father." *American Jewish Archives* 19, no. 1: 41–59.

"A Call to Detroit 1869." *American Jewish Archives* 19, no. 1: 34–40.

"In My Lifetime." *American Jewish Archives* 19, no. 1: 3–33.

1968

Documents selected and edited by Jacob Rader Marcus:

"Two Presidents and a Haberdasher 1948." *American Jewish Archives* 19, no. 1: 3–15.

"Cincinnati Celebrates 150 Years." *MOTOUR* [AAA Ohio Valley Magazine] (January): 16–18.

1969

The Americanization of Isaac Mayer Wise. Cincinnati: American Jewish Archives Pamphlet.

Impacts of Contemporary Life Upon Judaism. Cincinnati: American Jewish Archives Pamphlet.

Studies in American Jewish History: Studies and Addresses. Cincinnati: Hebrew Union College Press.

"The Beginnings of American Jewry," Part I. *The Jewish Digest* 16, no. 2: 49–55. Edited version of Syracuse lecture "The American Colonial Jew: A Study in Acculturation." The B. G. Rudolph Lectures in Judaic Studies (Syracuse University).

Documents selected and edited by Jacob Rader Marcus:

"No Better Jew, No Purer Man: Mayer Sulzberger on Isaac Leeser." *American Jewish Archives* 21, no. 2: 140–48.

1970

The Colonial American Jew, 1492–1776. 3 vols. Detroit: Wayne State University Press.

Foreword to *Studies in Judaica Americana*, by Rudolf Glanz. New York: KTAV.

"The Handsome Young Priest: Portrait of Gershom Seixas." *Hebrew Union College Annual* 40–41: 409–67.

An index to *Jewish Festschriften*, by Jacob R. Marcus and A. [T.] Bilgray. 2d ed. New York: Kraus. First published by Hebrew Union College (1937).

"The Quintessential American Jew." In *Forschung am Judentum: Festschrift zum 60,* 143–55. Bern, Switzerland: Geburtstag von Luther Rothschild. Reprint from *American Jewish Historical Quarterly* 58, no. 1.

1971

Introduction to *Critical Studies in American Jewish History.* 3 vols. Cincinnati: American Jewish Archives; New York: KTAV.

An Index to Scientific Articles on American Jewish History. Cincinnati: American Jewish Archives.

Mavo Le-Toldot Yahadut Amerikah Bitkufat Reshita. Jerusalem: Magnes Press.

"Money and Matrimony." *Jewish News* (Detroit) (17 September).

"The American Jew and China." *Southern Jewish Weekly* (Jacksonville, Fla.) (17 September).

"On the Passing of Nelson Glueck." *American Jewish Archives* 23, no. 1: 5.

Documents selected and edited by Jacob Rader Marcus:

"Early Days: The Story of Sarah Thal, Wife of a Pioneer Farmer of Nelson County," by Martha Thal. *American Jewish Archives* 23, no. 1: 47–62.

1972

Preface to *Roots in a Moving Stream: The Centennial History of Congregation B'nai Jehudah of Kansas City, 1870–1970,* by Frank J. Adler. Kansas City, Mo.: The Temple, Congregation B'nai Jehudah.

Jews in American Life. Rev. ed. New York: American Jewish Committee. First published in 1945. Second edition published in 1955.

Israel Jacobson: The Founder of the Reform Movement in Judaism. 2d ed. Cincinnati: Hebrew Union College Press. First published in *Central Conference of American Rabbis Yearbook* 38 (1928): 386–498.

"Money and Matrimony." *The Jewish Digest* (New York) 17, no. 7 (April): 45–46.

"The American Jew and China." *Jewish Civic Leader* (Worcester, Mass.) (30 March).

"The American Jewish Archives." *Reform Judaism* (19 September).

Documents selected and edited by Jacob Rader Marcus:

"Fighter for Women's Rights." *American Jewish Archives* 24, no. 1: 184.

1973

Introduction to *The Jews of Coro, Venezuela,* by Isaac S. Emmanuel. Edited with S. Chyet. Cincinnati: Monographs of the American Jewish Archives, no. 8.

The Rise and Destiny of the German Jew. 2d ed., with a Postmortem. New York: KTAV.

Introduction to *John Jacob Hays: the First Known Jewish Resident of Fort Wayne*, by Joseph Levine. Fort Wayne, Ind.: Indiana Jewish Historical Society.

"Coca Koller and Freud." *Jewish Exponent* (Philadelphia) (20 July).

Introduction to *An Analysis of Vatican 30*, by Lewis M. Barth. Monographs of the Hebrew Union College-Jewish Institute of Religion.

"19th Century American Unsure of Survival of Jewish State." *The Detroit News* (5 October).

A paper forthrightly called "The Jew was Forerunner of 2000 Journals in America." *B'nai B'rith Messenger* (6 April): 30, 34.

"Key 73 Recalls the Conversion Efforts of Zealots 150 Years Ago." *American Israelite* (March 15).

"The Jew of 1823: 150 Years of the American Jewish Press." *Detroit Jewish News* (23 March): 52.

"Month of March Marks 150 Years of American Jewish Press." *San Francisco Jewish Bulletin* (23 March): 5.

"Thank You God for Not Having Made Me a Woman." *Wisconsin Jewish Chronicle* (Milwaukee) (21 December).

Documents selected and edited by Jacob Rader Marcus:

"An Intimate Portrait of the Union of American Hebrew Congregations: A Centennial Documentary." *American Jewish Archives* 25, no. 1: 3–115.

1974

"After Twenty-five Volumes." *American Jewish Archives* 26: no. 1: 3–4.

Foreword to *A Century of Jewish Life in Dixie: The Birmingham Experience*, by Mark H. Elovitz. Tuscaloosa: University of Alabama Press.

Introduction to "The Hebrew Union College-Jewish Institute of Religion: A Centennial Documentary." Reprint from *American Jewish Archives* 26, no. 2: 103–243.

Historical Essay on the Colony of Surinam, 1788, edited by Jacob R. Marcus and S. F. Chyet. New York: KTAV.

"The Jew and the American Revolution." *American Jewish Archives*, 17 pp. Reprint in *The Torah*. National Federation of Jewish Men's Clubs, Inc. (Philadelphia) (Winter 1976): 5–15.

The Larger Task. Cincinnati: American Jewish Archives.

"Shed a Tear for a Transport." Reprint from *Raphael Mahler Jubilee Volume*. Tel Aviv: 53–61.

Foreword to *Beginnings on Market Street: Nashville and Her Jewry, 1861–1901*, by Fedora S. Frank. Nashville: Frank.

Early American Jewry. Two vols. in one. 2d ed. New York: KTAV.

Foreword to new edition of *A Jewish Tourist's Guide to the United States,* by Bernard Postal and Lionel Koppman. New York: Jewish Publication Society of America.

Jews and the American Revolution: A Bicentennial Documentary. Cincinnati: American Jewish Archives. Reprint from *American Jewish Archives* 27, no. 2: 103–257.

Memoirs of American Jews. Three vols. in two. 2d ed. New York: KTAV.

Foreword to *Unrecognized Patriots: The Jews in the American Revolution,* by Samuel Rezneck. Westport, Conn.: Greenwood Press.

Documents selected and edited by Jacob Rader Marcus:
"A Centennial Documentary: Hebrew Union College-Jewish Institute of Religion." *American Jewish Archives* 26, no. 2: 99–243.

1975

"Jews and the American Revolution: A Bicentennial Documentary." *American Jewish Archives* 27, no. 2: 103–257.

"Myron M. Meyer." *Central Conference of American Rabbis Yearbook* 85: 110–11.

"The Jews and the American Bicentennial." *UAHC General Assembly: Occasional Papers* (Dallas/Ft. Worth) (November): 6 pp.

1976

"Necrology for Samson Shain." *Central Conference of American Rabbis Yearbook* 86: 203.

The Jew and the American Bicentennial. Cincinnati: American Jewish Archives.

"Patriot and Prisoner during the Revolution." *The Detroit Jewish News* (20 February).

"HUC-JIR Salutes: The Coming Centenary of ORT." *ORT Quarterly* 18, no. 2 (Fall): 1.

"A Forgotten Federation Centennial." *The Detroit Jewish News* (24 December).

Documents selected and edited by Jacob Rader Marcus:
"The Founder of Christianity," by Felix Adler. *American Jewish Archives* 28, no. 2: 162–71.

"Adventures in America and the Holy Land." *American Jewish Archives* 28, no. 2: 126–41.

1977

Foreword to *First American Jewish Families: 600 Genealogies, 1654–1977,* by Malcolm H. Stern. New York: KTAV.

"Social Medicine in the Ghetto." Reprint from the *Jewish Spectator* (New York) 42: 23–30.

Foreword to *American Jewish Landmarks: A Travel Guide and History,* vol. 1. New York: Fleet Press Corporation, 1954, 1977.

"A Forgotten Centennial." *Jewish Chronicle* (Milwaukee, Wis.) (20 October).

"'Jewish Vignettes.' America's Most Important Jewish Document." *B'nai B'rith Messenger* (8 April): 25, 34.

"The Most Significant Document in the History of Jews in America." *The Detroit Jewish News* (1 April).

"America's Most Important Jewish Document." *Brotherhood* 11, no. 1 (September–October): 6–7.

1978

An Index to the Picture Collection of the American Jewish Archives. Cincinnati: American Jewish Archives Pamphlet.

Foreword to *Aspects of the Social, Political, and Economic History of the Jews in America,* by Rudolf Glanz. New York: KTAV.

Foreword to *Jewish Landmarks of New York: A Travel Guide and History,* by Bernard Postal and Lionel Koppman. New York: Fleet Press Corporation.

"Simon Cohen." *Central Conference of American Rabbis Yearbook* 88: 129–30.

"Genesis: College Beginnings." In *Jews in a Free Society: Challenges and Opportunities,* edited by Edward A. Goldman, 8–17. Cincinnati: Hebrew Union College Press.

1979

"Azkara." *Central Conference of American Rabbis Yearbook* (New York) 89: 199.

Documents selected and edited by Jacob Rader Marcus:
"History is the Record of Human Beings: A Documentary." *American Jewish Archives* 31, no. 1: 6–103.

1980

"Samuel Sandmel." *Central Conference of American Rabbis Yearbook* 90: 241–42.

"Presentation to Malcolm H. Stern." *Central Conference of American Rabbis Yearbook* 90: 177–78.

1981

The American Jewish Woman, 1654–1980. New York: KTAV/Cincinnati: American Jewish Archives.

Studies in the American Jewish Experience: Contributions from the Fellowship Pro-

grams of the Americans Jewish Archives, edited with Abraham J. Peck. Vol. 1. Cincinnati: American Jewish Archives. Second volume published by University Press of America (Lanham, Md.) and American Jewish Archives.

1982

Introduction to *Jew, Judaism, and the American Constitution,* by Milton R. Konvitz and Leo Pfeffer. Cincinnati: American Jewish Archives.

Dawn in the West. Cincinnati: American Jewish Archives Pamphlet.

"About this Issue." *American Jewish Archives* 34, no. 1: 1–2.

1983

"Editorial Note." *American Jewish Archives* 35, no. 2: 90.

1984

"Presentation to Edgar F. Magnin." *Central Conference of American Rabbis Yearbook* 93: 80–82.

1985

Foreword to *Dawn in the West,* by Allan Tarshish. Edited by Sefton D. Temkin. Lanham, Md.: University Press of America.

"In Memoriam: Maurice Jacobs, 1896–1984." *American Jewish Archives* 37, no. 2: 341–42.

Foreword to *A Treasury of Jewish Quotations,* edited by Joseph L. Baron. New York: J. Aronson.

Foreword to *Your True Marcus: The Civil War Letters of a Jewish Colonel,* edited by Frank L. Byrne and Jean Powers Soman. Kent, Ohio: Kent State University Press.

The Jews of Washington, DC: A Communal Anthology, edited by David Altshuler. Washington, D.C.: Jewish Historical Society of Greater Washington; Chappaqua, N.Y.: Rossel Books.

The American Rabbinate: A Century of Continuity and Change; 1883–1983, edited with Abraham J. Peck. Hoboken: KTAV.

1986

"Edgar Fogel Magnin." *Central Conference of American Rabbis Yearbook* 95: 298–99.

1987

Foreword to *Creative Awakening: The Jewish Presence in Twentieth-Century American Literature, 1900–1940s,* by Louis Harap. New York: Greenwood Press.

Foreword to *In the Mainstream: The Jewish Presence in the Twentieth-Century American Literature, 1950s-1980s*, by Louis Harap. New York: Greenwood Press.

Foreword to *Dramatic Encounters: The Jewish Presence in Twentieth-Century American Drama, Poetry, and Humor and the Black-Jewish Literary Relationship*, by Louis Harap. New York: Greenwood Press.

"Garry J. August." *Central Conference of American Rabbis Yearbook* 96: 260.

"In Honor of the 90th Birthdays of Sheldon H. Blank, Jacob Rader Marcus, and John J. Tepfer." *Central Conference of American Rabbis Yearbook* 96: 117–21.

1988

"A University that Would Revolutionize World Jewry." *American Jewish Archives* 40, no. 1: 1–4.

1989

United States Jewry, 1776–1985. 4 vols. Detroit: Wayne State University Press, 1989–1993.

Testament: A Personal Statement. Cincinnati: American Jewish Archives Pamphlet.

1990

To Count a People: American Jewish Population Data, 1585–1984. Lanham, Md.: University Press of America.

"Address." *Central Conference of American Rabbis Yearbook* 99: 111–14.

This I Believe: Documents of American Jewish Life. Northvale, N.J.: J. Aronson.

1991

Foreword to *Jews in the Caribbean: Evidence on the History of the Jews in the Caribbean Zone in Colonial Times*, compiled by Zvi Loker. Jerusalem: Misgav Yerushalayim, Institute for Research on the Sephardi and Oriental Jewish Heritage.

Preface to *Shloshim: After Thirty Years*, by Joseph R. Rosenbloom. St. Louis: Temple Emanuel Press.

1993

"Malcolm H. Stern." *American Jewish Archives* 45, no. 2: 299.

1994

Foreword to *Barnard and Michael Gratz: Their Lives and Times*, by Sidney M. Fish. Lanham, Md.: University Press of America.

Foreword to *Isaac Harby of Charleston, 1788–1828,* by Gary P. Zola. Tuscaloosa: The University of Alabama Press.

The Concise Dictionary of American Jewish Biography. Edited with Judith M. Daniels. 2 vols. Brooklyn: Carlson.

1995

The American Jew, 1585–1990: A History. Brooklyn: Carlson.

Maunderings of a Centenarian: An Informal and Illustrated History of the American Jewish Experience. Cincinnati: American Jewish Archives.

1996

The Jew in the American World: A Source Book, edited by Jacob Rader Marcus. Detroit: Wayne State University Press.

1997

"The Colonial American Jew." Reprinted in *The American Jewish Experience,* edited with introduction by Jonathan D. Sarna. 2d ed. New York: Holmes & Meier.

1998

"Light on Early Connecticut Jewry." Reprinted in *American Jewish History,* edited by Jeffrey S. Gurock, sponsored by the American Jewish Historical Society. New York: Routledge.

Sources

"A *Moment* Interview with Jacob Rader Marcus," by Elinor Grumet. *Moment Magazine* 6 (March and April 1981): A75-A85.

"America: the Spiritual Center of Jewry." *Jewish Community Bulletin* (Wheeling, W. Va.) 3 (1916): 4-5, 8.

"The Jewish Soldier." *HUC Monthly* (Cincinnati) 4 (1918): 115-22.

"Lost: Judaism in the American Expeditionary Forces, the Urgent Need for Welfare Workers." *American Hebrew* 104 (1919): 448, 456-57.

"Zionism and the American Jew." *American Scholar* 2 (1933): 279-92.

"Mass Migrations of Jews and their Effects on Jewish Life." *CCAR Yearbook* 50 (1940): 277-99.

"New Literary Responsibilities." *American Jewish Yearbook* 43 (1941): 784-91.

"The Program of the American Jewish Archives." *American Jewish Archives* 1 (1948): 2-5.

"Three Hundred Years in America." In *The Beth El Story, with a History of the Jews in Michigan Before 1850,* ed. Irving L. Katz, 151-64. Detroit: Wayne State University Press, 1955.

"Genesis: College Beginnings." In *Jews in a Free Society: Challenges and Opportunities,* ed. Edward A. Goldman, 8-17. Cincinnati: HUC Press, 1978.

"Pedagogue's Progress." Baccalaureate address delivered at State Teachers College of the State University of New York, Fredonia, New York, 9 June 1957. Cincinnati: American Jewish Archives, 1957.

"Testament: a Personal Statement." Cincinnati: American Jewish Archives, 1989; and *CCAR Yearbook* 99 (1989): 111-14.

Index

Abraham, Israel, 20
Academy for the Science of Judaism, 104
AJA (American Jewish Archives), xii, xix, 11, 26, 108–15
AJHS (American Jewish Historical Society), xv, 11, 109, 111
America: anti-Semitism in, 69–72, 122–23; father's survival struggle in, 3–4; Jewish role in history of, 108–15; Marcus's disappointment with, 149; migrations from Europe to, 4, 42, 65, 79, 90, 113, 117–20; Orthodox adjustment difficulties, 80; vs. Palestine as homeland, 68–69; as refuge from persecution in Europe, 39, 92–93
American Expeditionary Force. *See* World War I
American Israelite, The, 122
American Jewish Archives, 11
American Jewish Archives (AJA), xii, xix, 11, 26, 108–15
American Jewish Archives Journal, The, xii
American Jewish Historical Society (AJHS), xv, 11, 109, 111
American Jewish Periodical Center, 11, 26–27
American Jew, The (Marcus), 12
American Jewry: communal nature of, 52–53; decline of, 18–20; historical role of, 108–15; historical themes, xxi–xxix, 78–84, 101–2, 117–23; inspirational role of, 37–42, 45, 79, 97–98, 105; lack of support for soldiers, 56–57; leadership challenge of, xi, 39–40, 97, 99, 100–107; secular Jew issue, 44–45, 46, 47; social position of, 78–79, 124; and Zionism, 62, 64–65, 68. *See also* assimilation; institutions, Jewish
American Labor Party, 80
anti-Semitism: in America, 69–72, 122–23; and destruction of literature, 105; in

Europe, 63–64, 83, 84–85, 93–94, 119–20, 137; literary weapons against, 103; Marcus on, 20–21; and migration, 81–82, 88–89, 93–95; and personal integrity of Jews, 125; and social justice activism, 101
Arab culture in Spain, 89
Arabs in Palestine, 65, 74
archiving of Jewish history. *See* primary documentation
art music and Reform movement, 137–38
assimilation: archives as bulwark against complete, 115; and independence of Jewish culture, 88; intermarriage, 18, 72; and Jewish survival, 149; and loss of traditions, xvii, 40–41, 43–44, 45–46, 80–81; as reaction to discrimination, 71; Zionism as savior from, 72. *See also* secular Jews

Babylonia, 40, 86–87
Baeck, Leo, 7
Baer, Fritz, 7
Bahr, Hermann, 62–63
Balfour Declaration, 64
Baron, Salo W., xiii, 9
Barsimson, Jacob, 118
Bene Yeshurun Congregation, 138
Ben Israel, Menasseh, 91
Ben Zakkai, Jochanan, 149–50
Berlin, University of, xi, xiii, 6–7, 142
Beth Midrash Hagadol, 4
Bettman, Bernard, 14, 140
Board of Delegates of American Israelites, 121
Bohemia, anti-Semitism in, 137
Brandeis, Adolf, 120
Brandeis, Louis Dembitz, 120
Britain, support for homeland in Palestine, 64
Britt, George, 71